The Honour of God
and
Human Salvation

The Honour of God and Human Salvation

*A contribution to an understanding of
Calvin's theology according to his Institutes*

⮜✖⮞

Marijn de Kroon

Translated by
John Vriend and Lyle D. Bierma

T&T CLARK
EDINBURGH & NEW YORK

T&T CLARK LTD

A Continuum imprint

59 George Street
Edinburgh EH2 2LQ
Scotland

370 Lexington Avenue
New York 10017–6503
USA

www.tandtclark.co.uk

www.continuumbooks.com

Authorized English translation of
De eer van God en het heil van de mens
First edition Romen en Zonen, Roermond, 1968
Second edition © J. J. Groen en Zoon BV, Leiden, 1996
Additional material by the author copyright © T&T Clark Ltd, 2001

First published 2001

ISBN 0 567 08779 4

British Library Cataloguing-in-Publication Data
A catalogue record for this book is available from the British Library

Typeset by Waverley Typesetters, Galashiels
Printed and bound in Great Britain by Biddles Ltd, *www.biddles.co.uk*

Dedicated to the memory of
JEAN ROTT (+ Strasbourg 1998)

*'O if we were only truly committed to God! I
assure you: all the elements would sing to us and
we, we would get to hear in this world a melody
made in heaven, so utterly beautiful.'*

(Calvin)

Contents

Preface

IN 1996 J. J. Groen & Son, Publishers, Leiden, The Netherlands, decided to my surprise to reissue the Calvin study I first wrote as a doctoral dissertation in 1968, and asked me to add a chapter with a view to bringing the book up to date. I eagerly seized upon this request to rethink the basic thesis of the book and, in that context, to discuss the work of two American colleagues, the Calvin scholars Edward A. Dowey and William J. Bouwsma. Soon thereafter the Dutch Organization for Scientific Research (the NOW in The Hague) offered to make available the funds needed for an English translation. I am very grateful for their generous support. I take particular pleasure in the fact that the renowned Edinburgh publishing company of T&T Clark agreed to take on the project.

I was glad to comply with the publisher's request for an *index of subjects and names,* since it gave me an opportunity to add to the English edition of the book a significant substantial value of its own. In the *index of subjects* I list a large number of Calvin citations which have a special eloquence of their own in the book and therefore offer a suggestive impression of Calvin's thinking and a characterization of the special person the French reformer has been. I have done my best to reproduce his voice in such a way that it can be heard and understood.

On the occasion of the publication of the English edition of my book I am deeply indebted to many people. This applies first of all to my Dutch friends and colleagues. I want to mention in particular Professors Cornelis Augustijn and Willem van't Spijker, both of whom vigorously supported this project with their written recommendations. The former, moreover, carefully

ix

examined and criticized the numerous citations listed in the index of subjects. I am also very grateful to Professor Ian Hazlett (Glasgow) – with whom I was privileged to work in the Bucer-Forschungsstelle in Münster, Germany – for his effective support. A warm word of thanks is due as well to the two translators, John Vriend (text) and Lyle D. Bierma (notes), for the drive, competence and creativity with which they pursued their task.

I am sending off this English edition with the same two mottoes which accompanied the Dutch editions, a word from a prophet and a word from a church father:

'We are a planting of his glory' (Isaiah)

'The honour of God is the living human being' (Irenaeus).

Abbreviations

CO	*Ioannis Calvini opera quae supersunt omnia.* 59 vols. (= Corpus Reformatorum, vols 29–87). Brunswick and Berlin, 1863–1900.
CSEL	*Corpus scriptorum ecclesiasticorum latinorum.* Vienna, 1866ff.
DENZ	Denzinger, H., and A. Schönmetzer, *Enchiridion Symbolorum, Definitionum et declarationum de rebus fidei et morum.* 32nd edn. Freiburg, 1963.
DThC	*Dictionnaire de Théologie catholique.* Paris, 1909–50.
LThK	*Lexikon für Theologie und Kirche.* 2nd edn. Freiburg, 1957ff.
MSG	Migne, J. P. *Patrologiae cursus completus, series Graeca.* Paris, 1857–66.
MSL	Migne, J. P. *Patrologiae cursus completus, series Latina.* Paris, 1844–55.
NRSV	The Holy Bible, New Revised Standard Version.
OS	*Joannis Calvini opera selecta.* Edited by P. Barth and W. Niesel. 5 vols. Munich, 1926–62.
RGG	*Die Religion in Geschichte und Gegenwart.* 3rd edn. Tübingen, 1957ff.
WA	*Martin Luthers Werke.* Weimar, 1883ff.

Introduction

'A REDEEMED man who in all things and in all the choices of life is guided solely by the most heartfelt reverence for the God who is ever present to his mind and ever keeps his eye on him: there you have the true Calvinist.'[1] The thing that Abraham Kuyper describes in this solemn and somewhat stately manner is rooted in one of the most fundamental motifs of the Calvinistic confession: reverence before God's majesty. This, in an astonishing way, is what so deeply moved John Calvin. Also in the minds of those who cannot be called followers of the Genevan reformer the name of Calvin is firmly associated with the honour of God.

Up until about sixty years ago 'the honour of God' was studied as a principle to which all Calvin's ideas could be reduced. Contemporary scholars, however, have broken with this approach to Calvin's theology. Calvin is not the 'system builder' people so eagerly held him to be. On the contrary, he is much more a theologian with an 'existential' cast of mind, one who consistently thinks within the relation – the standing-out toward, *existere* – of God to human beings and human beings to God. The orientation of Calvin's theological thinking is bipolar.

Alexander Schweizer (in 1844) and Ferdinand Bauer (in 1847) were among the first scholars who tried to nail Calvin's thought down in a system.[2] To them the doctrine of predestination is

---

[1] A. Kuyper, *Het Calvinisme. Zes Stone-lezingen*, 3rd edn (Kampen, 1959), 58 (ET: *Lectures on Calvinism* [Grand Rapids, 1931], 72).

[2] A. Schweizer, *Die Glaubenslehre der evangelisch-reformierten Kirche*, vol. 2 (Zurich, 1844–5); F. Baur, *Lehrbuch der christlichen Dogmengeschichte*, 3rd edn (Stuttgart, 1867).

the central dogma of his theology, the starting premise in terms of which his thinking has to be explained and the principle to which everything has to be traced. With regard to the doctrine of predestination Paul Jacobs has provided a critical overview of this attempt, one that has been repeated several times.[3]

Otto Ritschl, as well, has to be counted among these 'system builders'.[4] He thinks he finds in Calvin's theological system a double God-image: that of the good Father and that of the severe righteousness-demanding God. Predominant, however, is the latter. He therefore calls the doctrine of God's unlimited righteousness the basic dogma and Calvin's focus on the honour of God the key which opens the door to an understanding of his theology.[5] Precisely because God's sovereign will predominates and is the all-controlling principle it is also Ritschl's view that the doctrine of predestination is central in Calvin.[6]

Martin Schulze, on the other hand, wants to introduce system in Calvin's theology on the basis of another principle. His work is a striking attempt to reduce all of Calvin's thought to his predominant interest in the future life.[7] In this connection he considers the *Jenseitsmotiv* as leitmotif and principle.[8]

In all the above authors the theme of God's honour is mentioned only indirectly. Among those who directly regard the honour of God as the first principle of Calvin's theology Emile Doumerque has to be mentioned first. In vigorous language he declares the sovereignty and honour of God connected with it

---

[3] P. Jacobs, *Prädestination und Verantwortlichkeit bei Calvin* (Neukirchen, 1937), 20–40.

[4] O. Ritschl, *Dogmengeschichte des Protestantismus*, vol. 3, *Calvins theologisches System* (Göttingen, 1926).

[5] Ibid., 178.

[6] Ibid., 163.

[7] M. Schulze, *Meditatio futurae vitae. Ihr Begriff und ihre herrschende Stellung im System Calvins. Ein Beitrag zum Verständnis von dessen Institutio* (Leipzig, 1901).

[8] So far as we know, there is not a single author who regards the strong christological aspect of Calvin's work as principle. In his well-known work *Die Theologie Calvins* (2nd edn [Munich, 1957]), W. Niesel sees Christ as central in the whole of Calvin's doctrine ('Jesus Christus beherrscht nicht nur den Inhalt, sondern auch die Form des calvinischen Denkens' [235]), but this dominant position is never elevated to the level of principle.

to be so much the dominant principle in the works of the Reformer that everything is logically based on it.[9] Pierre Imbart de la Tour, though he nowhere characterizes the honour of God as the first principle of Calvin's thought, places this theme so firmly at the centre of Calvin's theology that he feels impelled to observe that God does everything above all for the sake of his honour. The God of Calvin is a despot who is guided in all his actions by the motive of his own honour.[10] R. T. L. Liston, in his study on the sovereignty of God in Calvin, nowhere speaks of this sovereignty as of a principle but in fact to his mind also all the teaching of Calvin's *Institutes* is determined by Calvin's remarkable sense of God's majesty and his passion to render to God's high authority the honour due to it.[11] This author, accordingly, speaks frankly of the *system* of Calvin's theology.[12]

This systematization in terms of a first principle, from the perspective of which Calvin's entire oeuvre is said to proceed and becomes intelligible, may increasingly be viewed today as having been superseded.[13] In our opinion, it is one of the merits of the above-mentioned work of Jacobs that in it the conceptual framework usually followed up until then has been broken open and Calvin's theology is approached from within a different and broader perspective. He does not one-sidedly situate the doctrine of predestination in the light of God's sovereign will

---

[9] E. Doumergue, *Jean Calvin. Les hommes et les choses de son temps*, vol. 4, *La pensée religieuse de Calvin* (Lausanne, 1910), 34: 'La souveraineté de Dieu, l'honneur de Dieu, c'est le principe qui embrasse, contient, domine, caractérise, détermine tous les autres....' Ibid., 35: 'De ce principe fondamental tout ce qui est spécifiquement réformé peut être dérivé et expliqué.' Ibid., 362: 'des conséquences logiques'.

[10] P. Imbart de la Tour, 'Calvin', *Revue des deux mondes* 23 (1934): 166: 'Ce despote n'a d'autre fin que sa gloire.'

[11] R. T. Liston, 'John Calvin's Doctrine of the Sovereignty of God' (PhD diss., University of Edinburgh, 1930), 17: 'This emotional, irrational element may give us the key to the origin of Calvin's doctrine of God's sovereignty.' Liston speaks in this connection of an 'instinctive feeling'.

[12] Ibid., 88.

[13] Cf. A. M. Hunter, *The Teaching of Calvin: A Modern Interpretation* (London, 1950), 298–301; F. Wendel, *Calvin: The Origins and Development of His Religious Thought*, trans. P. Mairet (New York, 1963), 357–60; W. Dankbaar, *Calvijn, zijn weg en werk* (Nijkerk, 1958), 197.

but rather simultaneously forges a connection with human responsibility. God's sovereignty and human responsibility are not viewed as being parallel to or separate from each other but are considered above all in their mutual relationship. Thus the predestination of God obtains its ethical dimension; in other words, it becomes intelligible only in connection with the ethical conduct of human beings and the latter, conversely, raises the question of the decisive inner action of God and the decision of the divine will.[14]

In the development of this new approach to Calvin's theology one can observe a provisional end-point in the study of Karl Reuter.[15] Reuter consistently attempts, in a dogma-historical manner, to interpret Calvin's theological thought in terms of its bipolar structure.[16]

Also Alexandre Ganoczy repeatedly speaks of a bipolarity in Calvin's theology.[17] Yet, according to him, there are also fundamental principles by which Calvin's work is governed.

---

[14] Jacobs, *Prädestination und Verantwortlichkeit*, 41. Cf. p. 53.

[15] K. Reuter, *Das Grundverständnis der Theologie Calvins. Unter Einbeziehung ihrer geschichtlichen Abhängigkeiten* (Neukirchen, 1963), 9–28. Besides the aforementioned Jacobs, other authors also have taken note of this bipolarity in Calvin's thought. We mention by way of example W. Lüttge, *Die Rechtfertigungslehre Calvins und ihre Bedeutung für seine Frömmigkeit* (Berlin, 1909), 76–81 ('wechselseitige Beziehung' [79]); H. Barnikol, *Die Lehre Calvins vom unfreien Willen und ihr Verhältnis zur Lehre der übrigen Reformatoren und Augustins* (Neuwied, 1927), 104–5; P. Wernle, *Der evangelische Glaube nach den Hauptschriften der Reformatoren*, vol. 3, *Calvin* (Tübingen, 1919), 403.

[16] One could with good reason object to the use of the word *bipolarity*, which is drawn exclusively from the realm of physics. The word is used repeatedly in the recent works by Reuter and Ganoczy (cf. nn. 15 above and 17 below). If we follow their lead and speak of the bipolar structure of Calvin's theology, we mean to convey two things with this word: (1) Calvin wishes to maintain explicitly the difference between God and man: God remains God and man remains man. It is always a matter of *two*, and the two poles never flow together into one. (2) At the same time, however, in Calvin God and man, as two poles, relate to each other; there is a correlation. The word *bipolarity*, however, says nothing about the nature of this mutual relationship. How that is understood in Calvin's theology should become sufficiently clear in the course of this study.

[17] A. Ganoczy, *Calvin théologien de l'Eglise et du ministère* (Paris, 1964), 68–9, 74. Idem, *The Young Calvin*, trans. D. Foxgrover and W. Provo ('a profound bipolarity' [186]).

Such principles, according to him, are the honour of God, the figure of Christ, and the Word of God.[18]

The question of the place of God's honour in Calvin's work is one we will let him answer himself. Perhaps a modern person who has become increasingly sceptical about the wide range of speculations about *God in himself* will again be able to let Calvin speak for himself and to understand him.[19] God, after all, is a God *for* human beings. In his *Institutes* Calvin writes exclusively of that pro-human God. It is within the context of this correlation, this interactive existence, that Calvin conceives of the honour of God: it is the polar opposite of human sinfulness. Then, from within the enormous tension which this contrasting process generates the loving figure of the Lord emerges: mercy and justice kiss each other.

In the overall plan of our study I will attempt in chapter 1 to present an inventory of the ways in which Calvin speaks about God and human beings. In chapters 2, 3 and 4, I will examine those themes in his theology in which, in our opinion, the honour of God is most sensitively treated. I will, successively, discuss the place of the honour of God in the redemptive work of Christ (chapter 2). Next I will explore its role in the journey by which human beings arrive at salvation (chapter 3), and what it is in the case of the external means of grace (chapter 4). By means of this process I believe I will at the same time touch upon the key points of Calvin's entire teaching. In this way I hope simultaneously, at least in outline, to produce an accurate sketch of his theology.

I plan to listen to the answer to the question concerning the place of the honour of God in Calvin's work by a critical reading of the *Institutes* of 1559.[20]

[18] Ganoczy, *Young Calvin*, 188–94: 'The Principle of "Glory to God Alone [soli Deo gloria]"' (188); 'The Principle of "Christ Alone [solus Christus]"' (190); 'The Principle of the "Word of God [verbum Dei]"' (192).

[19] The 'God is dead' theology is an extreme example of this: the God of theological, abstract speculations has been declared dead. From the abundance of literature on this subject, cf. J. Sperna Weiland, *Oriëntatie* (Baarn, 1966), and for the anti-metaphysical tendency in contemporary theology, see H. M. Kuitert, *De realiteit van het geloof* (Kampen, 1967).

[20] The French edition of 1560 is neither an exact reproduction of the edition of 1559 nor an essential expansion of it. Cf. Doumergue, *Jean Calvin*, 4:10, 11.

In 1996, at the suggestion of the Dutch publisher, I added a new chapter to the second edition of my book (chapter 5, section 1). This gave me a second chance to summarize Calvin's theological ideas – this time in light of the terms 'perspectives' and 'structures'. This renewed reflection resulted in the three following sections.

In making a selection I limited myself to two studies, studies which I personally consider of great importance for Calvin's theology and for his person. I am referring to E. A. Dowey's study whose basic starting-point, the twofold knowledge of God, almost begs for a comparison with my book (section 2) and W. J. Bouwsma's portrait of John Calvin which in an astonishing way makes the man himself central (section 3). In the conclusion I return to my starting-point, 'the knowledge of God and the knowledge of ourselves', and in the section 'In search of God' I devote a number of pages to the majesty of God in connection with Calvin's self-knowledge (section 4). In this new conversation with Calvin I have above all tried to let him speak for himself – as is evident from the bibliographical index. With some boldness and freedom I have translated a fair number of quotations in such a way, that is, in contemporary words and a contemporary manner of speaking, that what Calvin intends to say may – hopefully – come alive. In my scheme these quotations fulfil a bridging function to an understanding of Calvin.

Whereas Calvin's oeuvre, besides his treatises and exegetical writings, contains more than 4,000 letters and 2,000 sermons, his *Institutes* in its final definitive form may be considered a compendium of the whole of his teaching. In this compendium his entire theology, at least materially (and not always in a succinct form), can be found. The *Institutes* constitute a *rocher de bronce*.[21] Yet Calvin's sermons and Bible commentaries, as especially Chapter V demonstrates, exhibit this rock in another light.

---

[21] Cf. Reuter, *Grundverständnis der Theologie Calvins*, 7: 'Die Institutio des Genfer Reformators steht wie ein rocher de bronce in der Zeit der Reformation. Aus allen seinen Veröffentlichungen führt der Weg zu ihr, selbst aus seinen Briefen, sobald es sich um die Frage nach dem Geist und Grundverständnis seiner Theologie handelt.'

We will quote Calvin in accordance with the text of the
Calvini opera in the *Corpus Reformatorum*. References to the
Institutes of 1559 will be given in terms of book, chapter, and
section, following which, in parentheses, the corresponding place
in the *Calvini opera* (CO) is mentioned.

I

⌘

The Knowledge of God and the Knowledge of Ourselves

JOHN Calvin opens his *Institutes of the Christian Religion* with the famous sentence: 'Almost the entire content of our wisdom, insofar as it must be considered true and profound, consists of two parts: the knowledge of God and the knowledge of ourselves.'[1] What does Calvin mean by that statement? To him the knowledge of God and the knowledge of ourselves are inseparable. God and humanity form the two poles between which our knowledge moves back and forth: we do not know God without knowing ourselves and do not know ourselves without knowing God. Although it is not easy to tell which of the two is prior to the other, Calvin first focuses his full attention on the human pole.[2]

No one can look upon himself or herself without immediately focusing upon God in whom we live and move.[3] In this context it becomes immediately clear to us that the attributes which make us somewhat important do not originate with ourselves. No: our entire being is subsistence in the one God; and all that we possess, indeed even our poverty, point to God.

With reference to this starting-point of Calvin, people have spoken of his 'anthropological principle' and a 'point of view of the human conscience'.[4] Although this is correct, it must not be forgotten that the attention Calvin pays to humanity always occurs in the context of his attention to God. Humans, he writes,

---

[1] *Institutes* 1.1.1 (CO 2:31).
[2] Ibid.
[3] Ibid.
[4] Doumergue, *Jean Calvin*, 4:14.

never achieve clear knowledge of themselves unless they have first looked upon God's face and then return from that contemplation to self-scrutiny. The two methods are used interchangeably and are inseparably interconnected in practice. In Calvin they constantly alternate: the one kind of knowledge leads to the other. And thus, from the very first page of the *Institutes*, God and humanity stand side by side and over against each other. Sometimes expressly but otherwise always tacitly, this bipolarity constitutes the background of Calvin's thinking. Undoubtedly God is the primary and all-dominating figure in this bipolarity but never in such a way that the other pole, the human figure, has totally disappeared from view. 'He recognized the bipolarity between the knowledge of God and the knowledge of self as the pivotal task of theological scholarship.'[5]

But how does he view the two poles? Who is God and who is the other, the human pole? In this first chapter we will attempt to answer this question in four sections:

1. God is a figure of awesome majesty; humanity is weakness and sin

2. God is a majesty of love; humanity is his image

3. Humanity must honour God

4. Tensions in Calvin's theology

1. God is an awesome majesty; humanity is weakness and sin

1.1. *God: an awesome majesty*

God is an awesome majesty. 'We see people, who were serene and strong when God remained absent, so shaken and appalled when he manifested his glory that they cringed in deadly terror. They are even so powerfully seized by fear that they still barely exist. . . .'[6] The way Calvin regards this awesome majesty of God comes to expression, first of all, when humans become conscious of God's *presence*, when, being confronted by that *majesty*, they begin to experience their own littleness and, in the light of God's unstained *purity*, acquire some sense of their own impurity.

[5] Reuter, *Grundverständnis der Theologie Calvins*, 20.
[6] *Institutes* 1.1.3 (CO 2:33).

That greatness is evident, further, from the *irresistibility of God's will* and from his all-effectuating *providence.* Finally, it comes to expression in Calvin's conviction that God is *unutterable* and *unimaginable.*

God's presence fills humans with dread, causes them to shudder,[7] fills them with fear,[8] fear before his judgment seat and wrath,[9] fear from which the ungodly cannot detach themselves[10] because they are so obsessed by it. It is fear which arises from the greatness of his majesty,[11] and is an inescapable power; fear which issues from God's severity which he daily displays to us,[12] and which is an unendurable fire.[13] This fear distresses hypocrites,[14] for God punishes those who despise him.[15] He is the avenger of his majesty.[16]

It is precisely in the light of that great majesty that we see our lowliness.[17] God's majesty prompts us to rightly see our lowliness. We dread it.[18] Really, Calvin says, no long proofs are needed for us to be convinced of the greatness of God.[19] It is a greatness which wreaks vengeance and appals us,[20] a greatness which is proclaimed by the firmament.[21] That world is a theatre of God's glory[22] and God's greatness comes through above all in humans, for they are a mirror of the glory of God.[23]

This awesome majesty reaches us as unstained purity which causes us to see our misery.[24] Calvin speaks of God's purity especially in connection with the Law. The Law must reform

---

[7] Ibid.
[8] *Institutes*, 'Prefatory Address to King Francis I of France' (CO 2:21).
[9] Ibid., 1.2.2 (CO 2:35).
[10] Ibid., 1.3.3 (CO 2:37).
[11] Ibid., 1.4.4 (CO 2:40).
[12] Ibid., 4.15.9 (CO 2:967).
[13] Ibid., 1.5.7 (CO 2:46).
[14] Ibid., 1.4.4 (CO 2:40).
[15] Ibid., 2.5.10 (CO 2:238).
[16] Ibid., 2.8.18 (CO 2:279).
[17] Ibid., 1.1.2 (CO 2:33).
[18] Ibid., 1.2.2 (CO 2:35).
[19] Ibid., 1.5.9 (CO 2:47).
[20] Ibid., 1.3.2 (CO 2:37).
[21] Ibid., 1.6.4 (CO 2:55).
[22] Ibid., 1.5.5 (CO 2:45): 'spectaculum gloriae Dei'.
[23] Ibid., 1.15.4 (CO 2:138): 'speculum gloriae Dei'.
[24] Ibid., 1.1.2 (CO 2:33).

people by the standard of God's purity;[25] it is a resumption of the journey to, to travel in the direction of the purity that is God himself. And when Calvin speaks of the good works people were intended to do, he invites us to compare ourselves to God's purity, to see what in the light of that purity there still remains of our innocence, 'for if the stars which shine most brightly at night lose their brilliance in the face of the sun, what do we think will happen to an even extraordinary moral soundness of man when it is compared with the purity of God?'.[26]

The awesomeness of God's majesty is succinctly expressed in his irresistible and all-powerful will. As much as possible we will let this theme – about whose background there have been so many studies and so much writing – speak for itself from Calvin's own writings. Then it will become clear that the irresistibility of God makes itself vividly felt in the activity of the divine will. That will of God is secretly present behind all his workings. Sometimes it makes use of secondary causes.[27] Another time God directly moves things by the finger of his might, but never in such a way that he would be untrue to the starting-point he once set for himself.[28]

That things are as they are is because he wills it. Simply for that reason and for no other: 'It is he who, everywhere diffused, sustains all things, nurtures and vivifies them in heaven and on earth.'[29] He keeps everything in existence. In Calvin, God's will characteristically causes all things. Nothing escapes its effect, for it is the cause, the most righteous cause, of all things.[30] The decree of God's will is fixed.[31] It cannot be frustrated.[32]

It is undeniable that precisely at the point of the will the greatness of God takes total control of humans. It is amazing that humans – however this is achieved – continue to exist, for God's

[25] Ibid., 2.8.51 (CO 2:303).
[26] Ibid., 3.12.4 (CO 2:556).
[27] Ibid., 1.17.6 (CO 2:159): 'causas inferiores'; cf. ibid., 1.17.9 (CO 2:161) and *Prael. Jon.* 4:6–8 (CO 43:275): 'has medias causas gubernat Dei consilium'.
[28] Cf. Hunter, *Teaching of Calvin*, 58.
[29] *Institutes* 1.13.14 (CO 2:102). Calvin is speaking here specifically of the Holy Spirit.
[30] Ibid., 1.17.1 (CO 2:154).
[31] Ibid., 1.17.2 (CO 2:156).
[32] Ibid., 1.16.6 (CO 2:149).

will is all-controlling[33] and that will must be the sole standard for guiding their life.[34] That will perseveres, also in regard to sin; also in the sinful conduct of people God's will manages to realize its goal. It is interesting to see how, for example in his commentary on Exodus, Calvin goes to the very limit to make God the author of everything that happens, barely even excluding sin.[35] Humanity can call sin its possession. The will of God is so all-controlling that no room is left for 'permission', the renowned theological invention by which, on the one hand, God is kept far from sin, while on the other his sovereignty is still honoured. However, in Calvin's opinion, the latter occurs in too small a measure because God's permission, precisely at the point of sin, threatens to detract from the powerful and exclusive dominance of the Lord's will.[36]

Finally, God's will is entitled to decide over life and death,[37] just as all things depend on his good pleasure,[38] *son bon plaisir*.[39] This last expression, used with a certain fondness, has the flavour of divine caprice; one may question, accordingly, whether it accurately conveys Calvin's thinking. True, speaking of the *predestination* of the reprobate, Calvin had the courage to formulate the following strong statement: 'For God's will is so much the highest rule of righteousness that we must consider right whatever he wills precisely *because* he wills it,'[40] but it would nevertheless be overly superficial to equate this with divine caprice. Such an adage immediately suggests to us the name of Scotus and the whole association with nominalism and *potentia absoluta*. It seems better, however, to discuss this additional complex of problems at the proper place, where we deal with predestination, which is ultimately a part of divine providence, and where

---

33 Ibid., 1.18.1 (CO 2:167).
34 Ibid., 1.2.2 (CO 2:35).
35 *Comm. Exod.* 3:20ff. (CO 24:50); cf. Reuter, *Grundverständnis der Theologie Calvins*, 146. For more on this see G. Beyerhaus, *Studien zur Staatsanschauung Calvins mit besonderer Berücksichtigung seines Souveränitätsbegriffes* (Berlin, 1910), 74ff.
36 *Institutes* 1.18.1 (CO 2:167): 'Tergiversando itaque effugiunt, Dei tantum permissu, non etiam voluntate hoc fieri.'
37 Ibid., 3.9.4 (CO 2:526).
38 Ibid., 3.22.1 (CO 2:287); cf. ibid., 3.22.3 (CO 2:689).
39 Cf. Hunter, *Teaching of Calvin*, 55.
40 *Institutes* 3.23.2 (CO 2:700).

the question of God's unconditional, supremely powerful and sovereign volition comes up in all its rigour.

Indeed, in the doctrine of divine providence, the omnipotence of the will of God is very prominent. That will is really the final premise of divine providence. It becomes clear, precisely in the doctrine of providence, that nothing escapes God's will. That will is active, at work, operative: 'Providence is not something by which God idly observes from heaven what takes place on earth but that by which he as it were keeps his hand on the rudder and leads all events.' Accordingly, it concerns action as well as seeing.[41] God is not idle but active. He does not just look on, but works.[42] He is the permanent governor, a perpetual builder; his activity also with respect to the entire process of cosmic events is ongoing. No: Calvin's God is not 'otiosus'. For all the rocklike immutability of his decrees and secret counsels, he is nevertheless above all the active God. What characterizes him is not rigid immutability but vigorous involvement in everything that concerns his creation, humans in particular. He is not a static entity but a dynamic personality who is directly and immediately at work dealing with humanity.

It is typical for Calvin that God exercises a special providence with respect to persons,[43] specifically to believers. God's providence displays a special accent, special care, and special guidance with respect to humanity. And the immediacy with which God relates to people is a genuine characteristic of Calvin's theology. It is integral to the attractiveness and existential authenticity of his believing reflection. It also characterizes the backdrop against which his reflection takes place, a relation of person to person, of God to humans and humans to God, and humans completely in the light of the self-revealing God. In the final analysis these are the two poles with which this theology is concerned.

Precisely because God is as great as he is pictured as being in the preceding pages, there is only one being who can adequately witness to him and may witness to him and that is God himself. 'He alone is competent to bear testimony concerning himself.'[44]

---

[41] Ibid., 1.16.4 (CO 2:147); cf. CO 8:347.
[42] Ibid., 1.16.3 (CO 2:146); cf. *Comm. Gen.* 2:2 (CO 23:31): 'esse in opere assiduus'.
[43] Ibid., 1.16.3 (CO 2:146), 1.17.6 (CO 2:159): 'singularis providentia'.
[44] Ibid., 1.11.1 (CO 2:74).

In this passage one clearly detects a defensive attitude vis-à-vis any other witness about God that would not proceed from himself. He alone may and can speak about himself. And precisely for this reason Scripture alone, as Word of God, is the authentic and responsible testimony about the great God. 'Let us then willingly leave to God the knowledge of himself', he says elsewhere, 'for he alone, according to Hilary, is a sufficient witness to himself, one who is not known except by himself.'[45] God's greatness is inexpressible.[46] It is a greatness to which we succumb.[47] His essence is so enormous that it cannot really be searched out by us nor should it be. It must be adored rather than investigated.[48]

Here we encounter Calvin's characteristic modesty as it pertains to theologizing. Over and over he urges us always to remain conscious of with whom we are dealing. Precisely when we think and speak about God, great modesty behoves us, though sometimes this feels like a sign of powerlessness. Let us just stop thinking and speaking about these things, for God is too great to be examined. His being is strong enough of itself, says Calvin, to overthrow the subtleties of speculation.[49] He is so great that he has to adapt himself to our speech.[50] Also this motif repeatedly returns in his thinking.

Even the order of the world, which deservedly excites our admiration, is as deep as an abyss.[51] For this reason alone humans should know themselves small and be modest.[52] But the requirement of modesty becomes even much more urgent when they see themselves in relation to God, when they begin to speak about God and his saving actions. One may speak of the triune God only with great caution.[53] It is pride and presumption to imagine

---

[45] Ibid., 1.13.21 (CO 2:107).
[46] Ibid., 1.5.9 (CO 2:48).
[47] Ibid.
[48] Ibid. (CO 2:47).
[49] Ibid., 1.13.1 (CO 2:89).
[50] Ibid. (CO 2:90).
[51] Ibid., 1.17.2 (CO 2:155): 'gubernandi admirabilis ratio merito abyssus vocatur'.
[52] Ibid., 1.17.13 (CO 2:165): 'ad eius altitudinem non pertingit nostra infirmitas'.
[53] Ibid., 1.13.21 (CO 2:107): 'multa cautione'.

God in terms of one's own understanding.[54] Over and over, therefore, Calvin admonishes us to be modest. Modesty belongs to the fixed rules of theologizing.[55] Curiosity in these matters is vain,[56] even unworthy of the Holy Spirit, foolish and reckless.[57] And when it concerns the mystery of the incarnation, the *cur Deus homo,* Calvin dismisses all the speculation about what that could have been: 'It is not lawful to inquire further',[58] for that is impious boldness. God, after all, wants us to 'avoid stupid questions'.[59] There is good reason to regard this defensive attitude as Calvin's resistance to Late Scholasticism which over-indulged itself in every conceivable subtle speculation. One is at the same time tempted to read this strong recommendation to practise modesty in theologizing as a means of silencing pesky questioners by warning and threatening them to refrain from impious presumption. Still Calvin's deepest inspiration seems to us to be of a genuinely religious nature. The willingness to be gladly ignorant is integral to all reflection that can truly be called believing,[60] and learned ignorance is better than pre-sumptuous knowledge.[61] Augustine, too, was a proponent of this ignorance.[62]

God's majesty is also far too great to be represented by material images. This above all is a desecration of his greatness.[63] God's greatness is insulted by the depiction of an artist.[64] Actually, all physical representation is inappropriate for him,[65] for he transcends what our eyes can see.[66]

---

[54] Ibid., 1.11.8 (CO 2:80): 'pro captu suo'.

[55] Ibid., 1.14.4 (CO 2:120): 'tenenda una modestiae et sobrietatis regula'.

[56] Ibid., 1.17.1 (CO 2:154): 'tenenda modestia'.

[57] Ibid., 1.14.16 (CO 2:128): 'nec Spiritu sancto dignum fuit, inanibus historiis sine fructu curiositatem pascere'.

[58] Ibid., 2.12.4 (CO 2:343): 'fas non [est] longius inquirere'.

[59] Ibid., 2.12.5 (CO 2:344): 'stultas quaestiones fugere'; cf. CO 2:700: 'improbitas'.

[60] Ibid., 1.14.3 (CO 2:119): 'libenter ignorare'.

[61] CO 2:680: 'docta ignorantia, temeraria scientia'.

[62] Augustine, *Ep.* 130.15.28 (*ad Probam*) (MSL 33:505; CSEL 44:72.13).

[63] *Institutes* 1.11.2 (CO 2:75).

[64] Ibid., 1.11.4 (CO 2:78).

[65] Ibid., 1.11.6 (CO 2:79).

[66] Ibid., 1.11.12 (CO 2:83).

Imbart de la Tour speaks in this connection of *la mystique de puissance*.[67] If by this he means an excessive emphasis on the power and greatness of God, he is misjudging Calvin. Calvin takes God with complete seriousness and therefore has to be impressed by God's majesty, a majesty which is, after all, overwhelming. It would be misleading and incorrect, furthermore, to associate Calvin with a certain kind of mysticism. We *can* say the following. God's greatness, in Calvin, is not something he learned from a book: 'this, I guess, is how God has to be', but a reality experienced in faith. This reality is attested by Scripture, a witness which, as we will say elsewhere, strongly resonated in him. *La mystique de puissance*, in Calvin, is the vital, lived-through, faith-based conviction that, whenever we speak and think about God, he comes toward us in an utterly surprising and amazing way.

1.2. Humans: weakness and sin

Calvin has an eye for the concrete individual, people as they are in their actual situation. This actual situation is characterized, to his mind, by lostness and salvation, radical lostness, just as salvation in Christ is radical, that is, reaching the very root. To speculate about matters outside of this salvific (or non-salvific) perspective is foreign to him or in any case a secondary interest which can only serve to illustrate the actual situation.

To view this actual situation as sharply as possible Calvin asserts that as a result of their sin people would simply no longer exist if God had not spared them.[68] But they do exist, which as such is already a sign of grace.

Further, it is not at all the case that the basic nature or *essence* of humans is sinful. 'How could God, who takes pleasure in the simplest work of his hands, have been angry at the noblest of all his creatures? God is disturbed at the corruption of the work of his hands more than at the work itself.'[69] Calvin, for that matter, does not speculate about the human essence or nature in the abstract. When he makes sombre and negative-sounding

---

[67] Imbart de la Tour, 'Calvin', 168.

[68] *Institutes* 2.2.17 (CO 2:199): 'quia nisi nobis pepercisset, totius naturae interitum secum traxisset defectio'.

[69] Ibid., 2.1.11 (CO 2:185): 'Sed operis sui corruptioni magis infensus est quam oper. suo.'

statements, it is incorrect to interpret those statements as Calvin's philosophy about basic human nature. Central to him is the human condition in its present reality, that is, as it is situated in the perspective of salvation. From this perspective – which is the decisive perspective – humans are lost without Christ.

In the light of God's awesome majesty (and true self-knowledge is only possible for humans in light of the knowledge of God) Calvin views humans as *weakness* and *sin,* as beings who by their sins violate the honour of God. Humans so constituted need to be convinced of their *littleness.*

It is unavoidable that, when people know themselves confronted by God's majesty, they are weak. In his prefatory address to the king of France, Calvin stated this fact impressively.[70] It sounds like a religious confession; and this is what it really is, for the text itself makes plain that Calvin speaks from within a concrete faith-perspective when he writes:

> For what is better and more consonant with *faith* than to recognize that we are stripped naked of all virtue in order that we may be clothed by God? That we are empty of all good that we may be filled by him? That we are slaves of sin that we may be freed by him? That we are blind that we may be illumined by him? That we are crippled that we may be led by him? That we are weak that we may be supported by him? That we deprive ourselves of all reason for glorying that he alone may excel in glory and we glory in him?

This kind of confrontation and comparison of God and humans is dear to Calvin. What is left of humans when they are confronted by God's purity and majesty?[71] In the face of God's highness we can only speak of our weakness.[72] That weakness, of course, gets its grubby fatal character from sin, which in fact marks the human situation. But this does not mean – and here another perspective breaks in – that humanity in its original state of integrity, when confronted by the mighty God, was not weakness. Even then he would have had no reason to boast: 'If even when man was not permitted to boast about himself when he by God's beneficence was adorned with the highest gifts, how then must he be humbled now that by his ingratitude he has been cast down from a high

---

[70] CO 2:13.

[71] *Institutes* 1.1.3 (CO 2:33): 'divina puritas'.

[72] Ibid., 1.17.13 (CO 2:165): 'nostra infirmitas'.

point of glory to a low point of disgrace.'[73] Ultimately this is the true misery, the real distance, and that which prompts us to speak of terrible weakness: namely, sin. This sinful weakness bears the stamp of guilt. To look for an excuse in the corruption of our nature is really to taunt God, says Calvin.[74] Not only do the gifts of God become impure to impure people – by themselves they cannot become impure for they come from God[75] – but because sin is the decisive factor by which humans become radically and fundamentally affected in their relation to God, Calvin dares to speak of a 'hideous deformity'.[76] It is for this reason also that he dares to speak of human corruption. And worst of all in all this is that God's honour is negatively affected by sin. 'Man annihilated the whole glory of God.'[77] Thus, from this kind of consideration (but this is the only decisive perspective), one has to repeat after Augustine that 'nothing is ours but sin'.[78]

Also in this light we must read Calvin when he speaks of our dullness which is insensitive to God's testimonies,[79] our coarseness which cannot encompass God's inexpressible glory.[80] What do little humans mean by trying to break into the inner recesses of divine wisdom?[81] In the face of that wisdom our wisdom turns into folly.[82] The reference here is, without any doubt, to that true wisdom, that is, the wisdom which leads to salvation, salvific wisdom, when with full concurrence he cites Chrysostom's saying: 'the foundation of our philosophy is humility'.[83]

---

[73] Ibid., 2.2.1 (CO 2:186): 'ab extrema gloria in extremam ignominiam'.

[74] Ibid., 2.1.10 (CO 2:184): 'ne in Deum ipsum naturae authorem stringamus accusationem'. Cf. ibid., 1.15.1 (CO 2:134).

[75] Ibid., 2.2.16 (CO 2:199): 'non quod per se inquinari possint, quatenus a Deo proficiscuntur'.

[76] Ibid., 1.15.4 (CO 2:138): 'horrenda deformitas'.

[77] Ibid., 2.1.4 (CO 2:179): 'exinanivit totam Dei gloriam'. Cf. ibid., 2.6.1 (CO 2:247).

[78] Ibid., 2.2.27 (CO 2:209); Augustine, Serm. 176.5 (MSL 38:952): 'nostrum nihil nisi peccatum'.

[79] Institutes 1.5.11 (CO 2:49): 'noster stupor'.

[80] Ibid., 1.13.1 (CO 2:90): 'mentes nostrae pro sua tarditate'.

[81] Ibid., 3.24.4 (CO 2:714): 'homuncio'.

[82] Ibid., 4.10.24 (CO 2:885): 'stultescere et nostram nobis ipsis et omnium hominum sapientiam oportet, quo solum illum sapere permittamus'.

[83] Ibid., 2.2.11 (CO 2:194): 'fundamentum nostrae philosophiae esse humilitatem' (Chrysostom, Homil. de profectu Evangelii [Paris, 1834–40], 3:360).

2. God is a majesty of love; humanity is his image

2.1. God: a majesty of love

To Calvin God is a loving father. But in a stunning way he also compares the affection of God with the love of mothers: 'The affection which he bears toward us is far more ardent and vehement than the love of all mothers.'[84]

In the first section of this chapter we first show how to Calvin God's love already speaks in the *creation* of which that love is the creating cause. This creation as such must already be for us humans a summons to *love in return*.

The love of God is evident, further, from his special *providence* on behalf of humans. God shows us the most brilliant sign of his love in his Son, *Jesus Christ*. But God's love is always the love of sublime majesty.

Finally, we note that in the love relation between God and humans, the latter are touched by the love of God down to the deepest level of their *subjectivity*: the whole human person is incorporated in this love relation.

God is a figure of majesty who loves. One already makes this discovery by listening to the testimonies of nature.[85] If, says Calvin, one asks about the motive which caused him to create and to maintain all this, one will find that it is only his own goodness. Indeed, even if this is the only cause, it should be more than enough to invite us to his love: after all, as the prophet teaches, there is not a single creature upon which his mercy has not been poured out.[86] His own goodness alone was for him the motive in creating them all and it is the only cause. One wonders whether in this saying there is a tacit protest against any additional causality, any co-authorship of some other agency, or can we say that Calvin simply wants to say that it was only goodness that prompted him to create the world?

Noting the whole of Calvin's discussion on this point, we have the impression that he meant especially the former but this is not to deny that God is viewed here as the person who, motivated by

---

[84] *Comm. Is.* 49:15 (CO 37:204–5): 'Nam affectus ipsius erga nos matrum omnium amorem ardore et vehementia longe exsuperat.'

[85] *Institutes* 1.5.6 (CO 2:46): 'naturae testimonia'.

[86] Psalm 145:9.

goodness, became a creating God. Here the word 'goodness' is used but with the rich import of 'love', for that goodness has to be for us more than sufficient reason to lure us to his love. The reference here is to the loving God, for we read further: 'There is not a single creature, as the prophet admonishes us, upon which his mercy has not been poured out.' It is precisely in the creation that he shows us his wonderful goodness.[87] That creation must be for us a summons to thanksgiving and answering love. 'Attracted by such glorious goodness and beneficence, let us apply ourselves to love and honour him with our whole heart.'[88] That is the calling of a human, who is a 'microcosm', 'because he is a rare example of God's power, goodness, and wisdom'.[89] The point is that this 'example' himself or herself learns to know and to enjoy God's love: 'No person will spontaneously and eagerly surrender himself in obedience to God except him who has tasted his fatherly love and feels drawn to love and honour him in return.'[90] It has to be said that in the light of these texts God comes powerfully to the fore as the lovable God who lures (*illicere*) and invites us to give him the answer of our heart (*toto pectore*). The idea, naturally, is to bind ourselves to him in obedience, but that must happen with eagerness (*libenter*), which is possible only if one has first tasted his fatherly love (*gustato paterno eius amore*). This is the foundation of a reciprocal love relation (*vicissim*). We are talking about God and human beings and this relation must fundamentally be a love relation. We are further struck by the fact that, according to Calvin, religion seizes people down to the bottom of their subjectivity. It is a matter of the heart. If one wants to charge that Calvin, in the context of his theological thought as a whole, has too strongly emphasized the Law (but precisely in this connection he dares to write: 'If we want to love properly, we must in the first place look toward God'),[91] one must always see this kind of text as the decisive background from the perspective of which all attachment to law at bottom receives another colour.

---

[87] *Institutes* 1.14.2 (CO 2:118): 'mirifica erga nos sua bonitas'.
[88] Ibid., 1.14.22 (CO 2:134).
[89] Ibid., 1.5.3 (CO 2:43): 'potentiae, bonitatis et sapientiae specimen'.
[90] Ibid., 1.5.3 (CO 2:43).
[91] Ibid., 2.8.55 (CO 2:306): 'si veram diligendi lineam tenere libet, . . . primum convertendi sunt oculi . . . in Deum'.

God's goodness is evident in a special way from his providence. God's governance is extended to all his works.[92] One must not restrict it, therefore, so that it only influences nature. That is to rob God of his honour and in that way his special goodness toward every individual is diminished.[93] This exceptional goodness of God leaps especially to the fore in the case of sinners. He pursues them with his mercy.[94] Anyway, we owe it to his immeasurable goodness when a person does no evil.[95] But this immeasurable goodness is never altogether seen apart from holy reverence toward God. There is always a concomitant note here of the fear-inspiring majesty which God is. Only in light of the fear of God's wrath[96] do we understand well what it is to live in God's mercy and can we receive that goodness with fitting gratitude. In this connection Calvin speaks of the redemptive work Christ has accomplished for us. Certainly it is not his concern here or anywhere else to settle the question what in God is primary: his fear-inspiring majesty or his awe-inspiring goodness. The question is: how should humans relate to God the Lord; what should be their attitude and their knowledge? Rather than telling us how God is in himself, he prefers to say how humans should relate to their divine partner. And his conclusion is that both sentiments, 'love' (*amor*) and 'fear' (*formido*), must shape their attitude. (Nor does he here want to determine which sentiment is the more important.) He does clearly indicate that apart from Christ we must consider God as being, in a way, hostile to us.[97] 'We can only embrace his benevolence and fatherly love in Christ.'[98]

Indeed, as will be explained at the proper place, Christ is never viewed apart from God's great majesty; yet he is the most brilliant sign of God's love. 'His face, full of grace and generosity, shines out in Christ.'[99] Christ's death is 'a model of measureless

---

[92] Ibid., 1.16.3 (CO 2:146); cf. ibid., 1.16.4 (CO 2:148).
[93] Ibid., 1.16.3 (CO 2:146): 'singularis erga unumquemque Dei bonitas'.
[94] Ibid., 1.5.7 (CO 2:46).
[95] Ibid., 2.3.5 (CO 2:214): 'immensa bonitas'.
[96] Ibid., 2.16.2 (CO 2:369): 'formido irae Dei'.
[97] Ibid.: 'nobis quodammodo infestus'.
[98] Ibid.: 'benevolentiam eius paternamque charitatem nonnisi in Christo amplexemur'.
[99] Ibid., 2.7.8 (CO 2:259): 'In Christo autem facies eius gratiae et lenitatis plena . . . relucet.'

mercy'.[100] In his suffering shines a goodness which can never be praised enough.[101]

It must strike the reader that in this kind of statement Calvin with fondness uses the word *suavitas*.[102] This gives a human accent to his discourse. It betrays his attention to humans in the sector of the God–humanity relation. Also the affectivity of the human subject is involved. 'In the present life', he writes, 'we begin, through various benefits, to taste the sweetness of the divine generosity.'[103] This, too, belongs to the encounter between God and us human beings: it impacts us so deeply that we humans can 'taste' God's goodness.

2.2. *Humanity as God's image*

The love of God is creative. This applies especially to human beings. The creative love of God has made him or her into his own image: a human being is the image of God.

We will now give a provisional sketch of what humanity as the image of God amounts to. In chapter 2 this sketch will be given its indispensable rounding off when we deal with Christ, the image of God *par excellence*. Here already we raise the subject of *the glory of that image*. We consider the *malformation* of that image by sin and the *remnants* left after the fall. We speak of the *restoration* of the image of God in humanity and the role it plays in the *new* life of the redeemed. We will then conclude this section with two distinct comments.

After the preceding section, in which we sketched humanity in its weakness and sin, the question may arise whether the furtherance of God's greatness and honour does not occur at the expense of humanity. Do we not get the impression that Calvin fails to do justice to humanity? This kind of question arises quite naturally; even Wendel writes: 'Calvin did not have a very high opinion of humanity itself even before original sin.' To support this question he cites a passage from the second book of the *Institutes*:

---

[100] Ibid., 2.16.11 (CO 2:377): 'immensae misericordiae specimen'.
[101] Ibid., 2.16.12 (CO 2:378): 'bonitas nunquam satis laudata'.
[102] Ibid., 2.7.7 (CO 2:258): 'suavior gratia'; ibid., 3.2.23 (CO 2:417): 'dulcedo et suavitas gratiae'.
[103] Ibid., 3.9.3 (CO 2:525): 'benignitatis suavitatem delibare'.

> Even if a man had remained free from all stain and perfectly sound, even then his state would have been too lowly for him to have been able to penetrate to God without a Mediator. Then what must we say now that by his deadly fall he plunged himself into death and hell, now that he is defiled by so many stains, now that he reeks as a result of his own depravity; in a word: now that he is covered with a whole range of curses?[104]

We would prefer to say that Calvin looks up to God in profound reverence and at the same time has a high view of humanity as well. This latter point will be well supported in what follows.

Both points are clearly registered. God is unbounded greatness. But humanity has its own glory and is certainly not unqualified worthlessness. Human greatness is circumscribed, created, and remains, and may remain, intact even before the great majesty of God. Precisely because both are as they are, there is demonstrable tension in the field of encounter between God and humanity. But this undoubtedly presupposes that humanity has its own given dignity and greatness. It is the age-old problem of the compatibility of God's existence as sovereign freedom alongside of and with the created freedom which defines humanity.

What is the source of human greatness and dignity? All the statements made by Calvin on this point tend toward a similar appraisal: humans are the image of God. This is their true greatness.[105] Among all God's works human beings are 'the noblest and most remarkable specimen of justice, wisdom, and goodness'.[106] By means of his exceptional gifts Adam gave expression to the glory of his Maker.[107] Humans are a mirror of God's glory.[108] By their body they make their Maker admirable. God's glory shines in their external form.[109] The soul, however, is the part in which the deity shines out most powerfully.[110] This microcosm,[111] this workshop and storehouse filled with an

---

[104] Ibid., 2.12.1 (CO 2:340); Wendel, *Calvin*, 215.
[105] *Institutes* 1.5.3 (CO 2:43).
[106] Ibid., 1.15.1 (CO 2:134): 'nobilissimum ac maxime spectabile iustitiae eius, et sapientiae, et bonitatis specimen'.
[107] Ibid., 1.15.3 (CO 2:138).
[108] Ibid., 1.15.4 (CO 2:138): 'speculum gloriae Dei'.
[109] Ibid., 1.15.3 (CO 2:136); cf. ibid., 2.25.8 (CO 2:739): 'in homine externo'.
[110] Ibid., 2.25.6 (CO 2:735): 'pars, in qua maxime refulget divinitas'.
[111] Ibid., 1.5.3 (CO 2:43).

inestimable abundance of goods, this person, ought to break forth into praises of his or her creator.[112] This image of God – remarkable again is Calvin's attention to people's inner experience – is extended to the human consciousness. Humans are endowed with a certain sense of divinity,[113] with a consciousness that a God exists,[114] a very strong suspicion that there is a God.[115] It is scarcely conceivable that one could limn human dignity in more positive, more appreciative and expressive terms. As a result of sin, however, this image of God, humanity, has become a 'hideous deformity'.[116] Strictly speaking – and that is how we must take this – this means a radical break, total decline, such a thorough malformation and deformation of the image of God that nothing but a few remnants are left. And even this is still surprising: 'if he had not spared us, the fall would have meant the destruction of our whole nature',[117] for that horrendous deformation is so hideous precisely because it most intensely touches what humanity is: its being the image of God. But Calvin is realistic enough to point out these remnants. They are the remnants left in Adam's descendants after his fall. The things Calvin sums up are glittering fragments; it sounds like a tribute to pagan antiquity but he does not hesitate to characterize them as gifts of the Spirit.[118] 'From these examples we can learn how many gifts the Lord left to human nature even after it was despoiled of its true good.'[119] Naturally we must be keenly aware that we are here on a different terrain! There is a world of difference between the level of being the image of God in which the intimate relation between God and humanity, the true good, the firm foundation of truth, comes to expression and the goods of human nature which God has left to fallen humanity. In this context Calvin appropriates Augustine's distinction:

[112] Ibid., 1.5.4 (CO 2:43).
[113] Ibid., 1.3.1 (CO 2:36): 'divinitatis sensus'.
[114] Ibid., 1.4.4 (CO 2:41): 'Deitatis sensus.'
[115] Ibid., 1.3.1 (CO 2:36): 'de numine impressio vehementissima'.
[116] Ibid., 1.15.4 (CO 2:138): 'horrenda deformitas'.
[117] Ibid., 2.2.17 (CO 2:199): 'quia nisi nobis pepercisset, totius naturae interitum secum traxisset defectio'.
[118] Ibid., 2.2.14–15 (CO 2:198).
[119] Ibid., 2.2.15 (CO 2:199).

For Augustine (with whose opinion, as we have said, the master of the Sentences and the Schoolmen are compelled to agree) was completely correct when he taught that just as the gifts of grace were taken away from man after the fall, so the natural gifts which remained were corrupt: not that the gifts as such can be defiled (seeing they come from God), but because they ceased to be pure to defiled man that he might not secure any renown from them.

The way back, redemption, is the way back to the restoration of the image of God. To restore this image of God is the purpose of regeneration. Just what the fullness of the image of God actually implies (*plena imaginis definitio*) is clearly evident only from the restoration of the corrupt nature. 'In fact this image consisted in the light of the intellect, in the integrity of the heart, and the soundness of all the parts.'[120]

We must fully highlight the role humanity as image of God plays in Calvin's thinking, for that role is crucially important.[121] The whole of the new life applied to us by Christ is controlled by it. The purpose of the law is to bring out God's image in us; it is to shape humanity in conformity with God's purity.[122] Humanity is God's image; the prohibition 'thou shalt not kill' is in part based on this.[123] The task of penitence, which in Calvin is given a place after regeneration, is precisely to bring about in us the reformation of the image of God.[124] And when in the *Institutes* (Book III, chapter 6) Calvin starts speaking about the Christian life, his fundamental starting-point lies in the newness of life by which the image of God is restored in us.[125] In this connection the Christian demand of mutual well-being is grounded in an appeal to humanity's being the image of God.[126] For God sees in his children 'the marks and lineaments of his own

---

[120] Ibid., 1.15.4 (CO 2:138): 'hunc regenerationis esse finem, ut nos Christus ad imaginem Dei reformet. . . . Unde colligimus imaginem Dei initio in luce mentis, in cordis rectitudine, partiumque omnium sanitate conspicuam fuisse'.

[121] On this see esp. T. F. Torrance, *Calvin's Doctrine of Man* (Grand Rapids, 1957).

[122] *Institutes* 2.8.51 (CO 2:303).

[123] Ibid., 2.8.40 (CO 2:295): 'Quia imago Dei est homo, et caro nostra.'

[124] Ibid., 3.3.9 (CO 2:440): 'ut imago Dei in nobis reformetur'.

[125] Ibid., 3.6.1 (CO 2:501).

[126] Ibid., 3.7.6 (CO 2:510): 'imago Dei in cunctis consideranda'.

face'.[127] They reflect their heavenly father in righteousness and holiness.[128]

a. In connection with the divine image in humans Calvin speaks of *participation*. On this topic we now want to make a few remarks.

At that time, I say, when he had been advanced to the highest degree of honour, Scripture attributes to him nothing other than that he had been created in the image of God [Gen. 1:27], thereby indicating that man was made happy, not because of his own goods, but by communion with God.[129]

It is clear from the immediate context that *'participatio'* is here contrasted with *'propria bona'*. The text is polemical; we detect in it a protest against the view that humanity owes it to its own excellence that it may be the image of God. This much is clear: the expression 'image of God' is by no means used in a favourable sense: Scripture only attributes to 'man' that he was created after God's image. This minimalizing use of the term 'image of God' is to be explained in light of the clearly charged intent of *Institutes* Book II, chapter 2. Calvin asserts that humans have been robbed of the freedom of their will and the affirmation is so precious to him because free will is the most stubborn stronghold in which humans could maintain something of their own ground for boasting. It needs to be utterly clear how important it is that humans be deprived of every shred of false glorying (*falsa gloriatio*). It is a polemical text. The two poles are not, in Calvin's mind, peacefully juxtaposed here, but he emphatically posits God's greatness to deprive humans of all reason to glory. It is as if he reluctantly admits that 'man' is the image of God: 'that, then, is all'. From other statements we know that something great lies behind this expression.[130] We scarcely need to say that we must avoid thinking of any notion of *participatio* in an Aristotelian sense. Calvin not only repeatedly distinguishes his own position from that of scholasticism,[131] but also his fierce

[127] Ibid., 3.17.5 (CO 2:593): 'notae et lineamenta vultus sui'.
[128] Ibid., 3.18.1 (CO 2:604): 'iustitia et sanctitate Patrem referentes'.
[129] Ibid., 2.2.1 (CO 2:186): 'quo scl. insinuat, non propriis bonis sed Dei participatione fuisse beatum'.
[130] See above, pp. 15ff.
[131] Cf. Hunter, *Teaching of Calvin*, 40–1; Ganoczy, *Young Calvin*, 210–12.

polemic against Osiander on the understanding of justification and regeneration sufficiently demonstrates that any *participation*-notion in essentialist fashion is foreign to Calvin.[132] He is utterly opposed to any form of *deification*. However, to translate *Dei participatio* by 'communion with God' seems to us to be too weak:[133] 'man' is happy as a result of *communion* with God. The use of the term *participation* is too striking to thus translate it in a weakened form. It simply means a 'partaking' here, even though one wishes to banish all trace of deification and is eager to abstain from all further philosophical speculation. The latter must not be allowed to influence the correct translation of the word. In another passage of the *Institutes* (Book I, 13, 14) Calvin states that we partake in God by the Spirit.[134] In Calvin's commentary on 2 Peter 1:4[135] we can find out how he would have us understand the expression.

b. Humanity as image of God is the most remarkable example of his glory. But this glory also shines through in the creation and in Holy Scripture. In the *Institutes* one can find beautiful statements concerning both. We will conclude our pieces on God and humanity with just a few comments on this subject.

The world has been created as a theatre of God's glory[136] and signs of God's glory also glitter in the individual parts of the world.[137]

The value and sublimity of Holy Scripture cannot be more graphically expressed than precisely in those words which suggest a close connection with God's greatness and majesty. Scripture has a majesty of its own,[138] for God speaks in it. This majestic

---

[132] Cf. Wendel, *Calvin*, 255–63.

[133] *Institutie*, trans. Sizoo, 1:255.

[134] Cf. *Institutes* 1.13.14 (CO 2:102): 'sic per ipsum in Dei participationem venimus'. Cf. *Institutie*, trans. Sizoo, 1:119.

[135] Cf. *Comm. II Petr.* 1:4 (CO 55:446–7): 'Notemus ergo hunc esse evangelii finem, ut aliquando conformes Deo reddamur: id vero est quasi deificari, ut ita loquamur. Caeterum naturae nomen hic non substantiam, sed qualitatem designat.' It is clear that Calvin's concern about the deification of humanity leads him to a cautious exegesis of this passage.

[136] *Institutes* 1.5.5 (CO 2:45): 'spectaculum gloriae Dei'.

[137] Ibid., 1.15.3 (CO 2:138): 'lineamenta quaedam gloriae Dei'.

[138] Ibid., 1.7.5 (CO 2:60): 'sua maiestas'.

character of Scripture comes to the fore repeatedly.[139] In Scripture the majesty of the Spirit is everywhere visible.[140] But this majesty as such is also – directly – called a heavenly majesty.[141] The Gospel and the Word of God have their own majesty.[142] It is a figurative way of speaking, of course, but there is inherent in it a splendid reality, an effulgence of divine majesty which is so real that Calvin more than once dares to speak of the Scriptures' own majesty. It is, of course, a given property; we would say: Scripture shares in the majesty of God. That majesty has been conferred on it and thus become its own. We are making this point with some emphasis to state clearly that, according to Calvin, a created entity (as Scripture is) can very well possess a value of its own without in any way diminishing God. In this discussion on Scripture we sense no tension whatever between the Creator and the creature (Scripture). If we cannot always say the same thing when referring to Calvin's discourse about God and humanity, this must not be attributed to the fact that he does not dare ascribe to persons a given value of their own, but rather to a somewhat aggressive anxiety to maintain the greatness and honour of God. It is, in fact, a characteristic human possibility to want to appropriate something from God for one's own honour. The apostle Paul was also familiar with that concern and that struggle.

3. Humanity must honour God

In the confrontation with the living God, who is awesome in majesty and most adorable on account of his love, human beings learn to know themselves. The content of this knowledge has been described in the two preceding sections. But we cannot confine ourselves to this knowledge. In the bipolarity between God and 'man' the latter is called to an attitude of trust and love, respect and obedience. In this section we want to devote special attention to these two postures.

[139] Ibid., 1.7.4 (CO 2:59): 'Dei maiestas'; cf. ibid., 1.8.1 (CO 2:61) and 1.8.1 (CO 2:62): 'divinum quidam spirare Scripturas'.

[140] Cf. ibid., 1.9.2 (CO 2:71), where especially the place of the Holy Spirit is emphasized.

[141] Ibid., 1.8.11 (CO 2:67): 'caelestis maiestas'. Cf. ibid., 1.18.13 (CO 2:69): 'dignitas et maiestas Scripturae'; and ibid., 3.20.14 (CO 2:639), where a *maiestas* is ascribed to the Word.

[142] Ibid., 3.2.10 (CO 2:405): 'Evangelii maiestas.'

In the first section we will discuss what the assignment of *honouring God* means to Calvin. In the second section we will explore the background of this thematic complex in Calvin; and finally, in a third section we will say a word or two about the *relation* between the *honour of God* and *human salvation*.

3.1. Honouring God

Minister: What is the chief end of human life?

Child: That men should know God by whom they were created.

M: What then is true and right knowledge of God?

C: When he is so known that his own proper honour is done him.

M: What is the right way of honouring him?

C: To put all our trust in him; to study to serve him all our life, by obeying his will; to call upon him, whenever any need impels us, seeking in him salvation and whatever good things can be desired; and lastly, to acknowledge him with both heart and mouth to be the only author of all good things.[143]

Appropriate to humans vis-à-vis the great and loving majesty which is God is an attitude of reverence, a posture of humble homage. The fitting response to self-revealing greatness, to glory making itself manifest, is honour. It is the reaction of spontaneous and sincere admiration to a value whose excellence and supremacy cannot be doubted.[144] Precisely because God's glory is greater than human words can express, Calvin insists, with unconditional severity, that the honour of that majestic Lord be inviolate. Consistently, in almost identical words, we hear the demand that God's honour must remain inviolate.[145] His name, which is most holy,[146] must be sanctified,[147] particularly as a sign of fear and veneration.[148] Because he alone is God, he alone can demand for himself the honour of the deity.[149] Calvin, accordingly, is opposed

---

[143] *Catèch. Gen.*, 1542 (CO 6:10).

[144] Cf. Doumergue, *Jean Calvin*, 4:27; Reuter, *Grundverständnis der Theologie Calvins*, 137.

[145] CO 2:11: 'quomodo Dei gloriae sua constet in terris incolumitas'. Cf. *Institutes* 3.4.27 (CO 2:478), 3.12.3 (CO 2:555), 3.13.1 (CO 2:559).

[146] *Institutes* 2.8.22 (CO 2:282).

[147] CO 2:16.

[148] CO 2:28.

[149] *Institutes* 1.11.1 (CO 2:75); cf. ibid., 1.12.1 (CO 2:87).

to the distinction between *latria* and *dulia*.[150] This is only one of the numerous passages in which he evinces meticulous concern to avoid transferring even one iota of divine honour to a creature. Nothing exists but to serve the honour of God. The domain of his honour has no boundaries. The story of it is told by the firmament;[151] infants proclaim it.[152] That honour is manifest even in sin. Even though the first human, misled by the devil, totally annihilated the honour of God,[153] yet his fall was to the glory of God![154] Thus also the glory of the Father shone in the man who was blind from birth.[155] And when it is impossible to respond, Calvin is inclined to say: that, too, is for the glory of God. God's glory is not only a manifestation of his greatness; it can also be the concealment of that greatness.[156]

To advance the honour of God was one of the primary manifestations of the original integrity of humanity.[157] This, accordingly, is the splendid task of the elect.[158] In his letters Calvin regularly reminds Christian witnesses to defend the honour of God:[159] 'Those who believe would rather have the whole world perish than that the minutest part of the glory of God be withdrawn.'[160]

For Calvin these powerful utterances were not just words. When it concerned the honour of God he was relentless.[161] He

---

[150] Ibid., 1.12.2 (CO 2:88): 'latriae et duliae ... distinctio, quo impune viderentur angelis et mortuis transcribi divini honores'.

[151] Ibid., 1.6.4 (CO 2:55).

[152] Psalm 8:3; *Institutes* 1.16.3 (CO 2:146); cf. ibid., 1.16.2 (CO 2:145).

[153] *Institutes* 2.1.4 (CO 2:179): 'Adam diaboli ... blasphemiis abreptus ... exinanivit totam Dei gloriam.'

[154] *Institutes* 1.15.8 (CO 2:143): 'ut ex illius lapsu gloriae suae materiam eliceret'.

[155] John 9:3a; *Institutes* 1.17.1 (CO 2:154).

[156] Proverbs 25:2: 'It is the glory of God to conceal things, but the glory of kings is to search things out' (NRSV). Cf. Hunter, *Teaching of Calvin*, 59.

[157] *Institutes* 2.3.4 (CO 2:213): 'praecipua pars rectitudinis Dei gloriae studium'; cf. ibid., 3.3.7 (CO 2:439).

[158] Cf. Reuter, *Grundverständnis der Theologie Calvins*, 227.

[159] Cf. Imbart de la Tour, 'Calvin', 171.

[160] *Comm. Gal.* 5:12 (CO 50:249): 'Nam quanto praestantior est Dei gloria hominum salute, tanto in sui amorem ac studium altius rapere nos debet ... ideoque malint totum mundum interire quam decedere aliquid gloriae Dei.' Cf. *Serm. Deut.* 13 (CO 27:266): 'Car si nous considerons que c'est de sa gloire, elle merite bien d'estre plus precieuse que tout le monde.'

[161] A. Lang, *Johannes Calvin* (Leipzig, 1909), 94.

defends his conduct relative to Ameaux's misstep with an appeal to the honour of God.[162] 'A dog barks when it sees that its owner is being attacked. I would certainly be a great coward if I saw that God's truth was being attacked and then remained silent, not uttering a sound.'[163] In the controversy with Servetus, the issue was basically the same. He was mercilessly ferocious precisely because he thought that God's honour was being violated.[164] This motive was also present in his *Petit traicte* of 1543: 'But the glory of God, which is the issue here, must be more precious to us than this decaying and transitory life, which, truth to tell, is only a shadow.'[165] And when on his deathbed he declared: 'I have never written anything against anyone out of hatred but always faithfully set forth what I deemed to be to the glory of God',[166] he, who so rarely spoke of himself, undoubtedly in all honesty revealed a motive which continually set him in motion and impressed upon the Genevan Reformer such a remarkably unusual but also such a sublime stamp.[167]

Next to honour to the supreme majesty stands the requirement of complete and unconditional obedience. In this respect as well the life of Calvin mirrors his doctrine. That obedience is the mark of true wisdom. 'Wisdom is the opposite of scholastic speculation and is characterized by obedient subordination to God.'[168] God's name compels obedience and disobedience violates his majesty.[169] At its core Adam's temptation was the test of his obedience.[170] 'It is enough', wrote Calvin in a farewell letter to Farel, 'that I live for Christ, who, both in life and in death, is gain to his own.'[171]

---

[162] Ibid., 122; W. Walker, *John Calvin: The Organizer of Reformed Protestantism, 1509–1564* (New York, 1969), 296.
[163] Letter to Marguerite of Navarre, 28 April 1545 (CO 12:ep. 634).
[164] Walker, *John Calvin*, 329.
[165] CO 6:576; cf. 'Prefatory Address to King Francis I of France' (CO 2:12).
[166] CO 9:893 (*Discours d'adieu aux ministres*).
[167] Cf. Lang, *Johannes Calvin*, 90.
[168] CO 34:278.
[169] *Institutes* 2.1.4 (CO 2:179), 1.7.4 (CO 2:59).
[170] Ibid., 2.1.4 (CO 2:178): 'obedientiae examen'.
[171] Letter to Farel, 2 May 1564 (CO 20:ep. 4104).

To our minds the same thing is perhaps less attractively but certainly as probingly stated, soberly and hard, by the expressions: 'the yoke of his majesty'[172] and 'the veneration of his majesty'.[173]

3.2. The background of this theme

It is not surprising that, in light of such abundant use of the term 'the honour of God' and the ascription of such an impressive role to the divine majesty described by it, people have inquired into the background and sources which explain why Calvin is so obsessed especially with this term. Not very convincing is the reference to the term 'gloire' which acquired such grand status among French kings. Also the influence of Roman civil law has been cited. According to Bohatec,[174] the term 'majesty' among Romans originally had sacral meaning.[175] Reuter refers to the *devotio moderna* which speaks of the mystical experience of God's majesty[176] and then continues: 'thus in Calvin both secular and spiritual ideas combine to form his biblical (though scantily documented) concept of the majesty God possesses'. The last, parenthetical, addition seems odd. In Scripture the concept of majesty hardly plays a modest role and the Reformer's entire oeuvre shows that this did not escape him. The Hebrew word *kabôd*, which encompasses the whole conceptual circle of glory, majesty, and splendour, is obviously significant.[177] It refers to something that gives weight, to someone who is impressive, to prestige and possessions, and so forth. In the New Testament, this even more expressly becomes the glory of the God of Jesus Christ, who proves himself to be a most devoted and passionate defender of the Father's glory.[178] Reuter does point with emphasis

---

[172] *Institutes* 2.8.13 (CO 2:275): 'sub divinae maiestatis jugum'.

[173] Ibid., 2.8.8 (CO 2:272): 'numinis sui cultus'. Sizoo, *Institutie*, 1:393, translates this as 'de dienst van zijn majesteit'.

[174] J. Bohatec, *Budé und Calvin. Studien zur Gedankenwelt des französischen Frühhumanismus* (Graz, 1950), 338; cf. ibid., 343–5.

[175] Cf. Wendel, *Calvin*, 126; O. Ritschl, *Dogmengeschichte des Protestantismus*, 3:174.

[176] Cf. Reuter, *Grundverständnis der Theologie Calvins*, 139.

[177] Zie *Bijbels Wdb.*, col. 613ff. Beyerhaus (*Studien zur Staatsanschauung Calvins*, 52–60) provides an important listing of the ways in which the idea of sovereignty is expressed.

[178] Cf. the Gospel of John.

(and convincingly) to the great influence exerted on John Calvin by some of his nominalistically-minded mentors, specifically John Major and his intellectual kin Gregory of Rimini and Bradwardine, and finally Duns Scotus. Although the spiritual background is very different, nominalistic, voluntaristic thinking shows striking resemblance to the ancient Eastern–Jewish conception of God's direct, sovereign and supremely powerful rule. It lies outside the scope of this study to demonstrate this in detail, but the God who hardens the heart of Pharaoh[179] and tests Abraham,[180] and does everything he wills to do is not too far removed from the God-image of nominalistic theology.[181]

This preconception (*Vorverständnis*), which stems from the Reformer's period of training at the College of Montaigu in Paris, combined with and fructified by the way the Bible speaks about God and the Father of Christ, seems to us to be the background of his striking view of God's majesty and the honour due to it. Christ 'breathed heart and soul the glory of the Father'.[182] This beautiful saying arises from the very heart of Holy Scripture.

3.3. *The relation between God's honour and human salvation*

'A cause more valuable and precious than your salvation: that is the glory of God and the advancement of the kingdom of Jesus Christ. Therein consists your salvation and that of the whole world.'[183]

'God so provided for our salvation that in faithfulness to himself he put his own glory in first place. To this end, accordingly, he created the whole world that it might be a theatre of his glory.'[184] In the same connection occurs also this striking text: 'But Scripture bids us contemplate in the will of God something

---

[179] Exodus 4:21; 7:3; 10:1, 20.

[180] Genesis 22:1.

[181] Cf. P. Vignaux, *La pensée au moyen âge* (Paris, 1938), 141ff.; idem, DThC 11:col. 717–84.

[182] *Institutes* 3.15.8 (CO 2:585): 'ille Patris gloriam toto pectore spiravit'.

[183] Letter of Calvin to the King of Navarre (CO 19:ep. 3664): 'voire d'une chose plus digne et precieuse, cest de la gloire de Dieu et de ladvancement de regne de Iesuschrist, ou consiste le salut de vous et de tout le monde'.

[184] CO 8:294: 'Sic Deo fuisse curae salutem nostram, ut sui non oblitus gloriam suam primo loco haberet, adeoque totum mundum hoc fine condidisse, ut gloriae suae theatrum foret.'

far different: namely, first righteousness and equity in the first place, then his concern for our own salvation.'[185]

These texts, which undeniably betray a certain tension between God's honour, his righteousness, and human salvation, may understandably give rise to the question of priority. Which comes through as the more important: God's honour or human salvation? *Justitia* has a broader and deeper meaning than the purely juridical term 'justice': it signifies the inviolable correctness and unassailable course of action of God, *the right order of God,* which is above all human criticism.[186] This is a firm foundation for his honour wherever and however he acts. The obvious meaning of the statement cited above is undoubtedly that God's honour is more important than human salvation. The passages cited betray Calvin's defensive reaction to the idea of making the salvation of humans separate and primary, regardless of and in isolation from the higher priority of God's greatness and honour. Once we have recognized the existence of this tension between divine honour and human salvation we have to admit that it is Calvin himself who forges the link by which all competition (let alone discrepancy) is eliminated.

God's honour is advanced above all by the elect; the church counts it among its tasks to realize it; even the reprobate make their contribution to this end (as we will see at length in chapter 3, section 3). If we view the matter from this angle and penetrate critically to the core of it the whole issue of the honour of God and human salvation has lost its acuteness. Human beings relate to the high God in such a way that to God's glory they contribute to their own salvation. Fundamentally there is no contrast but a concurrent structure. The basic affirmation – and it carries a hint of defensiveness – reads: God is greater than humanity.

But this implies that both poles, hence also the human pole, remain intact. In fact there is no problem of opposition between God's honour and human salvation.[187]

---

[185] *Institutes* 3.8.11 (CO 2:522): 'Scriptura in voluntate Dei considerare iubet . . . iustitiam primum et aequitatem, deinde salutis nostrae curam.'

[186] Cf. ibid., 3.23.8 (CO 2:705): 'Ubi mentionem gloriae Dei audis, illic iustitiam cogita.'

[187] Cf. *Comm. Eph.* 1:12 (CO 51:152): 'Ut simus in laudem gloriae ipsius. Quia demum illustratur in nobis Dei gloria, si nihil simus quam vasa eius misericordiae. Ac nomen gloriae *kat'exochèn*, peculiariter eam significat, quae

4. Tensions in Calvin's theology

In this section we will first of all offer an inventory of the primary 'tension-words' which characterize the divine–human relation in Calvin. In connection with these words, and also to conclude this chapter, we will criticize the opinion of several authors who say that Calvin's theological thought is filled with the tension of a double God-image.

4.1. 'Tension-words' in Calvin's theology

'Therefore we are robbing the Lord if we claim anything for ourselves.'[188] And in his first letter to Duchemin, which deals with the Catholic cult, a worship service in which no Protestant may join, Calvin writes as follows: 'The sacrilege of the mass consists in uncovering one's head before an image or in encouraging some superstition which can obscure the glory of God, profane the religion pertaining to him or in corrupting its truth.'[189] Doumergue comments on this threatening collision between God's honour and that of humankind as follows: 'those who accord too much to human beings diminish and lose them; those who accord too much (it seems) to God strengthen and save humans. This fact appears to defy all logic, all argument'.[190] Though it is not the most fascinating thing to do it is certainly, in our view, most illustrative, to note with special attention those words which speak of the relation between God and humans with an inner tension which betrays an almost painfully scrupulous concern to honour God's supreme greatness while at the same time ensuring that humanity remains intact. This is not meant as a complete inventory of all the possible words and expressions in which one senses friction, a tension in the relation between God and humanity; on the contrary, our intent is to give a faithful

---

elucet in Dei bonitate: nihil enim magis est illi proprium, in quo glorificari velit, quam bonitas.' It is hard to imagine a text in which the connection between God's honour and his goodness toward humanity could be any clearer. Cf. *Comm. Joh.* 8:54 (CO 47:213): 'gratia suae gloriae'; *Comm. Rom.* 9:22–23 (CO 49:188): 'praecipua eius laus est in beneficiis'. Cf. also Bohatec, *Budé und Calvin*, 341ff.

[188] *Institutes* 2.3.9 (CO 2:219).
[189] Letter to Duchemin, 1537 (CO 5:239–78).
[190] Doumergue, *Jean Calvin*, 4:39.

impression of the struggle in which Calvin was engaged when he sought to avoid doing even the least injustice to God in the polar interplay between God and humankind. Certain much-used words bear the stamp of struggle and tension, more of an adversarial relation than of a peaceful coexistence between them. Precisely at the point of God's sovereignty and of the honour which is due to him alone this tension-filled bipolarity is sharply in evidence.

We will focus on, and at the same time limit ourselves to, primarily three of the 'tension-words' which play a predominant role. Then we will note – together with the passages in which they are found – a few other similar key words, illustrated by examples.

4.1.1. God's greatness needs to be fully highlighted. Frequently, in various places and in numerous variations, we are menacingly warned not to *obscure* God and his honour. People have the capacity to do this and, according to Calvin, in fact do this – witness his protest (precisely at this point) against the church of Rome. In addition this language presupposes as its background a person-to-person situation in the God–human relation. The ignoble ability to obscure God's honour is a typically human capacity and thus, be it negatively and indirectly, witnesses to human greatness. That is how we may think; but to Calvin, of course, what stands out in this whole matter is humanity's smallness and coarseness which threatens God's honour. In by far the majority of cases he uses for this the word *obscurare* and occasionally *supprimere*, *obruere*, or *tenebras obducere*.

When in *Institutes* Book I, chapter 5, Calvin asserts that the knowledge of God shines forth (*lucere*) in the fashioning of the universe and the continuing government of it,[191] he says that there is not a single tiny spot in which you cannot discern at least some sparks of his glory (*emicare*).[192] A person is overwhelmed by the immeasurable power of the brightness (*fulgor*) of this beautiful work of art. Humans find God in their soul and body a hundred times over. It is an odious reality, but there do in fact exist those strange spirits who, to darken God's name, do not

[191] *Institutes* 1.5.1 (CO 2:41).
[192] Ibid., 1.5.1 (CO 2:42): 'scintillae gloriae'.

hesitate to misdirect all the seed of divinity spread abroad in human nature.[193]

At this point Calvin proceeds to discuss prevailing philosophical notions, specifically those of Aristotle, and it is interesting to see how he assesses them from the anxious perspective of whether they do or do not obscure God's glory.[194] To assume a motion in the soul corresponding to the several parts of the body need in no way obscure God's glory but rather illumines it. But if people so bind those capacities of the soul (*organicae animae facultates*) to the body that the soul cannot subsist without the body, then by praising nature they suppress (*supprimere*) and darken God's name! The same thing happens as a result of 'that jejune speculation (*ieiuna illa speculatio*) about the universal mind (here the author twice quotes Virgil). This is done even more clearly in the sacrilegious words of the filthy dog Lucretius . . . This means making an obscure God.'[195] Indeed, we always stand ready to transfer God's honour from him to ourselves:

> For as soon as we have enjoyed a slight taste of the divine from the contemplation of the universe, having passed by the true God, we raise up in his stead dreams and spectres of our own brains, and attribute to one thing or another rather than to the true source the praise of righteousness, wisdom, goodness, and power. We so obscure or distort his daily acts by mistakenly evaluating them that we snatch away from those acts their own glory and from their Author the praise that is due to him.[196]

Thus, throughout the *Institutes*, Calvin continues his struggle to fully bring God out into the light.

The whole glory of God is obscured by the ravings of heretics.[197] And although the brightness of God's glory shines in the angels,[198] there is a danger of lavishing unmeasured honours upon them, by which the glory of Christ is obscured.[199] That glory of Christ was

---

[193] Ibid., 1.5.4 (CO 2:43): 'totum divinitatis semen' (a striking expression).
[194] Ibid., 1.5.4 (CO 2:44).
[195] Ibid., 1.5.5 (CO 2:45): 'umbratile numen'.
[196] Ibid., 1.5.15 (CO 2:52).
[197] Ibid., 1.13.22 (CO 2:108): 'haereticorum deliria'.
[198] Ibid., 1.14.5 (CO 2:121).
[199] Ibid., 1.14.10 (CO 2:124): 'immodica elogia'.

hidden in darkness when the ceremonies of the Old Covenant were still in use.[200] Indeed, Calvin is conspicuously concerned about the glory of Christ. That glory threatens to be obscured in the cult[201] by a multiplicity and diversity of ceremonies in which we see the church entangled today![202]

Similarly a shadow threatens to fall over God's glory when people swear oaths,[203] or when the question of merit arises,[204] where Calvin says that the word 'merit' need not obscure God's grace! (On this matter, see chapter 2, section 6, and the important subject of justification, chapter 3, section 1.)[205]

There is no objection whatever in praying for each other provided only that the glory of Christ is not overshadowed.[206] And in interpreting the first petition of the Lord's Prayer Calvin wonders with a sigh what can actually be more base than that God's honour is obscured by our malice.[207]

Also in connection with predestination[208] and his discussion of the sacraments[209] (for these topics, see chapter 3, section 3, and chapter 4, section 2) we encounter, more than this same use of words, the same anxiety lest people stifle God's glory by the smoke of their malice.[210]

4.1.2. Most frequent is Calvin's use of the 'tension-word' *rob* which occurs in many forms (*eripere, prae-ripere, spoliare, fraudare*). In this context humans appear in relation to God in an unfavourable light. They are out to defraud God; they are thieves.

---

[200] Ibid., 2.7.17 (CO 2:266): 'Christi gloriam obscurare.'

[201] Ibid., 4.10.14 (CO 2:877): 'hic contendo ut is modus adhibeatur, qui Christum illustret, non obscuret' (a pleasing expression to modern, liturgically sensitive ears).

[202] Ibid., 2.8.33 (CO 2:290).

[203] Ibid., 2.8.26 (CO 2:286).

[204] Ibid., 3.15.2 (CO 2:500): 'obscurare Dei gratiam'. Cf. ibid., 2.17.1 (CO 2:386).

[205] Ibid., 3.13.1 (CO 2:560).

[206] Ibid., 3.20.19, 20 (CO 2:645).

[207] Ibid., 3.20.40 (CO 2:666): 'Dei gloriam obscuret partim nostra ingratitudo, partim malignitas.'

[208] Ibid., 3.21.1 (CO 2:679).

[209] Ibid., 4.16.32 (CO 2:1002): 'Dei beneficentiam obscurare.' Cf. ibid., 4.17.48 (CO 2:1049): 'Christi dignitatem obscurare.'

[210] Ibid., 1.4.4 (CO 2:41): 'malitiae caligo'.

They try to appropriate for themselves what belongs to God: his honour, his right, his kingdom.

Occasionally there is mention of robbing God of his right. This is the case in the passage cited above, where in keeping with Aristotle's view the faculties of the soul are so bound to the body that the soul could not subsist without the body.[211] That, says Calvin, is not only to nullify the immortality of the soul but also to rob God of his right. In the use of this terminology God appears on the scene as Creator. Creatures, human beings, are totally his possession. God alone is entitled to be lawgiver. Precisely at this fundamental point Calvin hurls severe accusations at the 'Papists': 'they rape the worship of God and despoil God himself, who is the sole legislator, of his right'.[212]

For if God is the sole legislator, then humans are not permitted to appropriate this honour to themselves.[213] We are not now talking of petty thievery, something really small: God is robbed of his own kingdom as often as he is served under laws of human invention.[214]

But in by far the majority of cases Calvin's reference is to robbing God of his honour. 'But what I have set down in the first place is to be retained: namely that God is robbed of his honour and that his service is violated if all that is proper to the Deity does not reside in him alone.'[215] Therefore, we are robbing the Lord if we claim for ourselves anything in will or accomplishment.[216] It is impious sacrilege to deprive God's majesty of its glory.[217] In that way the devil is the thief of God's honour,[218] as was the first human: he extinguished the whole glory of God.[219] And people still rob God of his honour when they strip him of his

---

[211] Ibid., 1.5.5 (CO 2:44): 'organicae animae facultates'.

[212] Ibid., 4.10.1 (CO 2:867): 'Taceo quod adulterant cultum Dei et Deum ipsum, qui unicus est legislator, suo iure spoliant.'

[213] Ibid., 4.10.8 (CO 2:872): 'id sibi honoris sumere'.

[214] Ibid., 4.10.23 (CO 2:884): 'Eripitur autem quoties humanarum inventionem legibus colitur.'

[215] Ibid., 1.12.1 (CO 2:87): 'honore suo ipsum spoliari, violarique eius cultum'.

[216] Ibid., 2.3.9 (CO 2:219): 'arrogare aut in voluntate aut in effectu'.

[217] Ibid., 2.8.11 (CO 2:273).

[218] Ibid., 1.14.15 (CO 2:127).

[219] Ibid., 2.1.4 (CO 2:179): 'exinanivit totam Dei gloriam'.

power[220] and we view ourselves as the inventors of so many arts and useful things. We consistently threaten anew to become thieves, especially where it concerns good works.[221] Robbing God of his honour is also the charge with which Calvin attacks the pope and the priests of the Roman Catholic church.[222]

We observe, finally, that in this terminology the figure of Christ plays a large role as well. If anything is detracted from his deity and humanity and people thereby undermine his mediatorship, he is at the same time deprived of all the attestations of honour with which Scripture honours him.[223] To him alone belongs the honour of the work of atonement he accomplished. Those who try to reconcile God with themselves by their own redemptive means seize that honour for themselves.[224] Christ's exclusive mediatorship also persists in the intercessions. Whereas Calvin very well knows how to situate the exclusivity of the intercessions above or alongside of the prayers which believers pray for each other, the mutual intercessions based on Paul's statement in 1 Timothy,[225] he is much more restrained with respect to the invocation of the intercession of the saints. At first blush this seems to be inconsistent, but Calvin fears that the honour of Christ is threatened when people address themselves to others in their intercessions.[226] When this prayer is addressed to others, sacrilege occurs.[227]

The urgency and emphasis with which Calvin fights against anything that robs God of his honour can also be inferred from the precise formulations he uses.[228] Even a little is too much and impermissible; no compromise is allowed or possible. Not even the slightest component may be taken from his honour.[229]

---

[220] Ibid., 1.4.2 (CO 2:39).

[221] Ibid., 3.15.3 (CO 2:581): 'boni authorem sua laude fraudamus'. Cf. ibid., 2.15.7 (CO 2:584): 'in laude bonorum operum Deo suffurantur'.

[222] Ibid., 4.7.25 (CO 2:843); cf. ibid., 4.18.2 (CO 2:1052).

[223] Ibid., 2.12.3 (CO 2:342–3).

[224] Ibid., 3.4.26 (CO 2:478): 'suae compensationes'.

[225] 1 Timothy 2:1, 2.

[226] *Institutes* 3.20.21 (CO 2:647): 'Christum inhonorant, et solius Mediatoris titulo spoliant . . . sua laude exuunt ac defraudant.'

[227] Ibid., 3.20.27 (CO 2:653): 'non sine manifesto sacrilegio orationem ad alios dirigi'.

[228] Ibid., 2.2.1 (CO 2:185): 'Rursum vel minutulum illi quippiam arrogari non potest et Deo praeripiatur suus honor.'

[229] Ibid., 2.3.10 (CO 2:220): 'portiuncula'.

It is an act of stealing the honour due to his gracious goodness.[230] Such small points especially characterize the greatness of the cause Calvin champions so relentlessly and with such great devotion.

4.1.3. As the third example we want to mention the complex of concepts connected with *the transfer of God's honour to another.* Actually this 'tension-saying' is very closely linked with the preceding one; it is, in fact, a continuation of it. At the same time, in the context of this transfer from one to another, the bipolar background comes more graphically to the fore than in the case of the preceding 'tension-word'. The creature here becomes even more clearly the counter-pole who stands there preening itself on that which is really from God. One can recognize this preening even in impersonal matters; or rather, impersonal things are elevated to a personal level on which they begin to show off with the honour that belongs to God.

These are idols (*idola*) to which the stolen honour of God is transferred, where even God's own works are mentioned as the rivals of his own personal honour.[231] In this connection Calvin's usage is quite extensive and varied: *transferre, conferre, transcribere, derivare, traducere.*

Those upon whom divine honour is illegitimately conferred constitute a diverse and colourful company. They are the idols: a piece of dead wood, says Calvin scornfully.[232] His definition of idolatry is sharp and on target: it is the practice of honouring the gifts instead of the giver himself.[233] (This is also the final reason why he is opposed to the distinction between *latria* and *dulia.* Also in the case of the latter the honour due to God is transferred to a creature.)[234] Indeed, angels can compete for divine honour, and become competitors to whom the honour of God himself or of Christ is transferred.[235] They may also be the dead to whom

[230] Ibid., 3.13.1 (CO 2:560): 'particula'.
[231] Ibid., 1.11.9 (CO 2:81), 1.5.15 (CO 2:52): 'laudem ab ipso fonte huc et illuc traducimus'.
[232] Ibid., 1.11.4 (CO 2:77), 1.11.9 (CO 2:81).
[233] Ibid., 4.17.36 (CO 2:1039): 'dona pro datore colere'.
[234] Ibid., 1.12.2 (CO 2:88).
[235] Ibid., 1.12.2 (CO 2:88): 'angelis et mortuis transcribi divini honores'. Cf. ibid., 1.13.11 (CO 2:99), 1.14.10 (CO 2:124).

people pray,[236] or the saints, a practice by which God's majesty is in large part suppressed and extinguished.[237]

Finally and, indeed, above all, it is living human beings themselves who try, like thieves, to attract to themselves the honour due to their Creator. Calvin attempts to repulse this attack on God's honour and his sovereignty (which lies behind it), no matter how little people would want to appropriate for themselves, with an impressive series of Bible texts.[238] Also in his exposition of the second commandment of the Decalogue this theme again recurs.[239] If ever humans stand empty-handed, then certainly in reference to salvation in Christ. All our salvation resides in him alone.[240] The honour of God may be transferred to no one or nothing else, neither to the Roman pontiff,[241] nor to the sacraments.[242]

Thus, in our opinion, the tension which characterizes the divine–human relation is evidenced especially in the use of these words and in the examples cited, all of which tell of obscuring and robbing God's honour and its transfer to creatures (this series could easily be expanded with still other striking 'tension-words'). We could, without any hesitation, call this usage typically Calvinian. This tension ('loadedness') is present and continually draws its inspiration and strength from Calvin's fervent conviction of God's supreme sovereignty, which powerfully controls the relation between God and humanity. On the other hand, it is fed by the experienced weakness and gross covetousness of the human partner when the latter takes his or her position before the generous God. Calvin's own time supplied him with enough examples, certainly, of intolerable human pretensions in matters which belong to God alone. Calvin all too often experienced humans as embodied weakness and admitted 'that I myself am a miserable creature . . .'.[243] Is this admission not one of all

---

[236] Ibid., 3.20.22 (CO 2:648).

[237] Ibid., 1.12.1 (CO 2:87): 'Dei maiestas supprimitur et extinguitur.'

[238] See ibid., 2.2.10 (CO 2:194).

[239] Ibid., 2.8.18 (CO 2:280), 2.8.25 (CO 2:285).

[240] Ibid., 2.16.19 (CO 2:385): 'salutis nostrae . . . ne vel minimam portiunculam alio derivemus'.

[241] Ibid., 4.7.25 (CO 2:843).

[242] Ibid., 4.14.12 (CO 2:950): 'Dei gloriam ad creaturas derivare.' Cf. ibid., 4.14.16 (CO 2:953).

[243] CO 9:891; cf. CO 21:166.

times? But the fact that this tension remains, that it is not resolved, at least is not smoothed out and always again makes itself felt, in other words, that the two poles continue to exist side by side and over against each other, that God does not absorb and sweep away the human person: that fact is as amazing as it is glorious. For Calvin at the same time continues to have a high view of human dignity, a dignity which is by no means foreign to the divine glory. At the same time, moreover, he does not reserve the word 'honour' exclusively for God alone. In a highly significant passage we read: 'So widespread is the use of the word "honour" . . .' (by which he means that it can also be said of humans).[244] This statement occurs when Calvin speaks of honouring our parents, posits such honour as a requirement and defends its legitimacy. One can, of course, simply characterize this as contradictory, but that is not the case either for Calvin or for the reader who listens to him with an open mind. Humans, typical examples of weakness before the high God but nevertheless human highness as God's own image, can become usurpers in relation to their Creator. This is the mystery but also the fact of sin. It is the ancient motive of wanting to be like God. This givenness, the divine majesty confronting the apostate, weak, but high dignity which is humanity: precisely this bipolarity, so defined, is the source of the tension and 'loadedness' we have cited. We will see that this tension permeates all of Calvin's theological thinking.

4.1.4. We will now pass in review a number of words and phrases which breathe the same tense atmosphere as the three listed above. Drawing on an abundance of passages we will illustrate the manner in which these expressions are used in Calvin.

> *Boasting in God alone.* He alone must excel in glory.[245] We must be divested of vainglory for no other reason than to learn to boast in the Lord.
>
> *Defiling* God's honour: by open blasphemies[246] or by absurd inventions.[247]

---

[244] *Institutes* 2.8.35 (CO 2:292): 'Sic enim late patet vocabulum honoris.'
[245] CO 2:13: 'ut solus ipse gloriosus emineat'. Cf. *Institutes* 2.2.11 (CO 2:194–5).
[246] CO 2:14: 'polluere'.
[247] *Institutes* 1.11.2 (CO 2:75): 'foedari'.

Promoting God's honour: in swearing an oath,[248] in self-denial,[249] by the justification of faith,[250] and especially in prayer.[251]

Trifling with God's honour: by our follies and a cult we ourselves have invented;[252] by an assortment of penitential practices and the mass.[253]

Desecrating God's honour: God's truth is *profaned* even by the most eminent people;[254] God's righteousness is desecrated by those who, apart from the law, apply themselves to good works.[255] Indulgences are a desecration of the blood of Christ.[256] The invocation of God is desecrated by praying for the dead.[257]

Against all human competition Calvin posits God *alone*: he *alone* is an adequate witness concerning himself.[258] He *alone* is deserving of the honour of the creation.[259] He is the unique and only God.[260] He *alone* affords us counsel.[261] In providence it is God's will *alone* which works and accomplishes all things.[262] The honour of our redemption is due to him *alone*.[263] He *alone* works in us the willing and the doing.[264] All the honour of the work is due to his grace *alone*.[265] By him *alone*

[248] Ibid., 2.8.28 (CO 2:287).

[249] Ibid., 3.7.2 (CO 2:506): 'ad gloriam eius promovendam'. Cf. ibid., 1.2.2 (CO 2:35).

[250] Ibid., 3.14.9 (CO 2:570): 'provehere'.

[251] Ibid., 3.20.28 (CO 2:655); cf. ibid., 3.20.35 (CO 2:662) and 3.20.43 (CO 2:668): 'studere'.

[252] Ibid., 1.4.3 (CO 2:40): 'cum Deo nugari'.

[253] Ibid., 3.4.28 (CO 2:479): 'cum Deo ludere et ineptire'. Cf. ibid., 4.18.8 (CO 2:1057).

[254] Ibid., 1.5.11 (CO 2:49): 'profanare'.

[255] Ibid., 2.8.5 (CO 2:270).

[256] Ibid., 3.5.2 (CO 2:491): 'sanguinis Christi profanatio'.

[257] Ibid., 3.5.10 (CO 2:500): 'profanatio invocationis Dei'.

[258] Ibid., 1.11.1 (CO 2:74): 'Deus ipse solus est de se idoneus testis.'

[259] Ibid., 1.16.2 (CO 2:145).

[260] Ibid., 1.12.3 (CO 2:89).

[261] Ibid., 1.14.13 (CO 2:127): 'ipsius est solius et concilium et robur et animos et arma subministrare'.

[262] Ibid., 1.18 (CO 2:167–74).

[263] Ibid., 2.3.6 (CO 2:215–16).

[264] Ibid., 2.3.9 (CO 2:219).

[265] Ibid., 2.3.12 (CO 2:222): 'tota laboris laus'.

our life will be successful.[266] In bearing our cross we must trust in God *alone*.[267]

Violating God's honour: God's honour is violated when a visible form is attributed to him,[268] when the law is transgressed,[269] when the true service of worship is violated.[270] His majesty is dishonoured by images when he is depicted in art,[271] as well as in the veneration of saints.[272]

God's honour *is ripped to shreds*: when other gods are set up next to him.[273]

God's honour is *diminished*: God's honour is not diminished when Christ is called Mediator,[274] but it is when a limitation is imposed on God's providence,[275] or when an oath is sworn without sufficient reason.[276] This occurs as well when people in any way detract from either the deity or the humanity of Christ,[277] or when the doctrine of predestination is withheld from people by silence.[278] This saying also frequently comes back in connection with the Lord's Supper.[279]

Dividing God's honour. We may not divide the honour due to God with the angels,[280] nor with people.[281] Nor must we attempt to divide the work of conversion between God and humans.[282] Nor may we in this manner divide the honour

---

[266] Ibid., 3.7.9 (CO 2:512): 'sola Dei benedictio'.

[267] Ibid., 3.8.3 (CO 2:517).

[268] Ibid., 1.11.1 (CO 2:74): 'corrumpere Dei gloriam'.

[269] Ibid., 2.8.59 (CO 2:308): 'violare'.

[270] Ibid., 4.10.1 (CO 2:867): 'adulterare'.

[271] Ibid., 1.11.2 (CO 2:75): 'maiestatis suae dedecora'. Cf. ibid., 1.11.4 (CO 2:78): 'contumelia'.

[272] Ibid., 1.12.1 (CO 2:87): 'supprimere et extinguere'.

[273] Ibid.: 'divinitatis gloria dissecatur'.

[274] Ibid., 1.13.26 (CO 2:113).

[275] Ibid., 1.16.3 (CO 2:146): 'indigne extenuatur singularis bonitas'.

[276] Ibid., 2.8.26 (CO 2:286).

[277] Ibid., 2.12.3 (CO 2:342).

[278] Ibid., 3.21.1 (CO 2:679).

[279] Ibid., 4.17.25 (CO 2:1024).

[280] Ibid., 1.14.12 (CO 2:116).

[281] Ibid., 2.2.9 (CO 2:193): 'inter Deum et hominem laudem boni operis partiri'.

[282] Ibid., 2.5.9 (CO 2:237).

of good works between God and humans.[283] In the doctrine of predestination we must not create a split between God's will and grace on the one hand and our works on the other.[284]

In conclusion we want to refer to a passage in which the divine–human relation is expressed in a remarkable way. It pertains to God's providence where God is characterized as the principal giver and author.[285] Evidently Calvin here leaves open the possibility that another receives honour as well. Striking also is that humans are called instruments of providence.[286] In this connection Calvin uses the term 'subservient'. This, then, refers to the human deliberations employed in divine providence.[287]

4.2. A double image of God?

To speak, side by side, of God's dreadful majesty and of a loving, caring Father feels contrived, but it was not in any way our purpose to suggest that there is a duality in God. From the above discussion it should also be clear to the reader that such a contrast is far removed from the thinking of Calvin. Nevertheless, it has been held against him that his work is marked by a split between two mutually contradictory images of God.

By way of illustration we will cite in this connection A. Ritschl, who posited such a contrast in Calvin's image of God.

The idea of God which dominates the doctrine of predestination, the idea of an all-powerful will, capricious, devoid of law, which is its own end and seeks its honour by the contradictory means of election and reprobation, is completely different from the idea of God which is developed in the first book and dominates the system as a whole. The good will, kind and just, which represents God reaches its own

---

[283] Ibid., 3.15.3 (CO 2:581). In connection with self-denial Calvin does concede that there is a division (ibid., 3.7.4 [CO 2:508]), but this division does not apply to the honour of God.

[284] Ibid., 3.24.1 (CO 2:712); cf. ibid., 3.22.6 (CO 2:692).

[285] Ibid., 1.17.9 (CO 2:161–2): 'Denique Deum in acceptis bonis reverebitur et praedicabit ut praecipuum authorem: sed homines ut eius ministros honorabit.'

[286] Ibid., 1.17.9 (CO 2:162): 'legitima divinae providentiae instrumenta'.

[287] Ibid., 1.17.4 (CO 2:157): 'subservire'. Cf. p. 150 below for what is said about this in connection with the church.

proper end in the way of finality, in creation and the direction of the world, hence as providence.[288]

But also his son, O. Ritschl, exaggerates. He proceeds to work in an almost equally unCalvinian way when he tries to point out rankings and priorities in God.[289] According to him, the doctrine of God's unrestricted 'justice' is a fundamental dogma and Calvin's concept of divine love is not superordinate to that of the justice of God.[290] 'To Calvin's religious sensitivity the essence of God's being is not primarily love but immeasurable self-glorification through the unrestricted revelation of his freedom, a freedom that is not bound by any law.'[291] Such speculation as to how God's being may be structured shows little understanding of John Calvin's true interest.

Imbart de la Tour sometimes speaks of two poles: wrath and compassion, dread and confidence, between which 'Calvin's mysticism' is said to move.[292] Corresponding to these two poles, he writes, is a double affection[293] from which springs the prayer of believers, but he takes care not to extend the idea of a duality to the being of God himself. Hunter, too, speaks of two lines in Calvin's thinking about God but the judgment of this author is much more balanced and more nuanced.[294] According to him, too, the idea of sovereignty is dominant, but it comes to expression in different attributes:

> from different centres of His being, he represents the sovereign divine will as operating now as justice, now as mercy or love or wrath. . . . The various impressions he gives us of God's activity produce the sense of a composite photograph in which the features are so blurred . . . as to represent no definite personality.[295]

---

[288] A. Ritschl, *Geschichtliche Studien zur christlichen Lehre von Gott*, Jahrbücher für deutsche Theologie, vol. 13 (Gotha, 1868), 1008.

[289] O. Ritschl, *Dogmengeschichte des Protestantismus*, 3:179; cf. also ibid., 178, where the author speaks 'von einem starken und erhabenen Ethos' in God. However, this is 'dem Pathos, das Calvins Begriff von der gloire de Dieu ohne weiteres eigen ist . . . untergeordnet'.

[290] Ibid., 174.

[291] Ibid.

[292] Imbart de la Tour, 'Calvin', 167.

[293] Ibid., 169.

[294] Hunter, *Teaching of Calvin*, 50.

[295] Ibid., 51.

But Calvin is very well aware that, if we knew everything about God, there would be no inner contradiction at all. 'It is the part of faith to believe that behind the veil mercy and judgment kiss one another.'[296] We must be thoroughly conscious of the fact that our knowledge of God is most fragmentary. God is inaccessible[297] and it has not been given to us to know what God is in himself (*quis sit apud se*) but only what he is toward us (*sed qualis erga nos*).[298] All this is true and a faithful rendering of Calvin's thinking. Still, when Hunter speaks of 'two lines in his thinking about him',[299] there is the threat of oversimplification and of subsuming everything under those two headings. It is a great temptation (but all too simple and mistaken) to think that all of Calvin's thinking was controlled by those two components. Imperceptibly, his theology is then again still understood dualistically. We believe that the work of the Reformer himself adequately refutes any suggestion of a dichotomy between two distinct images of God. By way of illustration we will cite a few pronouncements of Calvin which clearly argue against a dualistic understanding of his God-image.

> God is so highly exalted in majesty that we must be moved by profound reverence every time we think about him. Then we must worship him in humility, knowing that we are nothing and that he is above all. Nevertheless, he does not keep us from recognizing that his power is near to us and that his arms reach out very close to us to help.[300]
>
> God is awe-inspiring in his majesty but his goodness is as infinite as his power.[301]

---

[296] Ibid., 53.
[297] *Institutes* 3.2.1 (CO 2:398): 'imo quum in scholis de fide disputant, Deum eius obiectum simpliciter vocando, evanida speculatione (ut alibi diximus) miseras animas rapiunt. . . . Nam quum Deus lucem inaccessam habitet [I Tim. 6:16], Christus occurrere medium necesse est'.
[298] Cf. *Serm. Job* 1:6–8 (CO 33:57): 'Brief, iamais nous ne cognoistrons Dieu tel qu'il est, mais nous le cognoistrons en telle mesure qu'il lui plaira de se manifester à nous, c'est à dire, selon qu'il cognoist qu'il nous est utile pour nostre salut.' Cf. *Institutes* 1.10.2 (CO 2:73): 'animadvertamus . . . commemorari eius virtutes, quibus nobis describitur non quis apud se, sed qualis erga nos: ut ista eius agnitio vivo magis sensu, quam vacua et meteorica speculatione constet'.
[299] Hunter, *Teaching of Calvin*, 50.
[300] CO 29:199.
[301] *Sermon sur Deut.* 32 (CO 28:695).

God is called holy that we would know how he manifests himself to us when he dwells among us. It is not merely the case that his majesty compels respect (for he does after all fill us with awe) but he also deigns to show us his special care. Therefore the experience of his presence fills us with inestimable joy.[302]

In fact, God's love and majesty always go together.[303]

The thesis of a double image of God in Calvin's teaching is more fundamentally and perhaps more clearly refuted when we point to the significance of the Covenant in his theology.[304] The God who displays his majesty in the heavens becomes a Father to people in the Covenant. The Covenant forges a bridge from the awesome majesty before which the earth trembles when his voice is sounded to the Father who has bound himself with bonds of love to his people.[305] Scripture also makes clear that God's honour is integrally connected with his covenant. He is a jealous God who gives his honour to no other.[306] That honour also consists in the unbreakable love and faithfulness by which God, as a bridegroom, remains bound to his people, the unfaithful bride.[307]

Calvin's theology is a theology of the Covenant.[308] Federal theology does not begin with Cocceius but can already be found germinally in Calvin.[309] Repeatedly, accordingly, he speaks of the covenant of grace.[310]

---

[302] CO 36:254.

[303] Cf. Bohatec, Budé et Calvin, 340.

[304] For this suggestion I am especially indebted to Prof. S. van der Linde.

[305] Cf. Psalm 8:2; 76:8, 9; Hosea 11:4.

[306] Cf. Joshua 24:19; Isaiah 48:11.

[307] Cf. Isaiah 50:1; 54:5; 62:5; Jeremiah 2:2; 3:7; Ezekiel 16:8; Hosea 2:18–22.

[308] Cf. W. van den Bergh, Calvijn over het genadeverbond (The Hague, 1879).

[309] Ibid., 6–13. Cf. Jacobs, 'Föderaltheologie', in RGG, 1:1518–20.

[310] The term foedus gratiae seldom appears in Calvin; more often it is the expression foedus gratuitum (e.g. Institutes 2.7.1 [CO 2:253]). According to van den Bergh (Calvijn over het genadeverbond, 12–13, 131–4), in Calvin the covenant of works is included in the covenant of grace. The covenant has an important place in Calvin's theology, but unlike in the later federal theology of Cocceius, the covenant concept does not take on the character of a system that dominates his thought. Cf. G. Schrenk, Gottesreich und Bund im älteren Protestantismus vornehmlich bei Johannes Coccejus (Gütersloh, 1923), 44–8.

This covenant of grace encompasses the Old as well as the New Testament. These two testaments agree in essence and content.[311] The foundation of the unity of the two testaments is Christ.[312] Calvin also clearly states in what this covenant of grace consists. It is the adoption of people to be children of God.[313] The One, however, who effects this adoption is the Holy Spirit. He is the Spirit of our adoption to be children of God.[314] In the Old Covenant already he is called the Spirit of rebirth.[315] There his grace is already active in a special way in the elect.[316]

If we may call the covenant of grace the bridge which connects God's majesty with his fatherly love, the Holy Spirit may be called the great bridge-builder. And if God seeks his honour in the Covenant with his people, then the honour of the Holy Spirit lies particularly in this covenant of grace. It is he, after all, who brings about our adoption, to be children of God.

Thus the Holy Spirit is the bridge-builder, not only in the sense that he constructs the bridge between God and human persons by which the latter become children of God and God becomes their Father, but also in the sense that he forges and maintains the link between the immeasurable majesty and the loving Father. By the Spirit it becomes possible to speak of the one God as the Father of immeasurable majesty.[317] As a result of Calvin's doctrine of the

---

[311] *Institutes* 2.10.2 (CO 2:313): 'Patrum omnium foedus adeo substantia et res ipsa nihil a nostro differt, ut unum prorsus atque idem sit.' Cf. H. H. Wolf, *Die Einheit des Bundes. Das Verhältnis von Altem und Neuem Testament bei Calvin*, 2nd edn (Neukirchen, 1958).

[312] The *substantia et res* in which the two covenants are unified is Christ. Cf. Wolf, *Einheit des Bundes*, 24–67. Cf. also Chapter II, Section 2 (The Law of the Old Covenant), pp. 62ff. below.

[313] *Comm. II Cor.* 1:20 (CO 50:23): 'Promissio qua nos sibi Deus in filios adoptat, omnium est prima'; *Institutes* 2.6.4 (CO 2:251): 'gratuitum foedus quo Deus electos suos adoptaverat'. Cf. van den Bergh, *Calvijn over het genadeverbond*, 30; Wolf, *Einheit des Bundes*, 23.

[314] *Institutes* 3.1.3 (CO 2:395): 'vocatur Spiritus adoptionis: quia nobis testis gratuitae Dei benevolentiae qua nos Deus Pater in dilecto unigenito complexus est, ut nobis esset in Patrem'.

[315] *Comm. Gen.* 4:22 (CO 23:100).

[316] *Comm. Gen.* 21:20 (CO 23:305): 'adest enim electis suis quo peculiari spiritus gratia gubernat'.

[317] 'Pater immensae majestatis' (from the hymn *Te Deum*).

Holy Spirit, therefore, it becomes impossible to speak of a duality in his image of God.

Finally we note that the covenant idea in Calvin's theology brings to clarity, decisively and persuasively, the reciprocal relation between God and human beings. Several pronouncements of Calvin bear explicit witness to this bipolarity in connection with the covenant of grace.[318]

---

[318] *Comm. Gen.* 17:2 (CO 23:235): 'gratis descendo ad mutuum foedus'; *Prael. Ez.* 16:59 (CO 40:391): 'requiritur enim mutua fides in foederibus'. Cf. van den Bergh, *Calvijn over het Genadeverbond*, 29, 36, 44. This reciprocity is most strongly expressed, in our judgment, in *Comm. Psalm.* 132:12 (CO 32:348): 'Nam conditio, sub qua paciscitur Deus, innuit non aliter ratum fore Dei foedus quam si homines bona fide respondeant. Unde sequitur effectum gratiae promissae pendere ab eorum obedientia.'

II

⟨◈⟩

God's Honour
and Salvation in Christ

PROCEEDING from Calvin's principle of the interdependence
of our knowledge of God and of ourselves, we took inventory
in chapter 1 of how Calvin spoke of the divine–human relation.

In this chapter and subsequent chapters we will turn our
attention to specific topics in his theology.

In this connection we will be deliberately selective. We will be
especially interested in those topics in which the theme of God's
honour in its relation to human salvation is treated most pointedly
and sensitively. Hence our selection will be determined by the
thematics of the divine–human bipolarity.

In pursuing this aim, we will, for practical reasons, as much
as possible follow the order in which these topics occur in the
Institutes. We believe that, by following this method, we can
simultaneously produce a sketch of Calvin's theology as a
whole.

In close connection with the 'tension-words' in Calvin's theology
to which we called attention in chapter 1, we will discuss the theme
of 'free will' in the first section of this chapter. In section 2 we will
devote a separate discussion to the Law, because at its crucial
centre, in the Decalogue, it almost automatically raises the question
concerning the role of God and man as this comes to expression
in the two tables of the Ten Commandments. At the same time
this Old Testament theme constitutes a good introduction to
Christ about whom we speak in the four remaining sections of
this chapter.

Bipolar tensions can be shown to exist in the divine–human
relation in connection with the figure of Christ as well. Section 3
will treat the figure of Christ in the light of God's majesty, while

45

section 4 will discuss the doctrine of the satisfaction which humanity owes to this divine majesty.

The figure of the incarnate Son of God, however, at the same time displays a high form of divine–human concurrence, inasmuch as Christ is incomparably the image of God. This is the topic treated in section 5. In close connection with it, the last section of this chapter deals with the merit of Christ which can be viewed as a practical consequence of Christ's being image of God.

1. Free will: an idol

Humanity's deep lostness, its deformed state (*deformitas*), comes to unique expression in Calvin's discussion of human free will. It is a complicated topic, one that was highly controversial in the sixteenth century. Dogma-historically one could devote more than one study to the subject.[1] On it Calvin himself already accumulated an impressive amount of material which not only reflects the vehemence of the controversy but also its great scope. It is not easy to follow the line of his impassioned argument. In everything he says one senses the topicality of the subject in his days, but it is quite possible that it is still topical today. All these points of consideration, however, are of secondary importance.

Calvin views the theme of free will (*liberum arbitrium*) as one of the foci in which the tension between the divine and the human pole is clearly articulated and thought through. It is our task to point out the points of friction. The sovereignty of God is vigorously highlighted as solely salvific and solely determinative. The human being threatens to become a puppet. One wonders whether all human initiative is not completely lost. Does God not take everything into his own hands? Reading and re-reading *Institutes* Book II, chapter 2.2–5,[2] one gets the impression that Calvin himself did not achieve full clarity either. Indeed, he categorically denies free will. This cannot be doubted, but in what light, what context, and what perspective? One encounters statements in which, from a different perspective (but a diversity of perspectives is nowhere clearly distinguished!), humanity, also fallen humanity, keeps its free will. But in the latter case Calvin

[1] Barnikol, *Lehre Calvins vom unfreien Willen.*
[2] *Institutes* 2.2.2–5 (CO 2:185–90).

would rather not speak of free will. He would rather abolish a term that is so susceptible to misunderstanding.[3] He fails to achieve a consistent and harmonious position.[4] Urgent questions remain unresolved. Everything betrays Calvin's struggle with a problem which, especially since Luther and Erasmus, was very much in discussion and in whose solution one saw expressed, as in a mirror, one's own Catholic or Reformational confession. Of interest to us is how, in this cluster of problems, God and man are related to each other – undoubtedly more (or so at least it seems) as opponents than as allies – and how humanity maintains itself and relates to its divine 'counterpart' (*Gegenüberstand*). In other words, how does the divine–human bipolarity present itself here?

The following is a survey of the points which successively arise in answering this question.

1. The double danger of slothfulness (*desidia*) and false boasting (*falsa glorificatio*).

2. The twofold perspective that is crucial in the issue of free will.

3. Augustine's distinction between the loss of the supernatural gifts (*exinanitio* of the *supernaturalia*) and the corruption of the natural gifts (*corruptio* of the *dona naturalia*).

4. The consequences of this for human reason and free will.

5. The distinction between compulsion (*coactio*) and necessity (*necessitas*) in connection with free will.

6. The threat to God's honour.

7. A comparison with the doctrine of the Roman Catholic church.

From the moment the issue of free will is raised one encounters the tension which dominates the juxtaposition of God and man. Now

> the best way to avoid error will be to consider the perils that threaten man on both sides. (1) When man is denied all uprightness, he immediately takes occasion for inertia from that fact; and, because he is said to have no ability to pursue righteousness on his own, does not concern himself about it as though he has nothing to do with it.

---

[3] Ibid., 2.2.8–9 (CO 2:192–3): 'magno Ecclesiae bono futurum si aboleatur'.
[4] Cf. Reuter, *Grundverständnis der Theologie Calvins*, 163.

(2) On the other hand, nothing, however slight, can be credited to man without depriving God of his honour, and without man himself falling into ruin through presumptuous self-confidence.[5]

These are the two dangers to be avoided: on the one hand, there is slothfulness (*desidia*) which paralyses a person and renders him or her inactive. We would like to describe this attitude as one of resigned acquiescence, the acquiescent passivity of a person, inasmuch as any initiative is completely superfluous and inappropriate, because vis-à-vis God, the great counter pole, all initiative is not only powerless but also incorrect. This is something Calvin wants to avoid. Man must yearn (*aspirare*) for the good he lacks and for the freedom (*libertas*) of which he has been deprived, and this aspiration needs to occur despite the fact that he is 'hedged about on all sides by a most miserable necessity'.[6] If anywhere, then certainly from this opening passage we feel the tension which dominates Calvin's language when he tries to combine necessity (*necessitas*) with a nevertheless truly human aspiration. At the same time it is clear that the warning against slothfulness arises from a pastoral concern that is rich in experience. Behind this sort of warning one can even discern the threatening background of libertinism against which the Reformer had to fight so hard. A couple of lines further down this warning against human slothfulness and apathy is even repeated. It was for this reason, among others, that the early ecclesiastical writers extolled human powers so highly 'to avoid giving fresh occasion for slothfulness to the flesh which of itself is already so slack toward the good'.[7] It is beyond dispute, moreover (and this is an important statement by Calvin), that humankind must not be deprived of anything that is its own.[8] This, again, is a forceful attempt to uphold humans in their full dignity.

Still, in Calvin's entire discourse about free will, this danger of human slothfulness plays a much smaller role than another and greater concern (and here, in all its weight, the accent falls on the other pole): the concern for God, his unblemished goodness and

[5] *Institutes* 2.2.1 (CO 2:185).
[6] Ibid.: 'miserrima undique necessitate circumseptus'.
[7] Ibid., 2.2.4 (CO 2:188): 'deinde carni suapte sponte nimis ad bonum torpenti novam desidiae occasionem praeberent'.
[8] See below, p. 51 (esp. n. 21)

honour. In its proper place we will be able at greater length to designate this leitmotif as the stronger of the two. We briefly refer to it here already to make even clearer that the theme of the honour of God is involved in this discussion from the start.[9] Such a tension-filled text is actually typical of all of Calvin's treatment of human free will. It is not an accident, therefore, that by way of an initial rounding-off of his discussion he praises the humility which must be a fundamental characteristic of all authentic religious reflection and discourse. The first phase of his discussion of free will ends, as it were, in a sermon on humility. In this connection he eagerly quotes statements made by Chrysostom and even more eagerly and wholeheartedly Augustine,[10] and he himself finds a beautiful con-cluding formulation: 'For as our humility is his loftiness, so the confession of our humility finds his mercy ready to heal.'[11] The latter part has a warm sound: people face a majesty that is merciful.

Precisely in order to gain insight into how people in some fashion still remain on their feet despite the clear denial of free will, we must, particularly in this matter, point out a diversity of perspectives in light of which certain statements are made. This undertaking is not without risk, for Calvin nowhere in so many words makes a distinction in perspective. Still, while remaining faithful to the text, we believe we can everywhere discern from the words themselves a salvific perspective in light of which strong statements gain validity and can alone gain validity.

Before we attempt to flesh out this line of thought, however, we must first briefly note here what we mean by the term 'salvific perspective'. In this term we have in mind the premise and pers-pective which looks at man in terms of his deepest destiny and final value. That is the destiny and appraisal which he has vis-à-vis the God of salvation, the God who becomes his father. The salvific perspective is nothing other than the vantage-point from which we regard man in his relation as child to the Father, the relation which is possible and real in Christ *the* Son. It is to view him in the intimate relation of person to person which is characterized, at least in this life, by the theological virtues of

---

[9] Ibid., 2.2.1 (CO 2:185): 'Rursum vel minutulum illi quippiam arrogari non potest, quin et Deo praeripiatur honor.'

[10] Ibid., 2.2.11 (CO 2:195).

[11] Ibid.: 'Siquidem ut nostra humilitas, eius est altitudo: ita confessio nostrae humilitatis miserationem eius in remedium paratam habet.'

faith, hope and love. This salvific perspective is the level of pure grace. It is the human being (being human is already a gift of God), but then in a completely new and decisive relation to God who becomes his God and Father. This salvific perspective is the only decisive viewpoint from which Holy Scripture looks at man. Theology can serve to make clear that every person is called to enter into this high and intimate communion with God. The strange thing is that the person who breaks off this unique relation still continues to exist.[12] We will make this comment merely in passing, but the fact is there and thanks to this *fact of experience* one can speak about man in terms of his actual condition, the person who lacks the perspective of salvation. In Calvin, with astonishing consistency (we think), the salvific perspective is everywhere decisive (think, for example, of the relation between the Old and the New Testament; this alone – we will simply posit this point without elaborating it – is a strong indication of his Christocentric way of thinking). In addition, but as a subordinate reality, he is nevertheless conscious of the fallen human being who is and remains human, yet no longer has a salvific future. These are the two perspectives from which Calvin looks at humanity. Precisely in order to determine the place of humans before God when the discussion concerns free will and the loss of it, it is important to make and use this distinction.

'And, indeed, the familiar saying which they have taken from Augustine pleases me: that the natural gifts were corrupted in man through sin and that man was stripped of his supernatural gifts.'[13] Thus Calvin aligns himself with a distinction in perspective which was still current in the theology of his time. He also explains what is meant by the latter set of gifts: the light of faith (*fidei lux*) and the righteousness (*iustitia*) which were said to be sufficient to secure the heavenly life and eternal bliss. The corruption (*corruptio*), not the loss (*exinanitio*), of the natural gifts, is clearly postulated from the start. This applies, in the first place, to reason (*ratio*). This is a natural gift (*donum naturale*) and has not, there-fore, been destroyed in its entirety.[14] The soundness of the mind

[12] See above, p. 9.

[13] *Institutes* 2.2.12 (CO 2:195); cf. ibid., 2.2.4 (CO 2:189): 'naturalia dona corrupta, supernaturalia ablata'.

[14] Ibid., 2.2.12 (CO 2:196): 'Sic voluntas, quia inseparabilis est ab hominis natura, non periit.'

(*sanitas mentis*) and the true uprightness of the heart (*rectitudo cordis*) have been stripped away. The decay of reason and the sickness of the mind at least implies (but this is a lot) that they are completely impotent with respect to salvation, powerless and worthless from the perspective of salvation.[15] When it concerns the knowledge of God and his fatherly favour in our behalf, 'the greatest geniuses are blinder than moles'.[16] In divine matters their insight is totally blind and dulled, he says elsewhere.[17] This is confirmed by Scripture. True knowledge is lacking.[18]

It is clear that the decay (*corruptio*), if we may so put it, does not pertain to the gift *as such*. For the human intellect, even despite its injured state, is still ornamented by God with eminent gifts.[19] The works of pagan authors testify to this fact and teach us how many gifts God has still left to human nature even after it 'was despoiled of its true good'.[20] Again, though we speak of decay in this connection, it is not because the gifts themselves have gone bad but because they are gifts of defiled people (the humans who as it concerns their salvation have fallen away from God; note how this last perspective is decisive).[21]

We have spoken fairly extensively about the place of reason, because this is the framework and approach in which the burning issue of free will comes up. In chapter 2.26[22] Calvin finally says: 'Now we must examine the will in which freedom of decision (*arbitrii libertas*) especially resides.'[23]

But when he makes this statement a great deal has already been said about free will. Also, this theme is overshadowed by Augustine's saying about the corruption of the natural gifts and

---

[15] Ibid., 2.2.18 (CO 2:200): 'humana ratio, ubi ad regnum Dei venitur . . .'.

[16] Ibid.: 'talpis caeciores'.

[17] Ibid., 2.2.19 (CO 2:201): '[humanam rationem] in rebus divinis caecam prorsus esse et stupidam'.

[18] Ibid., 2.2.12 (CO 2:195): 'vera notitia'.

[19] Ibid., 2.2.15 (CO 2:198): 'mens hominis, quantumlibet ab integritate sua collapsa et perversa, eximiis tamen etiamnum Dei donis vestita est et ornata'.

[20] Ibid., 2.2.15 (CO 2:199): 'talibus exemplis discamus quot naturae humanae bona Dominus reliquerit, postquam vero bono spoliata est'.

[21] Ibid., 2.2.16 (CO 2:199): 'Non quod per se inquinari possint [i.e. dona naturalia], quatenus a Deo proficiscuntur: sed quia polluto homini pura esse desierunt.'

[22] Ibid., 2.2.26 (CO 2:207).

[23] Ibid.

the loss of supernatural gifts. In any case, mention has already been made, precisely in the immediate context of reason (*ratio*), that some kind of volition has been left. So the will, because it is inseparable from human nature, did not perish.[24] This is graphically evident as well as interesting in the issue of the *intermediate things* (*res mediae*). These indifferent matters which have nothing to do with the kingdom of God (the redemptive perspective) fall under the heading of human free judgment.[25] But true righteousness is usually referred to God's special grace and spiritual regeneration.[26] Man, accordingly, is not robbed of his will but of the soundness of his will,[27] and Calvin appropriates the saying of Bernard of Clairvaux where the latter says: simply to will as such inheres in the nature of humanity; to will ill arises from a corrupt nature; to will well arises from grace.[28]

Pursuing this reasoning logically one would expect: people are powerless to will anything that is conducive to salvation (the *true good* is parallel to *true righteousness*, of which reason is incapable), but in the sinful situation in which fallen man finds himself he may indeed will the good without its having any effect with respect to his salvation in Christ. The gate of the kingdom of God remains closed.

Thus – still under the impression of the many good things of which reason in the state of sin (*ratio in statu peccati*) is capable – one might reason. One gets the strong impression, however, that man's free will is more thoroughly crippled than his reason. It is the servant of sin, *cannot* confine itself to the good; man no longer has a free will with respect to good and evil. From a labyrinth of texts we will quote a few strong pronouncements.

'Man will then be spoken of as having a free will, not only because he has free choice equally of good and evil, but because

[24] Ibid., 2.2.12 (CO 2:196).

[25] Ibid., 2.2.5 (CO 2:190): 'Sub libero hominis concilio.' This is essentially the same as the *liberum arbitrium*.

[26] Ibid.: 'veram autem iustitiam ad specialem Dei gratiam et spiritualem regenerationem referre'. Cf. ibid., 2.4.6 (CO 2:227).

[27] Ibid., 2.3.5 (CO 2:213): 'non voluntate privatus est homo ... sed voluntatis sanitate'. Cf. ibid., 2.3.6 (CO 2:215).

[28] Ibid., 2.3.5 (CO 2:213): 'simpliciter velle, hominis: male velle, corruptae naturae: bene velle gratiae' (Bernard of Clairvaux, *Tractatus de gratia et libero arbitrio* 6.16 [MSL 182:1040]). Wendel (*Calvin*, 190), points out differences in nuance with the literal text of Bernard.

he does evil by will, not by compulsion.'[29] This last point is a typical attempt to uphold in man the feature that he does not choose evil because he is forced to consent to it but that it actually happens by necessity. The ingenious distinction between compulsion (*coactio*) and necessity (*necessitas*), which will be reviewed later, is a striking sign of how little man still is before the sovereign God. The only positive thing he still has of his own and can do is to commit evil without being compelled to do so. 'It is indisputable that man has no free will for good works, unless he be helped by grace, indeed by special grace, with which the elect are endowed through regeneration.'[30] In a statement like this last one the greatness of Another breaks into the littleness of the one: there can only be a truly free will for good in a person if God's power grants it; in other words, there is no free will unless it is made free by God.[31] Thus in the word 'grace' used here there is already a (passing) reference to the One who completely controls the problematics of free will: the sovereign God who alone brings the elect to regeneration and true freedom. Although this is perhaps exegetically debatable, Calvin consistently applies Romans 7 to the elect.[32] Apart from grace, there simply cannot be such consultation between evil and good as Paul so incisively describes it in that chapter. In the final analysis, is it not the case (let it still be stated in the form of a question), that in the above quotation the good, of which only the divinely liberated will is capable by grace, is situated in the perspective of salvation? As far as Calvin is concerned, we can abolish the term 'free will'. Such an abolition would be a real boon to the church.[33] If the term actually stands for so little, why decorate such a slight matter with so proud a title?[34] In this connection it is striking that, when

[29] *Institutes* 2.2.7 (CO 2:191): 'Voluntate, non coactione'; cf. ibid., 2.2.5 (CO 2:190).

[30] Ibid., 2.2.6 (CO 2:190): 'extra controversiam erit, non suppetere ad bona opera liberum arbitrium homini, nisi gratia adiuvetur'.

[31] Ibid., 2.2.8 (CO 2:192): 'non libera, sed a Deo liberata voluntas'.

[32] Ibid., 2.2.27 (CO 2:208): 'Quis in se tale dissidium habeat, nisi qui Spiritu Dei regeneratus, reliquias carnis circumfert?' Cf. *Comm. Rom.* 7:14–25 (CO 49:128–36).

[33] *Institutes* 2.2.8–9 (CO 2:192–3).

[34] Ibid., 2.2.7 (CO 2:191): 'quorum attinebat rem tantulam adeo superbo titulo insignire?'

he is speaking of the moral achievements of pagans, Calvin is much more restrained and sceptical than when he discusses their intellectual and cultural achievements.[35] Some people obviously pointed especially to the virtues of pagans to argue that, with reference to the free will's power to do good, things were not as bad as the Reformer actually made them out to be. Calvin's response to this is deep distrust toward all external human virtues.[36] Supposing, however, that the gifts of Camillus (the pagan example of sanctity) were as genuine as they are made out to be, they are not the common gifts of nature but the special gifts of divine grace.[37] As he then continues his 'vote of no-confidence', Calvin puts down the standard that is precious and decisive for him: 'Besides, the chief part of purity is lacking where there is no zeal to bring out God's glory. . . .'[38]

Actually this statement alone already touches Calvin's deepest intentions, intentions which govern his discussion of free will. It is one of the most sensitive points in which his zeal for the honour of God (*studium gloriae Dei*) is given free rein, as it were; one of those points at which the tension within the bipolarity of God and man is maximal. 'Free will' seems to be for him an irritating and dangerous expression which has the ring of a challenge to God, the domain to which man withdraws himself from the sovereign God, a place of refuge from the perspective of which he repeatedly, stubbornly and incorrigibly, indulges in deceptive self-glorification (*falsa glorificatio*).

One instinctively gets this impression as one encounters the many points of friction which mark the divine–human relation especially on the level of free will. Altogether they serve as so many evidences of Calvin's struggle to let the sovereign God have full scope vis-à-vis man with his so-called free will. As it pertains

---

[35] Cf. ibid., 2.3.3, 4 (CO 2:211–13) with ibid., 2.2.2, 15 (CO 2:186–87, 198–9).

[36] Ibid., 2.3.4 (CO 2:212): 'vitia sub virtutis imagine'. Indeed, the estimation of the pagans by other authors, even a long time later, is no more flattering. Cf. C. Hazart, SJ, *Triomph vande waerachtige Kercke* (Antwerp, 1673), 102: 'Wat sal ick segghen van d'Heydenen? Allegaer saemen waeren sy uytghestort als onverstandighe beesten tot haere vleesschelijcke wellusten.'

[37] *Institutes* 2.3.4 (CO 2:212): 'speciales Dei gratiae'.

[38] Ibid., 2.3.4 (CO 2:213): 'Adde quod praecipua pars rectitudinis deficit ubi nullum est illustrandae Dei gloria studium.'

to neutral works, Calvin still wants to speak softly and comparatively about God and the will of man.[39] But this changes totally when it concerns human initiatives in relation to whatever good or evil.

As one of these points of friction we want to mention the remarkable distinction between compulsion (*coactio*) and necessity (*necessitas*). This is not an invention of Calvin. Luther already employed it.[40] Calvin eagerly adopts[41] and defends it, as in the following passage:

> Now, when I say that the will deprived of freedom is of necessity either drawn or led into evil it is strange that this seems a hard saying to anyone, since there is nothing absurd in it and it does not differ from what the saints have also taught. But it offends those who know not how to distinguish between necessity and compulsion. But if anyone asks them whether God is not necessarily good and the devil is not necessarily bad, what would they reply? For God's goodness is so connected with his divinity that it is just as necessary for him to be good as it is for him to be God.[42]

Our concern is not to undertake a critical examination of the validity of this distinction. It seems to us rather ingenious and contrived, however acceptable and correct the comparison between God's will and the devil's sounds. What makes this kind of distinction so interesting, however, is the deeper background which comes through in it. God's sovereignty advances right into the fortress of human decision and conduct, whereas human capability shrinks down into dreadful human powerlessness. In this *necessitas* God's all-controlling causality indirectly shines out to the limit. Why is the human will not able to make a choice for whatever good a person might fancy? Why does that person necessarily opt for evil? Because God abandons them, because God's grace is lacking in them, because without God they are unable to do any

---

[39] For example, in ibid., 2.5.7 (CO 2:228): 'Velis nolis, animum tuum a motione Dei potius quam ab electionis tuae libertate pendere, . . . experientia reputare coget.'

[40] Luther, *De servo arbitrio* (WA 18:634); cf. Bucer, *Metaphrases epistolarum Pauli* (1536), 100f.

[41] *Institutes* 2.2.5 (CO 2:190): 'Hanc distinctionem ego libenter recipio.' On the topic of psychological freedom and ethical lack of freedom, cf. Barnikol, *Lehre Calvins vom unfreien Willen*, 10.

[42] *Institutes* 2.3.5 (CO 2:213–14); *Institutie*, trans. Sizoo, 1:300.

good. In line with this, and in the same conceptual framework, we would read the word *compulsion* (*coactio*) which is absent in this tragic event. In the context of Calvin's intense concern to give all honour to God and to keep him far from any blame for sin, the word *compulsion* undoubtedly first of all conceals in the first place Calvin's firm intention to make a person responsible for the evil that necessarily happens. *Not by compulsion* means: (1) God is not to blame and (2) the person is guilty. This last motif will play a comparable role in Calvin's view of the predestination of the reprobates.[43] At the same time this phrase 'not by compulsion' conceals a piece of human initiative, human responsibility, and human accountability. To say this, you may be sure, is not Calvin's primary intent! Nevertheless it *is* being said, be it implicitly. So it becomes clear that man is not totally absorbed by the superiority of God's sovereignty and the power of his creative grace. There remains an incomprehensible core of human decision and human insight, even if it be on the sinister level of sinful, culpable, human powerlessness. In the final analysis Calvin cannot meet the challenge of harmonizing God's sovereignty, or even combining it, with the meagre remnant of human initiative. But even here the concern of his theology is the divine–human relation.

Actually all of Book II, chapter 5, in which he refutes an assortment of objections, witnesses to the same struggle. It is interesting to read how he comments on Augustine when the latter speaks of the Spirit of God who is the Helper of those who work and even adds: 'the name "Helper" indicates that you, too, do something'.[44] One must not understand this, according to Calvin, as though he attributes something separate to us; but in order not to reinforce our slothfulness he links the works of God to ours . . . a combination, therefore, of God's works with ours, not in order to credit anything to human capability, but – negatively – in order not to drive humans toward total inertia. The familiar risk of human slothfulness again surfaces here; this possibility of slothfulness, however, again implies the involvement or non-involvement of persons in the event of the working of God's Spirit. This possibility

[43] Chapter 3, pp. 138–9, of this study.
[44] Augustine, *Sermons* 156 C, 11.11 (MSL 38:855f.); *Institutes* 2.5.15 (CO 2:243).

of laziness is left to them and by implication something of the human input which is evidently not compelled. Here, too, one senses how this is left to man by God's sovereign will.

A linking of God's works to ours, indeed. But never in such a way that some kind of authorship on the level of grace would befall to man and he would have reason to boast of it. In this respect no mixture (*mixtura*) is permissible, for any mixture people attempt to make of the power of free will with the grace of God is nothing but a corruption of grace – 'just as if one were to mix wine with muddy, bitter water'.[45] It is again all the more evident from this splendid formulation on what level Calvin's defence is directed in the matter of the free will of man: it is the level of grace, the plane of salvation. Man may not claim the praise due to the good done by the will, for in reality it is God who is at work. Still *ours* is the will, *ours* the zeal and *ours* the mind which God directs toward the good. Man is here pushed back very far, radically and resolutely, from the good the will does here. Still it is *our* mind (etc.), which is involved and activated.[46]

Thus, simultaneously, it is really our will, our zeal, and our thinking, which are at work. In this formulation one senses the laboured effort to give both God and human beings a place in the good the free will accomplishes. Not one of all these attempts, however, is completely satisfactory. One itches to ask more questions, for also Calvin does not degrade the fallen, enslaved will to the status of a mere automatism. This was already true of the fallen, enslaved will which without compulsion (*non coactione*) chooses to do evil. Even much less can this be said of the liberated will.[47] Here the will, liberated and continually spurred on and stimulated by grace, is fully honoured. That is possible at this point because by now the danger that a person would pride himself or herself on their moral achievements and capability has been effectively banished. *That* danger is Calvin's greatest concern and the source of his intense distrust when people speak of human free will. His struggle is directed against the will which, detached

---

[45] *Institutes* 2.5.15 (CO 2:243): 'perinde ac siquis lutosa et amara aqua vinum dilueret'.

[46] Ibid.: 'Nostra est mens, nostra voluntas, nostrum studium' – with a clear emphasis on the possessive pronoun.

[47] Ibid., 2.3.14 (CO 2:223): '[significat], hominem non ita trahi ut sine motu cordis, quasi extraneo impulsu feratur: sed intus sic affici ut *ex corde obsequatur*'.

from God and his grace, is supposed to be able to achieve the good on its own strength and would boast about it. Actually this struggle is an extension and consequence of the divine demand of the Decalogue: 'You shall not have strange gods before you.' The free will is one of the most popular and beloved idols. Calvin's deepest intent in these militant chapters, accordingly, can be captured in the phrase: the idol of the free will.[48] The sin of the natural man which consists in wanting to be equal to God is concretized above all in the idolization of free will. From this perspective Calvin's whole struggle is an attempt to honour the divine–human relation precisely in its most basic character as the Creator–creature relation.

Calvin's zeal to accord to God the Creator the place that is due to him also when human free will is at stake finds its expression in the ever-returning demand to give the glory to him alone. This motif keeps coming back as a monotonous refrain.[49] Not even one tiny particle of the glory of God may be taken from him,[50] just as the apostle would rather ascribe all the credit of his labour to grace alone.[51] Also this repeated stress on the glory of God which is at issue here is nothing but an unbroken attempt to do justice to God's sovereignty. It is another version of the 'idol of the free will' approach. It is characterized by the same purpose and intensity as was present when Calvin sought to prevent persons from stealing any part of God's honour and place. That honour is nothing other than the response people owe to God vis-à-vis the true place which is his due. It is the answer a person gives when conscious of standing before the great God. It is the heartfelt answer of the liberated will when it sees itself confronted by the God of all salvation.

Although it actually lies outside the scope of the present study, it is nevertheless worthwhile comparing what Calvin says about human free will to some pronouncements made on the subject by the Roman Catholic church. Following Hans Küng's example,

[48] Ibid., 2.5.11 (CO 2:239): 'liberi arbitrii simulacrum'.

[49] Ibid., 2.3.6 (CO 2:216): 'quasi diceret ne tantillum quidem restare homini in quo glorietur, quia totum a Deo est'.

[50] Ibid., 2.3.10 (CO 2:220): 'nec . . . portiuncula de eius laude decerpenda erat'.

[51] Ibid., 2.3.12 (CO 2:222): 'totam laboris laudem uni gratiae transcribit'. Cf. 1 Corinthians 15:10.

we would like to compare the teaching of the *Institutes* with a few dogmatic utterances of the Catholic church.[52] Calvin's statement (title, chapter 2 of Book II): 'Man has now been deprived of freedom of choice and subjected to miserable servitude'[53] seems diametrically opposite to Trent's condemnation: 'If any one says that, since Adam's sin, the free will of man is lost and extinguished . . . let him be anathema.'[54] But the Second Council of Orange is just as radically opposed to the above pronouncement by the Council of Trent:

> On the things that belong to man no one has anything of himself but lies and sin. But whatever man has in the way of truth and righteousness comes from that source for which we in this desert must thirst, so that we, being bedewed from there as with a few drops, should not perish on the way.[55]

Now compare the words: 'no one has anything of himself but lies and sin' to the superscription of chapter 3 of Book II of the *Institutes:* 'From man's corrupt nature nothing comes forth but what is damnable.'[56]

In the preceding pages we have already expressly pointed out the double perspective that is demonstrable in Calvin's discussion of free will. It is not necessary to repeat this at length. We can illustrate its presence from two statements: (1) 'The will did not perish because, in spite of sin, man continued to exist.'[57] This by itself is already a fact of grace, as Calvin clearly states (cf. what has been said above about the *intermediate things*). (2) A second statement reads: the human will is completely powerless in relation

---

[52] H. Küng, *Rechtfertigung: die Lehre Karl Barths und eine katholische Besinnung* (Einsiedeln, 1957), 172–97.

[53] *Institutes* 2.2 (CO 2:185): 'Hominem arbitrii libertate nunc esse spoliatum et miserae servituti addictum.'

[54] 'Si quis liberum arbitrium post Adae peccatum amissum et exstinctum esse dixerit . . . A.S.' DENZ 1555 (815).

[55] 'De his, quae hominum propria sunt. Nemo habet de suo nisi mendacium et peccatum. Si quid autem habet homo veritatis atque iustitiae, ab illo fonte est, quem debemus sitire in hac eremo, ut ex eo quasi guttis quibusdam irrorati non deficiamus in via.' DENZ 392 (195).

[56] *Institutes* 2.3 (CO 2:209): 'Ex corrupta hominis natura nihil nisi damnabile prodire.'

[57] Ibid., 2.2.12 (CO 2:196): 'Sic voluntas, quia inseparabilis est ab hominis natura, non periit.'

to the good. Man has no free will. In relation to any good at all? *No: for the will to do good, in Calvin, is always anchored in the perspective of salvation.* For that matter, Trent does *not* say either that the free will is able to will the good apart from grace. The fact that man simply continues to exist after the advent of sin is already an instance of grace, thanks to Christ the 'author of nature'. Trent, too, has a very radical view of sin as something deserving of death.[58] The fact that any will is left at all, that the freedom of choice has not been entirely lost and extinguished, is by itself a fact of grace. But Calvin more explicitly places the will to do good in the light of grace. In other words, he does not know the possibility that the still-surviving will could choose the purely natural good because this good does not in fact *exist*. To will the good is always to will for salvation. The salvific perspective clearly extends to all willing-for-good. We will substantiate this fact in the following points.

1. Both at the beginning and the end Calvin's discourse on free will is expressly situated in the perspective of salvation: 'except out of the Lord's mercy there is no salvation for man';[59] and at the end of chapter 5 the clear conclusion is: 'man has utterly died as far as the blessed life is concerned'.[60]

2. 'Thus there is left to man such free will ... that except through grace can neither be converted to God nor abide in God.'[61] This phrase 'except through grace' is added each time there is mention of any will toward good.[62]

We recall the texts cited above: a person has no free will to perform good works 'unless he be helped by grace'.[63] When he deals with the virtues of pagans, Calvin even more strikingly puts them in the context of salvation. If there should ever be a clear

[58] DENZ 1511 (788).

[59] *Institutes* 2.2.3 (CO 2:211): 'Nullam esse homini salutem nisi a Domini misericordia.'

[60] Ibid., 2.5.19 (CO 2:246): 'Dei verbum ... penitus interiisse docet *quantum ad beatae vitae rationem.*' Cf. ibid., 2.5.19 (CO 2:247): 'gratuita *unde salus dependet*'.

[61] Ibid., 2.3.14 (CO 2:224): 'Ita homini tale relinquitur liberum arbitrium ... quod nec ad Deum converti nec in Deo persistere *nisi per gratiam* possit.'

[62] Cf. ibid., 2.3.5 (CO 2:214), where it is generally stated: 'immensa eius bonitate fieri ne male agere possit'.

[63] Ibid., 2.2.6 (CO 2:190): 'nisi gratia adiuvetur'. Cf. ibid., 2.2.8 (CO 2:192): 'a Deo liberata voluntas'.

suggestion of a *natural moral goodness* anywhere, then we might expect it to be here. But, as we saw above, this is not the case.[64] Either we are looking at 'lofty appearance' or at 'the special graces of God'.[65] We must think in this connection of the remarkable achievements of pagans, achievements which could not have been attained without the assistance of the Spirit of God.[66] Thus Calvin consistently links all will to do good with the grace of God. In other words: it is possible only because of human salvation in Christ.

3. For this must be said in general and may be said particularly with reference to Calvin's theology: Every grace is Christian grace and only Christian grace. Any good theology can make this clear but it may be said especially of Calvin, inasmuch as he, in a remarkable way, attributes *everything* to salvation by Christ. This is the basis for the far-reaching unity he posits between the Old and the New Testament. This alone already is strong warrant for speaking of Calvin's Christocentric thinking. This is also the final reason why in his thought all the moral good which the human will might possibly achieve must be touched by the saving action of Christ. It is the ability to will *for salvation*.

4. Finally, we would have to cite the Scripture passages which all occur in a salvific context, from the *new heart* in Ezekiel,[67] to the persistent use of New Testament verses, among which especially Philippians 2:13; 2 Corinthians 3:5 and also Ephesians 2:10 stand out.

Now when the Council of Orange II so radically states that man has nothing of himself but lies and sin, it is speaking on this level: from the perspective of salvation in Christ and with an eye to the unique fellowship with God which is only possible in him. It is not at all surprising, for that matter, that this council speaks along these lines.[68] Orange took the text cited straight from Augustine, under whose influence, specifically on the point of free

---

[64] See above, pp. 52ff.

[65] *Institutes* 2.3.4 (CO 2:212): 'speciales Dei gratiae'.

[66] Ibid., 2.2.16 (CO 2:199): 'Neque tamen interim obliviscamur haec praestantissima divini Spiritus esse bona.'

[67] Ezekiel 36:26; *Institutes* 2.3.6 (CO 2:215).

[68] For a dogmatic appraisal of the statements of Orange II, see Küng, *Rechtfertigung*, 177, along with the secondary literature cited there.

will, Calvin also was writing. Calvin[69] as well as Orange II reacted to all possible forms of Pelagianism.

But when, so many centuries after the Council of Orange, Trent posits that after the fall into sin human free will has not been lost and extinguished, this has to be understood of human freedom to choose. It is the free will which can choose in indifferent matters, of which Calvin states that they have nothing to do with the Kingdom of God.[70] Of *this* free will (*liberum arbitrium*) Calvin also says that it is integrally bound up with the human nature which has not been lost as a result of the fall.[71]

In addition it must be said of Trent as well that it views the continued existence of human nature *after* sin and the continued existence of a human free will as integral to that nature, as a fruit of grace. For Trent asserts, along with Calvin, that sin deserves death.[72] Also, according to Trent, it is astonishing that human beings did not completely perish after the fall.

There is no contradiction, accordingly, between Orange II and Trent. Both speak of free will, but each speaks from a different perspective. This twofold perspective, as we saw, is also present in Calvin's line of argument.

So we believe we have found in the *Institutes* what Küng asserted with respect to the whole of Reformational theology: there is no essential difference in view between what Calvin posits in relation to man's free will and what the Roman Catholic church teaches on the same point. Without wanting to pursue this topic further, we believe that the ecclesiastical decrees against Baius, read in the right perspective, do not in any way alter this picture.[73]

2. The Law of the Old Covenant

Before we speak of Christ – who stands for a unique and incomprehensibly exceptional union of God and man, a union in which the two poles not only achieve intense coexistence but in an

---

[69] Cf. *Institutes* 2.2.21 (CO 2:203); 2.5.1 (CO 2:230); 2.3.13 (CO 2:222): 'aetatis nostrae Pelagiani'.

[70] Ibid., 2.2.5 (CO 2:190); see above, p. 52, n. 24.

[71] Ibid., 2.2.12 (CO 2:196); see above, p. 59, n. 56.

[72] DENZ 1511 (788).

[73] Ibid., 1927 (1027). Cf. Küng, *Rechtfertigung*, 177, with the view of G. C. Berkouwer, *Man: The Image of God*, trans. D. Jellema (Grand Rapids, 1962), 162ff. On this question see also Le Bachelet in DThC, 1:cols. 38–111, and P. Smulders, 'Bajanismus', in LThK, 1:cols. 1196–8.

incomprehensible manner attain existence in one person – we will first direct our attention to the Law of the Old Covenant.

In order properly to contextualize this subject of the Law we must first of all bring out the Christological aspect of the Old Covenant in Calvin's thought. Then we will discuss the place of God and man in their mutual relationship as it comes to the fore in the function of the Law in general and in the commandments of the Decalogue in particular.

A discussion of the Law of the Old Covenant can be viewed as an introduction to Christ and is actually already a discussion of Christ, be it in the concealed manner which marks the old dispensation. In no way, therefore, is there a dichotomy between what is said here about the Old Covenant and its fulfilment in Christ. As we commented earlier, the line of thought which brings unity in the redemptive order of both is highlighted in Calvin. That line is Christ. The Old Testament is Christian. 'The covenant of grace is contained in the Law.'[74] There is actually no essential distinction between it and the covenant of Christians.[75] The difference consists only in the manner of its implementation (the *modus quo*). It is a difference between the plain and clear reality over against a similar reality but then clothed in images and told in a childlike manner.[76] 'The Old Testament fathers had Christ by the pledge of the covenant.'[77] God never took delight in any cult which had no relation to Christ.[78] Neither did God show his good will to the ancient people apart from that Mediator. These statements are strongly supported by a number of Scripture passages, especially from the Old Covenant. From this it even follows that God cannot be gracious to the human race apart from the Mediator who is Christ.[79] The faith of the fathers under the Law was directed toward him.[80] In order

---

[74] *Institutes* 2.7.7 (CO 2:253): 'gratia Iudaeis oblata'; *Comm. Rom.* 8:15 (CO 49:149): 'in lege foedus gratiae continetur'. On this see also above, p. 43.

[75] Ibid., 2.10.10–23 (CO 2:319–29).

[76] Ibid., 2.11 (CO 2:329–40); cf. ibid., 2.10.2 (CO 2:313): 'administratio variat'.

[77] Ibid., 2.10.23 (CO 2:328): 'Patres scl. Christum in foederis sui pignus habuerunt.'

[78] Ibid., 2.6.1 (CO 2:248): 'nisi qui in Christum respiceret'.

[79] Ibid., 2.6.3 (CO 2:250): 'Hinc iam satis liquet, qua non potest Deus propitius humano generi esse absque Mediatore, sanctis Patribus sub Lege Christum semper fuisse obiectum, ad quem fidem suam dirigerent.'

[80] Ibid., 2.6.3 (CO 2:251): 'lectores volo admonitos, spem omnium piorum non alibi unquam fuisse repositam quam in Christo'.

to look out upon their deliverance, the Jews, guided by all these predictions, had to turn their eyes directly to Christ.[81] We deliberately underscore the central place in the entire economy of salvation here in order not to yield too quickly to the temptation of pointing out in Calvin's theology, apart from Christ, a principle to which all of his believing reflection could be reduced. It seems to us more correct – let this be said here already and by way of precaution – to point out a number of pivotal points on which the whole of Calvin's thinking seems to rest.

Also the Law exists in the shadow of the figure of Christ. The superscription of Book II, chapter 7, still only weakly indicates this truth ('the law was given, not to restrain the folk of the Old Covenant under itself, but to foster hope of salvation in Christ until his coming').[82] But already very quickly it is openly and clearly stated: 'Now, from the grace offered the Jews, we can surely deduce that the law was not without Christ.'[83] By no means devoid of Christ. He was represented to the people of the Old Covenant in a double mirror:[84] in the tribe of the Levites and in the offspring of David, nor does Calvin forget Romans 10:4 where Christ is viewed as the end of the law. Certainly the first thing that strikes us in Calvin's view of the Old Testament and the Law is this Christological aspect and it seems to us to be dominant precisely on this point of the Law. It is very much a question whether this fact comes sufficiently into its own in the assessment of Lang[85] and Ritschl.[86] Any 'legality' (*Gesetzlichkeit*) which they consider an objection to and a mistake in Calvin's theology, after all, fundamentally comes to stand in another light as a result of this Christological starting-point.[87]

---

[81] Ibid., 2.6.4 (CO 2:251): 'oculos ad Christum convertere'.

[82] Ibid., 2.7 (CO 2:252).

[83] Ibid., 2.7.1 (CO 2:253): 'Iam ex gratia Iudaeis oblata certo colligitur legem Christo non fuisse vacuum.' Cf. *Comm. Rom.* 10:4 (CO 49:196): 'Imo quidquid doceat lex, quidquid praecipiat, quidquid promittat, semper Christum habet pro scopo.'

[84] *Institutes* 2.7.2 (CO 2:254): 'in duplici speculo'.

[85] Lang, *Johannes Calvin*, 67, 93.

[86] O. Ritschl, *Dogmengeschichte des Protestantismus*, 3:164: 'Calvins Neigung zur Gesetzlichkeit . . . in der man zutreffend seinen Grundfehler erkannt hat.'

[87] *Institutes* 2.8.55 (CO 2:306): 'si veram diligendi lineam tenere libet . . . primum convertendi sunt oculi . . . in Deum'.

Having given prominence to this very important Christological aspect, we now focus our attention on the question: how are God and man related in Calvin's views on the Law?

In line with our purpose in this study we will consciously confine ourselves to this question. But it is not saying too much if we claim that the Law in the restricted sense, the Decalogue, actually already invites us to take this approach when it presents the commandments on two tables, both of them having a specific focus, namely God and man respectively. Before we focus on the moral law, however, the question can be raised whether in Calvin's general reflections on the Law nothing jumps out that is notable for the bipolarity that is central to our study. In our opinion, that is clearly the case. Calvin speaks about the threefold use of the moral law.[88] We will review all three uses.

'The first part is this: while it shows God's righteousness, that is, the righteousness which alone is pleasing to God, it reminds, informs, and lastly convicts and condemns every person of his own unrighteousness.'[89] This seems to us a significant beginning. God and man are placed side by side and over against each other, our attention is directed toward both, but first toward God. His righteousness (*iustitia*) is highlighted and in this light human unrighteousness (*iniustitia*) stands out. It is the same relational focus we have signalled before. For that matter, we find here no low-key observations, for the words go beyond factual information (*certiorem facere*). In the light of God's righteousness, the law shows up every person's own unrighteousness. It penetrates our conscience (again that attention to the inner experience of man) and finally pronounces its condemnation. The findings to which, in God's light, the Law brings people are far from flattering. And we cannot escape the impression that Calvin parades the dark secrets of the human soul with a certain amount of pleasure. Blinded and drunk with self-love, feebleness and impurity, vanity, man is puffed up with insane confidence and illusion – all in all, a sombre array of errors which a person would never have discovered had he measured himself by the standard of his own

---

[88] Ibid., 2.7.6–12 (CO 2:257–62). A. Göhler (*Calvins Lehre von der Heiligung* [Munich, 1935], 117) notes that Calvin sometimes also speaks of a twofold use of the law.

[89] *Institutes* 2.7.6 (CO 2:257): 'prima est, ut dum iustitiam ostendit . . . suae unumquemque iniustitiae admoneat'.

judgment. Calvin continues this exploration of the deep and tortuous hiding places for some time and for a moment it seems as if God is lost from view, and the Law is highhandedly playing judge in its own right. But then it again becomes evident that all those evils gain a final malignity by collectively raising a fist against God. Man uses his inferior talents, his fictitious acts of righteousness,[90] to elevate himself against the grace of God. Again, the aggressive atmosphere which was noted earlier in the divine–human relation is not lacking here either.

Thus the Law teaches man to judge his own misery;[91] it is a mirror in which we see the reflection of our own misery.[92] It is undeniable that Calvin, in indulging in this kind of reflection, finds himself in good company.[93] It is natural that he should also interpret the familiar passage from the Letter to the Galatians in this fashion.[94] But Calvin continually has before his mind the reciprocal activity that occurs between God and man. God's righteousness reveals human unrighteousness, indeed, but the latter in turn increasingly brings out the irreproachable righteousness of God.

> For, since all of us are proved to be transgressors, the more clearly it reveals God's righteousness, conversely the more it uncovers our iniquity. These statements . . . have great power to commend God's beneficence all the more gloriously. . . . Thereby the grace of God . . . becomes lovelier. . . .[95]

Here again it is clearly evident how great a role God's glory – here evidently in the manner of his beneficence (*beneficentia*) and his sweet grace (*suavis gratia*) – plays in the interpersonal relation between God and man. Calvin next ends the account of this first function of the Law with a plethora of quotations from Augustine.[96]

---

[90] Ibid.: 'factitiae iustitiae'.

[91] Ibid., 2.7.3 (CO 2:255): 'suam miseriam aestimat'.

[92] Ibid., 2.7.7 (CO 2:258): 'Ita Lex instar est speculi cuiusdam, in quo nostram impotentiam . . . contemplamur.'

[93] Romans 3:20.

[94] Galatians 3:19–29 (CO 50:214–23).

[95] *Institutes* 2.7.7 (CO 2:258): 'ad illustriorem divinae beneficentiae commendationem'.

[96] Ibid., 2.7.9 (CO 2:259): 'Sint omnes parvuli, et reus fiat omnis mundus coram Deo' (Augustine, *In ps.* 118, *sermo* 27.3 [MSL 37:1581]).

The second function of the Law is that of the disciplinarian, the *paidagogos,* who with a hard hand restrains those who do not want to listen. Note that Calvin clearly poses the demand that humans must obey God's law heart and soul. In this context there is no chance that people will be spoken to in their hearts. They are afraid of punishment; God actually does not interest them; in fact, if they could – though this sounds somewhat exaggerated – they would prefer to eliminate him. Here man is openly hostile to God. One cannot really speak of religion in this connection. The law is basically no more than a bridle to restrain man in human society.[97]

Keeping the Law reluctantly is of course sinful. This idea, which is so powerfully present in Luther, pervasively entered Reformational thought. This view is also implicitly present in Calvin. Only the regenerate, after all, are able sincerely and spontaneously to listen to God's commandments. Only they belong to the beloved children of God.

For this last category of people too, those in whose hearts the Spirit of God also exerts power and dominion, the Law has its proper function.[98] For them the idea is to learn and to obey God's will ever better. Here too, in standing together with man, regenerate persons, God holds his own place. It is his will that must be obeyed. For the renewed humans the flesh is like an idle and stubborn donkey which has to be whipped into line from time to time. But here we are clearly dealing with a cordial relationship. Here indeed justice is done to man's interior being. Such a person relates to the Law with all his heart;[99] Calvin cites Psalm 19:8ff. where the Law is celebrated as rejoicing the heart and enlightening the eyes. . . . Here certainly human dignity is fully honoured. The human being is genuinely open to the Other. Indeed, here Calvin uses the word 'lovable', a quality which belongs to the Law, and which has to come from the Mediator.[100]

---

[97] *Institutes* 2.7.11 (CO 2:261): 'Alii opus habent fraeno.'

[98] Ibid., 2.7.12 (CO 2:261): 'quorum in cordibus iam viget ac regnat Dei Spiritus'. For a comparison with Luther's conception of the law, see Berkouwer, *Sin,* trans. P. Holtrop (Grand Rapids, 1971), 149–86 ('Sin and the Law'). See Luther, *Von den guten Werken* (1520; WA 6:204–76). On this question cf. also W. Joest, *Gesetz und Freiheit: Das Problem des Tertius usus legis bei Luther und der neutestamentlichen Parainese,* 2nd edn (Göttingen, 1956).

[99] *Institutes* 2.7.12 (CO 2:261): 'toto animi studio'.

[100] Ibid., 2.7.12 (CO 2:262): 'oblectatio et suavitas'.

Is not this cordial mutual orientation of God and man the source of a high ethic, a strong incentive to make progress in the knowledge of God and a life that corresponds to it?[101] Authentic Calvinism cannot be denied an active drive toward high-minded ethical conduct. So much for what concerns the intent of the Law in general. Now for something about the Decalogue, the ten commandments of God in the strict sense.

We noted earlier that the distribution of the Ten Commandments over the two tables of the Law automatically raises the question concerning the divine-human relation. The two poles are discussed more or less separately. The focus of the Lawgiver seems to be distinctive in each case. For our reflection the question is relevant what the place of God is when the issue is the commandments of the second table where human relations play a role; another question is: how does man conduct himself when, as in the first few commandments, God's unicity and greatness come so powerfully to the fore? We will refrain from a detailed discussion (that would require a separate study). We will limit ourselves to a few salient points, hoping that thereby the character and atmosphere of Calvin's discussion as a whole will nevertheless come into its own.

'. . . Now we have taught that we cannot conceive him in his greatness without being immediately confronted by his majesty, the majesty which binds us to his service'.[102] Of course, in connection with the commandments of the first table of the Law, if anywhere, it is to be expected that God's majesty will be set forth on a grand scale. The light in which the deity is viewed here, accordingly, is expressly that of his majesty. Calvin continually resorts to this manner of speaking.[103] The Lord alone wants to be pre-eminent among his people,[104] with a clear emphasis on this *alone,* and so the purpose of the first commandment is described.[105] True religion is characterized by reverence before

---

[101] Ibid.: 'novos facere progressus in puriorem divinae voluntatis notitiam'.

[102] Ibid., 2.8.1 (CO 2:266): 'docuimus non posse ipsum pro sua magnitudine a nobis concipi quin statim occurrat eius maiestas'.

[103] Cf. ibid., 2.8.4 (OS 3:346, lines 5, 21) and 2.8.11 (OS 3:352, lines 20, 35).

[104] Ibid., 2.8.16 (CO 2:277): 'Dominus in populo suo solus vult eminere.'

[105] Ibid., 2.8.13–16 (CO 2:257–79).

that majesty.[106] That fear before God is something Calvin takes with utter seriousness. God is an avenger of his majesty who visits the misdeeds of the fathers upon the children to the third and fourth generation.[107] In this connection he speaks of God's 'righteous curse',[108] thus reconciling God's causality with his moral purity. But also God's mercy – be it in passing – is given full scope.[109] This is particularly clear from the promise: 'On the other hand the promise is offered of extending God's mercy unto a thousand generations. . . .'[110]

In this connection Calvin returns to the beginning of his *Institutes* where he posits the knowledge of God and the knowledge of man – inseparably bound together and interwoven – as the starting-point of true wisdom. In the Law he again sees greatness and littleness standing side by side in mutual bondedness. God is given his place as Creator and Father and therefore we are duty bound to show him honour, reverence, love and fear. In that way the majesty of God becomes clearly visible to us. It is the identical God-image we sketched earlier (chapter 1); it arouses love and instills fear. This majesty is reflected in the Law (Calvin does not hesitate to speak of the majesty of the Law).[111] The supreme purity of God radiates from the penalty clause, his amazing beneficence from the promise.[112] It is this majesty man faces. It is this majesty he discerns when the Law confronts him. One could say that the function of the Law is to make humans conscious of who God is and what they themselves are in the light of that deity: the true nature of the bipolar divine–human relation becomes clear to them.

The worship of the divine majesty[113] is not only the main content of the first commandment and is not only central there but actually also in – rather, serves as starting point for – the commandments of the second table. 'Accordingly, in the first table,

[106] Ibid., 2.8.16 (CO 2:278); cf. the definition of *religio* in ibid., 1.3.2 (CO 2:35): 'fides cum serio Dei timore coniuncta'.
[107] Ibid., 2.8.18 (CO 2:279).
[108] Ibid., 2.8.19 (CO 2:280): 'iusta Dei maledictio'.
[109] Ibid., 2.8.21 (CO 2:282): 'misericordiae amplitudo'.
[110] Ibid., 2.8.21 (CO 2:281): 'in mille generationes Dei misericordia'.
[111] Ibid., 2.8.13 (CO 2:275): 'Legis maiestas.'
[112] Ibid., 2.8.4 (CO 2:269): 'summa Dei puritas, mira benignitas'.
[113] Ibid., 2.8.11 (CO 2:273): 'numinis sui cultus'.

God instructs us in piety and the proper duties of religion, by which we are to worship his majesty. The second table prescribes how *on account of the fear of his name* we ought to conduct ourselves in our relations with people.'[114] In other words: how people conduct themselves among themselves is determined by the 'fear of his name'.[115] Now what is the human profile which emerges in the Decalogue, specifically where the focus is on him and on the duties of love which relate to people?[116] In fact, God also plays the key role in the second table of the Law. The commandments are really the commandments *of God* and the power of his Person does not for a moment give way to the duties of love (*officia charitatis*). These commandments completely cover the love which God, for his own sake, enjoins upon people.[117] Whereas the version of 1536 still reads 'on account of himself' (*propter se*), in the text cited the emphasis on the God who commands is very strong. It is not correct to flatly translate it by the phrase 'according to his command'.[118] It is God who is speaking here. It is he to whom, in the final analysis, human behaviours have to be referred. Here too, he is the *legislator* who claims us *in toto*.[119] The fear and awe before God everywhere constitute the decisive background from which the command issues. Observe, says Calvin, who it is who commands and realize that it is a serious matter in any way to violate the divine majesty. It is God who is the reason for the moral conduct of persons.[120] You must not lie because God detests lying.[121] When a human being truly fears and loves God, he does not speak evil of others,[122] nor does his covetousness reach out to another man's house.[123]

Still, confronted by the commanding Ruler, humans are not reduced to things. The aim of the Law is a person who gives

[114] Ibid., 2.8.11 (CO 2:274): 'propter nominis sui timorem'.
[115] Ibid.
[116] Ibid., 2.8.9 (CO 2:273): 'officia charitatis'.
[117] Ibid., 2.8.12 (CO 2:274): 'charitatem quam propter seipsum nobis erga homines mandat'.
[118] *Institutie*, trans. Sizoo, 1:396.
[119] *Institutes* 2.8.44 (CO 2:297): 'legislator qui nos totos possidere debet'.
[120] Ibid., 2.8.59 (CO 2:308): 'Atqui oportuerat considerare, non simpliciter quid praecipiatur, sed quisnam sit ille qui praecipit.'
[121] Ibid., 2.8.47 (CO 2:300).
[122] Ibid., 2.8.48 (CO 2:301).
[123] Ibid., 2.8.50 (CO 2:303).

himself or herself wholeheartedly, for that is the deep level on which the Law wants to address humankind. All the powers of the soul are directed toward the love for God.[124] *And thus human beings are simultaneously raised up and built up to be the image of God.* This is even called the goal of the Law.[125] Whereas the Law was first the exposer of human powerlessness in light of God's greatness, it is now viewed, positively, as formative and constructive in line with God's own readiness to serve. This is the *humane* task of the Law. It draws people toward God; it is growth in the direction of God's image, doubtlessly a growth in love, because especially the commandments revolve around the *officia charitatis.* The surprising use here of the image of God in describing the work of the Law brings God and man close together and, in this process of coming together, being human is increasingly viewed positively as being the image of God.[126]

The fact that, precisely on the level of the commandments for man, the commanding God does not set aside and ambush man as competitor but respects him, in our opinion, is nowhere more evident than in the commandment in which we are commanded to honour our parents. There is no objection whatever against the word 'honour', 'for the word has a wide meaning in Scripture'.[127] Indeed, God shares his name with others.[128] 'The names "Father", "God" and "Lord" so belong to him alone that as often as we hear any one of these our mind ought to be struck with an awareness of his majesty.' Hence those persons

> with whom he shares the names, he illumines with a spark of his own splendour, so that each may be honoured in accordance with his position. Thus, in him who is our father it is fitting that we should see something divine, because he does not bear the divine title without cause. He who is a 'prince' or a 'lord' has some share in God's honour.

Participes . . . spectabiles . . . cum Deo communio ('participants . . . distinguished persons . . . some share with God'): most

---

[124] Ibid., 2.8.58 (CO 2:308): 'nisi ergo omnes animae potentiae in Dei timorem intenduntur, iam discessum est a Legis obedientia'.

[125] Ibid., 2.8.51 (CO 2:303): 'Lex spectet ut hominis vitam ad divinae puritatis exemplar formet . . . ut imaginem Dei quodammodo sit in vita expressurus.'

[126] Ibid., 2.8.40 (CO 2:295): 'quia imago Dei est homo'.

[127] Ibid., 2.8.35 (CO 2:292): 'Sic enim late patet vocabulum honoris in Scriptura.'

[128] Ibid.: 'suum cum illis nomen communicat'.

remarkable language, in our opinion, which manifests a profound unity and communion with God. However dominant the place of God may be in the commandments of the second table of the Law, they are enriching, upbuilding and value-creating, and situate people in an intimate relation to their God. Here, in the bipolar relation, a high measure of rest and unity has been attained. Human highness does not stand in the way of divine highness: 'It is unworthy and absurd that their eminence (as parents), which depends on God's highness and should lead us to it, should serve so as to pull down the highness of God. . . .'[129] This is the basis for a legitimate and authentic honouring of *people*. We recall here a statement of the *Institutes* of 1560 in which the honour of God and that of humans also coexist peacefully:

> We will bring honour to God by recognizing him as the principal author of all good; but we will also honour humans as servants and dispensers of those benefits and believe that he wants us to be in debt to them, because he has shown himself to be our benefactor through their hands.[130]

3. The mediator in the light of God's majesty

The bipolarity of God and man reaches a never-suspected meeting point in Jesus Christ. In him the two poles come so close together that this meeting becomes a unity, the unity of one Person. Two come together in such a way that we can speak of one: Christ. It is truly a *human being* who is so taken up into the unity of the person who is Christ and who was a human being in soul and body.

> For Jesus Christ is not only man as it concerns his body but he is equally man in his soul. We see how he was subject to emotions, to fear, and sadness. If he then was prepared to assume a human soul, why should he not also possess the attributes which naturally belong to a soul?[131]

It is truly God who entered into this incomprehensible oneness of the one person Christ: Christ, aside from being truly human, is

[129] Ibid., 2.8.38 (CO 2:294): 'Indignum enim et absonum est ut ad deprimendam Dei celsitudinem eorum eminentia polleat, quae ut ab illa pendet, ita in illam deducere nos debet.'

[130] 1560 *Institutes* (CO 3:261–2).

[131] *Sermon sur Luc* 2:50–2 (CO 46:487f.).

also truly God. This was necessary for him to be our Mediator. To this divinity of that human Mediator the *Institutes* graphically testify as follows:

> It was his task to swallow up death. Who but he who is Life could do this? It was his task to conquer sin. Who but he who is Righteousness itself could do this? It was his task to destroy the powers of the world and the air. Who could do this but he who is a power greater than the world and the air? Now where does life, righteousness, lordship, and the power of heaven lie but with God alone? Therefore our gracious God, when he willed that we be redeemed, made himself our Redeemer in the person of his only-begotten Son.[132]

'Those who despoil Christ either of his divinity or his humanity diminish his majesty and glory, or obscure his goodness.'[133] This witness to Christ has nothing special in it. It has been the believing conviction of Christianity from early times to the present. But can we also perhaps detect in Calvin's Christology something that betrays special attention to God and man separately and to the relation between the two? In other words, does Calvin also pursue his interest in the divine–human relation, to which we have repeatedly called attention, into the bosom of Christ's own existence? We believe this is the case.

In this section we plan to discuss how the existence of Christ was first of all illumined by Calvin from the vantage-point of the majesty of God. Second, we believe that the bipolarity of God and man present in the figure of Christ comes to expression in Calvin's special interest in the distinctiveness of the deity and the humanity in the one person of the Lord.

'The situation would surely have been hopeless had not the very majesty of God descended to us, since it was not in our power to ascend to him. Hence, it was necessary for the Son of God to become for us "Immanuel", that is, God with us.'[134] Indeed, if anyone should inquire into the necessity of Christ's mediatorship, the first reply must be a heavenly decree[135] so as to

---

[132] *Institutes* 2.12.2 (CO 2:341).

[133] Ibid., 2.12.3 (CO 2:342): 'Qui ergo Christum sua aut divinitate, aut humilitate spoliant, eius quidem vel imminuunt maiestatem et gloriam, vel bonitatem obscurant.'

[134] Ibid., 2.12.1 (CO 2:340): 'Deplorata certe res erat nisi maiestas ipsa Dei ad nos descenderat: quando ascendere nostrum non erat.'

[135] Ibid.: 'manavit ex caelesti decreto'.

eliminate any possibility of any causality apart from God. By this means, moreover, the final answer has already been given to curious and superfluous questions in this regard. Having thus given priority to the creative initiative of God, Calvin then proceeds to point out the various *motivations* which underlie the mediatorship of the Son of God. The first to be mentioned is this: Who could accomplish this work? One of Adam's children, all of whom are terrified at the sight of God? No; neither could one of the angels . . . ; in other words, precisely because God's majesty is so great, what was needed is a Mediator such as Christ is. We could never have looked, face to face, at God's glory, were it not hidden behind the veil of a human being. Though this is the first time this motif is asserted, it is certainly not the last. Then follow the other motivations all of which are listed as elements of comprehensibility – elements implied in this heavenly decree.

For us this mediatorship means a pledge, a security. For to make us, from being the children of humans, into the children of God is possible precisely because the Son of God took upon himself that which is ours . . . ; so, on the one hand, he could become the spotless Lamb of God, on the other a sinner subject to the curse.[136] Also inherent in this mediatorship is a possibility of 'satisfaction', about which we will talk later. All this is true, but we can agree with Reuter when he says: 'the first reason for this is certainly to be found in the *experience* of the . . . majesty of God; the other in the idea of the total remoteness and incomprehensibility of God'.[137] To look at Christ's mediatorship from the angle of God's majesty means, to Calvin, that apart from Christ, the Mediator, God's greatness cannot be known. Although his greatness can be distinguished from Christ's redemptive mediatorship, in fact the two coincide, to know God as he appears to us in the incarnate Son of God *is* salvation. It is striking that Calvin sees Christ's mediatorship in the light of God's

---

[136] *Comm. Gal.* 3:13 (CO 50:210). This argument of convenience, which views Christ's incarnation as the *arrha* of our salvation (*Institutes* 2.12.2 [CO 2:341]), betrays Calvin's pastoral concern for humanity. Although first the majesty of the divine pole serves to make the incarnation comprehensible, nevertheless in the second place Calvin immediately focuses his attention on the other pole, man, whose certainty of salvation is guaranteed in the incarnation.

[137] Reuter, *Grundverständnis der Theologie Calvins*, 130.

majesty. Not only does he start with the motif[138] 'that Christ, to perform the office of mediator, had to become man', but this view is strongly and continually accented in other places as well.

'. . . Faith . . . disappears unless he himself as mediator intervenes. . . . Moreover, God's majesty is too lofty to be attained by mortal men who are like little worms crawling upon the earth.'[139] In this connection he cites Irenaeus to the effect 'that the Father, himself infinite, becomes finite in the Son, for he has accommodated himself to our little measure lest our minds be overwhelmed by the immensity of his glory'.[140] Trusting in their Mediator, Christians 'now freely dare to come forth into God's presence'.[141] So great was the distance between our uncleanness[142] and God's perfect purity, and so lowly was our condition that we would never have achieved access to God without a Mediator[143] – the God who dwells in unapproachable light.[144] 'In Christ, God in a sense makes himself small in order to come down to our level of understanding.'[145]

---

[138] *Institutes* 2.12.1 (CO 2:340).

[139] Ibid., 2.6.4 (CO 2:251): 'altior quoque est Dei maiestas quam ut ad eam penetrent mortales'.

[140] Ibid., 2.6.4 (CO 2:252): '[Pater] . . . in Filio . . . se ad modulum nostrum accommodavit, ne mentes nostras immensitate suae gloriae absorbeat.'

[141] Ibid., 2.7.1 (CO 2:254): 'Mediatore suo freti, libere in Dei conspectum prodire audent.'

[142] Ibid., 2.12.1 (CO 2:340): 'inter nostras sordes et summam Dei munditiem dissidium'.

[143] Ibid.: 'humilior tamen erat eius conditio quam ut sine Mediatore ad Deum penetraret'.

[144] 1 Timothy 6:16; *Institutes* 3.2.1 (CO 2:398): 'Nam quum Deus lucem inaccessam habitet, Christum occurrere medium necesse est.'

[145] *Comm. 1 Petr.* 1:20 (CO 55:227): 'Hinc apparet, non posse nos Deo credere, nisi per Christum, in quo se Deus quodammodo parvum facit, ut se ad captum nostrum submittat.' Cf. *Comm. 1 Tim.* 6:15–16 (CO 53:625f.): 'si nous scavions que Dieu habite une clarté inaccesible, cela seroit bien pour nous humilier, sçachans bien que nostre esprit ne peut nullement approcher à Dieu. Pource que nous ne pouvons pas monter iusque à luy, il nous fait la grace de descendre à nous, afin de nous elever à soy; mais devant qu'il nous y attire, il s'abaisse c'est à dire, il se fait petit'; *Prael. Hos.* 3:5 (CO 42:264): 'Ostendit enim nunc Deum a nobis quaeri non posse, nisi in mediatore Christo. . . . Nam Deus lucem inaccessam habitat: deinde quanto spatio nos ab ipso distamus? Ergo nisi Christus se medium nobis offerat, qua via possemus ad Deum accedere?' Cf. finally *Comm. Joh.* 1:18 (CO 47:19): 'quum nuda Dei maiestas in se sit abscondita, nunquam potuisset comprehendi, nisi quatenus se in Christo manifestavit'.

So Calvin strongly ties Christ's mediatorship to God's greatness, but, at the same time, in connection with Christ and his
single personhood he never forgets who God really is and what
being human is. While these two poles uniquely and incomprehensibly unite themselves in the unity of the person of Christ,
they still remain distinct; in other words, the bipolar background
continues to cast a shadow over Calvin's Christology. Not that
this fact produces tension (that is putting it too strongly); still less
does it detract from the unity in Christ. It is absolutely not the
case that the deity of Christ and his humanity are separated from
each other. But the distinctiveness of each is certainly strongly
underscored by Calvin. Also in the event of the incarnation God's
transcendent greatness remains inviolate. His majesty is not
diminished by it. This would happen in any form of the deification
of or contamination by human nature.[146] According to Wendel,
this strong accentuation of the distinction between the divine
and the human nature of Christ is an important aspect of
Calvin's theological thought in which he is perhaps most
original.[147] This *extra-calvinisticum* is the background behind the
conflict over the real presence of Christ in Holy Communion and
also explains Calvin's fear of all forms of the *communicatio
idiomatum* between the two natures of Christ. It is nothing other
than an expression of Calvin's great concern to uphold the divine
pole in undiminished greatness vis-à-vis all that is human, even
when it pertains to Christ. It is an aspect of the bipolarity between
God and man.

4. Satisfying God's majesty

In the doctrine of the atonement (*satisfactio*) God's justice acquires
the hard sound of a demanding justice which has not been satisfied.
God here is the offended majesty who demands satisfaction. The
divine–human relation is formulated here in terms which sound
juridical. The doctrine of satisfaction presupposes a bad relation

---

[146] *Conf. Trin.* (CO 9:706): 'sic autem coniunctam humanitate asserimus ut
sua utrique naturae solida proprietas maneat; et tamen ex illis duabus unus
Christus constituatur'.

[147] Wendel, *Calvin*, 220: 'What mattered above all to Calvin was to avoid
anything that might be interpreted as a confusion of the divinity with the humanity,
even at the centre of the personality of Christ.'

between God and man which demands rectification. Someone has been ill done by, an act which demands restitution. An irregularity has to be corrected; a debt has to be paid. God, here, is the creditor; the debtor is humankind.

Just as God's majesty made Christ's mediatorship necessary lest little man be swallowed up by God's presence, so also God's Son had to become man to compensate for the injustice done, to pay a debt to satisfy God's 'injured' majesty. Hence 'satisfaction' is one of the 'comprehensibility moments' with which Christ's mediatorship is surrounded. It is clear that this reasoning proceeds, more than the previous one, from the situation of fallen man, from the fact of indebtedness which has to be corrected or satisfied.

Thus God's majesty comes at humans with its demands, indeed even its threats, for the reader is struck by how often in this context there is mention of God's wrath, of a terrifying majesty (*horribilis maiestas*) before which culpable persons must tremble, the wrath of God which has to be appeased.[148] However remarkable this sort of statement may sound, however strange this approach may seem at first sight, Calvin not only knows it but it occupies an important place in his thought. He, like others, expressly approaches the seriously disturbed relation between God and humankind from the angle of the satisfaction that is required, and for that reason we too have to pay attention to it here.

Proceeding from the terrifying majesty of God, we will note down a number of words and expressions which focus on the imperative demand of satisfaction. Thus, in the first place, we get an image of a purely juridical doctrine of satisfaction in Calvin.

Next we will illumine the interior of his juridical formulations by which the fatherly love of God becomes visible. In this connection we sketch the problem of how the two – justice-demanding satisfaction and fatherly love – can comport with each other in the one God.

Finally, we will compare Calvin's doctrine of satisfaction with that of Anselm as it comes to expression in his *Cur Deus homo*.

Although the motif of satisfaction comes to the fore in several places,[149] we will confine ourselves to the most significant pericopes, namely those in which the doctrine of satisfaction is

---

[148] *Institutes* 2.16.1–6 (CO 2:367–74).
[149] Ibid., 2.12.3 (CO 2:341).

discussed *ex professo* in the context of Christ's death and resurrection. This is more than enough for us to gain an impression of the particular way in which Calvin views this matter. Sometimes it looks like a lawsuit between God and man in which the latter, found guilty, proves powerless to satisfy the demands of his divine creditor, until a third party intervenes, offering satisfaction in man's place and redressing the injustice done. He is our advocate who intervenes on our behalf, the link between God and us.[150] We will try to bring out the place of God and man in some detail and to describe it in order thus, from within this angle, to gain insight into the divine–human relation in Calvin.

How did Christ abolish the breach between God and people and acquire for us the righteousness which would make God well-disposed toward us? Calvin's answer is: by his entire life which was one single course of obedience. In this connection, then, what is the function of Christ's death? This death indicates more precisely the manner in which God desired to save us (*modus salutis*).[151] And if this construal requires further explanation, there turns out to be a 'necessity of justice' hidden behind the way Christ desired to save us.[152] Indeed, Calvin calls 'satisfaction' another key focus of our reconciliation with God. The important point was 'that man, who by his disobedience had become lost, should by way of remedy counter it with obedience, satisfy God's judgment and pay (*persolvere*) the penalties for sin'.

> Accordingly, our Lord appeared as true man, putting on the person of Adam, in order in his place to obey the Father, to present our flesh as *the price of satisfaction* (*in satisfactionis pretium*) to *God's righteous judgment* and, in that same flesh, to *pay* (*persolvere*) the *penalty* we had deserved. In short, since neither as God alone could he undergo death, nor as man alone could he overcome it, he coupled human nature with the divine that he might submit the weakness of the one nature to death; and that, to atone for sin, he might wrestle with death by the power of the other nature, so winning the victory for us.[153]

---

[150] *Serm. Tim.* 1:9,10 (CO 54:60): '. . . Iesus Christ . . . a esté envoyé comme lieutenant de Dieu son Père'.

[151] *Institutes* 2.16.5 (CO 2:371): 'Scriptura tamen, quo certius definiat modum salutis, hoc morti Christi quasi peculiare ac proprium adscribit.'

[152] Wendel, *Calvin*, 218–19.

[153] *Institutes* 2.12.3 (CO 2:341–2).

Expressed in this passage, at least in outline, is the entire relation-ship which underlies the doctrine of satisfaction. Here too, the self-knowledge of Calvin is a permanent point of comparison by which he tests his own statements. 'No one can look into himself and seriously consider what kind of person he really is without meeting God, who is angry with him and ill-disposed toward him. . . . God's wrath and curse always press down upon sinners. . . .'[154] In sum: the condition of humans is wretched and ruinous; they are subject to the curse and live with the prospect of dreadful destruction. It is for such that the Mediator came, took their place, bore their punishment and *paid* their debt.[155]

It is repeatedly said that God's judgment is just. Satisfaction comes through in such words as 'expiation' (*expiare*) and 'peace-offering' (*piaculum*) by which God is given satisfaction and the proper sacrifice is made. The word 'rightly' (*rite*), as is clear from what follows in the text, is of special importance. It has the sense of meeting some requirement 'in the proper manner', 'correctly', 'with juridical accuracy'. Precisely *this* suffering and *this death* which Christ underwent meet the demands of a satisfaction which is in all respects correct and in order. So we read in the 1539 edition of the *Institutes*: 'It was not sufficient for him to undergo just any death; no, such a death was chosen by which he would properly observe to the end all the parts of our redemption.'[156] If he had been murdered by criminals or killed in an insurrection by a raging mob, in such a death there would have been no form whatever of proper satisfaction.[157] He was condemned by Pontius Pilate precisely because actually we humans should have been condemned. He brought about atonement, whereas in fact that task rested upon us. It is our acquittal (*absolutio*) that the guilt (*reatus*) was laid upon the head of the Son of God. The words used here have a peculiarly businesslike, commercial feeling to them; *compensatio*: something had to be adjusted, counter-balanced, offset. The righteous wrath of God (*iusta Dei ultio*): this adjustment threatened to be brought about by the

---

[154] Ibid., 2.16.1 (CO 2:368): 'semper incumbit ira Dei et maledictio'.

[155] Ibid., 2.16.2 (CO 2:369): 'poenam in se recepisse et luisse'.

[156] 1539 *Institutes* (CO 1:526): 'non satis erat ipsum quamlibet obire mortem: sed quo rite omnibus redemptionis nostrae partibus defungeretur, genus mortis deligendum fuit'.

[157] *Institutes* 2.16.5 (CO 2:372): 'nulla satisfactionis species'.

vindictiveness of a righteous God.[158] But what in the Old Testament was redressed by *ashamoth* (propitiatory sacrifices) is now accomplished by Christ, who is the fulfilment of the ancient custom. He has become our *asham* to perform a perfect expiation.[159] He is the sacrifice who makes satisfaction (*hostia satisfactoria*), the sacrifice to which our guilt is transferred and imputed (*translatitia imputatio*).

It would not be hard to expand this list of expressions which have a juridical 'feel' to them. In our opinion, however, this is enough to show that the doctrine of satisfaction situates persons before God as the accused before a court of law. We hear the call for righteousness and the demand for the redress of injustice done. That demand is made across the board: everything must be made right, and properly so (*rite*). This can serve as our first finding: the divine–human relation is viewed soberly, objectively, and juridically. And when it is so considered, man collapses; viewed in this light he cannot stand. He is a person condemned.

But this initial impression is incomplete and therefore gives a false picture. It does not describe the whole divine–human relation; in fact it only touches the periphery. The interior of the relation is more revelatory, and from that perspective alone there emerges a decisive view of humankind, precisely when we speak of satisfaction.

This interior side of satisfaction is clearly and even strikingly described by Calvin. On the one hand, it is the obedience of the son of God, an obedience which illumines his entire life and finally ends in the crowning event of his death on the cross. His obedience takes the place of our disobedience. That alone is what gives value to his sacrifice (*sacrificium*). 'And naturally, in the case of his death, his voluntary submission to it is primary, for a sacrifice would have contributed nothing to righteousness unless it were brought from the heart (*sponte*).'[160] He came to do his Father's will.[161] Truly, this obedience was no everyday example of love

---

[158] Cf. 'iusta Dei maledictio'. Ibid., 2.8.19 (CO 2:280).

[159] Ibid., 2.16.6 (CO 2:373): 'iusta expiatio'.

[160] Ibid., 2.16.5 (CO 2:371): 'quia ad iustitiam nihil profuisset sacrificium nisi sponte oblatum'.

[161] Psalm 40:9.

toward us.[162] Here the most beautiful dimension of the interior shines out. The true background of atonement-by-satisfaction is demonstrated by decisive passages about God's mercy, passages from which it is evident that the doctrine of satisfaction can only be understood in that light. Satisfaction is subservient to God's mercy and in such a way that by it alone we really learn to know God's love.

> In short, we are incapable of understanding deeply enough what it means for us to live in God's mercy. Neither can we be grateful enough for it. We must first be struck and alarmed by the fear of God's wrath and by dread of eternal death. As sacred doctrine teaches us, we must learn to see that in a certain sense (*quodammodo infestus*) God is hostile toward us. His hand threatens to destroy us. We can only grasp his goodness and fatherly love in Christ.[163]

When as a result of our own wickedness we were sinners, we nevertheless remained God's creatures. This fact was owing to his mercy. His love toward us remained, said Augustine. In a marvellous, that is in a divine, way he continued to love us, even when he hated us.[164] We believe that this last citation, quoted from the middle of the discourse on satisfaction, approaches the core and final depth where our comprehension stops. We do not see the divine manner of it (*modus divinus*); what we see and articulate is our failure to which the divine answer of righteousness has to come. When we speak of the righteous wrath and vengeance from the side of God, that is nothing but the certain knowledge that our culpability has to draw a punitive answer from God because he is righteousness itself. But this does not exhaustively describe the divine depth of his attitude. This is most nearly approximated (and that, clearly, is how we must read Calvin) by love (*charitas*). How this can be squared with vengeance (*ultio*), wrath (*ira*), and curse (*maledictio*) escapes us. We can say, however, that from the perspective of God the interior of satisfaction is

---

[162] *Institutes* 2.16.5 (CO 2:371): 'non vulgare fuit amoris erga nos incomparabilis specimen'.

[163] Ibid., 2.16.2 (CO 2:369): 'beneficentiam eius paternamque charitatem nonnisi in Christo amplexamur'.

[164] Ibid., 2.16.4 (CO 2:370): 'Proinde miro et divino modo et quando nos oderat, diligebat.' Cf. *Prael. Jer.* 29:6 (CO 38:585): 'Ubi autem eripimus Dei ei ius suum et arbitrium, perinde est ac si nollemus admittere eius gratiam.'

determined by fatherly love. On top of this, satisfaction leads us to the recognition of that love.

Is it the case, then, that the doctrine of satisfaction with all of its juridical vocabulary is no more than a pedagogical means to illustrate the love of God? No: the God who inspires dread (*formido Dei*) is not a figure of speech: this language reflects reality. It does not mean anything other, however, than the relentless order of God which comes to man as a dreadful demand, for God's essence is righteousness which simply *has to* burn away all unrighteousness. God's glorious holiness has to be negatively defined with words like wrath, vengeance, and the like. In these terms as well an attempt is made to express something of God's greatness. But ultimately they point to God's love. How that is remains unclear. The divine mode (*divinus modus*) in which everything in God flows together escapes us. It is not at all accidental in this connection that Calvin touches upon this human incapacity to understand. Immediately following the text which speaks of God's mercy and his dreadfulness we read: 'and although this statement is tempered to our feeble comprehension, it is still correct'.[165] And after speaking of the hostile God from whom we live in separation, he immediately adds: statements like these are accommodated to our intellectual capacity.[166] The idea of atonement by satisfaction is one of those starting-points which lie within the reach of our ability to comprehend. But we must not fancy that the 'divine manner of conduct' is thereby made plain and clear and can be exhaustively understood by us.

Of course, it is not hard to read the name of Anselm, the author of *Cur Deus homo*, between many of these lines. He is the theologian who elaborated at length the theory of satisfaction and who actually made it classic. At the same time this has made him for many people the representative of a juridical doctrine of salvation. It is well to know that B. Willems has convincingly challenged this assessment of Anselm.[167] One cannot confine

---

[165] *Institutes* 2.16.2–3 (CO 2:369): 'non potest animus noster vitam in Dei misericordia . . . excipere, nisi formidine irae Dei . . . . Atque hoc tametsi pro captus nostri infirmitate dicitur, non tamen falso'.

[166] Ibid., 2.16.2 (CO 2:368): 'Huius generis locutiones ad sensum nostrum sunt accommodatae.' Cf. ibid., 1.13.1 (CO 2:90); ibid., 1.17.13 (CO 2:165).

[167] B. Willems, 'De verlossing als menselijke werkelijkheid', *Tijdschrift voor Theologie* 5 (1965): 39–42.

Anselm, any more than Calvin, within the narrow framework of a juridical doctrine of satisfaction. It is noteworthy that Anselm, too, reserved a large place for the obedience of Christ by which the proper relation between God and man (*ordo debitus*) is restored.[168] Also in Anselm righteousness has a much wider meaning than juridical righteousness. Righteousness is God's very essence.[169] 'Your mercy therefore proceeds from your justice and you spare evil ones out of justice.'[170] Here the author taps the same source from which Calvin drew his deepest inspiration: 'we have been reconciled to him who already loved us with whom we were enemies on account of sin'.[171] This throws fresh light on the divine–human relation as this relation is according to a well-understood theory of satisfaction. The accused who is unable to pay up is at the same time beloved by the Accuser. The latter is the only reason why the accused is still on his feet. Even in the doctrine of satisfaction the relation between God and man is not juridical. The bond which exists between the person of God and the person of man is a bond of love which keeps people alive and

---

[168] *Cur Deus homo* 2.17: 'non necessitate, sed libera potestate animam suam posuit'. Cf. ibid. 1.9: 'Non ergo coegit Deus Christum mori, in quo nullum fuit peccatum sed ipse *sponte* sustinuit mortem . . . propter obedientiam servandi iustitiam.' According to Anselm, this very obedience unto death is to the *honour of God*: 'Nihil autem asperius aut difficilius potest homo *ad honorem Dei* sponte et non ex debito pati quam mortem . . . cum se morti tradit *ad honorem illius*.' Ibid., 2.11.

[169] Ibid., 1:13: 'summa iustitia, quae non est aliud quam ipse Deus'.

[170] *Proslogion* ch. 9.

[171] *Institutes* 2.16.4 (CO 2:370): 'iam nos diligenti reconciliati sumus, cum quo propter peccatum inimicitias habebamus'. It is worth noting that besides the themes already mentioned of God's righteousness and obedience to his majesty, the will of God also plays an all-embracing and shaping role in Anselm's treatise *Cur Deus homo*, just as it does in Calvin. 'Quaecumque itaque timetis aut desideratis, eius voluntati subiacent, cui nihil resistere potest' (*Cur Deus homo* 1.6). 'Nonne Dei omnipotentia regnat ubique?' (ibid., 2.12). For Anselm, too, God is the exalted majesty, to whom humanity can give no satisfaction unless Christ comes between them. Even though the Bishop of Canterbury, for purposes of his debate with the pagans, intends to argue *remoto Christo*, in fact his exposition is permeated with Christ, and his *rationes* call for Christ. Nevertheless, it would be going too far, in our judgment, to infer from these remarkable points of agreement a common background, the same *Vorverständnis* of both theologians (the feudal social structure of the Middle Ages), as a way of explaining their striking conception of the majesty of God. On this question cf. M. Wilks, *The Problem of Sovereignty in the Later Middle Ages* (Cambridge, 1963).

is ultimately aimed at salvation. The adjustment which is posed as a demand is a demand of fatherly love which, in his resourcefulness, restores the *ordo debitus* (the right relation) in the Only-begotten and thus raises the divine–human bipolarity to the height and splendour God had in mind from the start.

5. Christ: the image of God

To what height and splendour is the relation of God to man and of man to God lifted up? On what level does the bipolarity of God and man end up and how is it brought to the degree of intimacy and intensity God intends? In the preceding pages we learned that the sovereign God, even when he rightly takes a demanding position toward culpable humanity, is ultimately driven by mercy. In other words, the deepest meaning of the divine–human relation (*ordo debitus*) does not come to expression in a juridical doctrine of satisfaction. Indeed, this order, in its ultimate significance, is a relation on the level of mercy (*ordo misericordiae*) which, upholding and maintaining man, does not let him go but keeps him on his feet over against an all-powerful Partner. Now we may learn how this *ordo misericordiae* expands to the level on which humans become the image of God. How does this process unfold? Answer: In the Son of God, who became man and who is the image of God *par excellence*. Earlier already, when we spoke about humans, we said a thing or two about the high quality of the status of being the image of God in which they may stand vis-à-vis God. We will not repeat this. What happens here is a sequel to and a rounding off an earlier beginning. Soteriologically we will now complete the story. It is the story of redemption, told in the single dynamic concept – intensely vital and personal – that is concealed in the image of God. This too, is a way of approaching Calvin's theological thinking and we are convinced this approach is legitimate.[172] Also the *Corpus Reformatorum* offers a long list of references which convey some idea of the importance of the image of God in Calvin's theology.

---

[172] The space given to the image of God in treatments of Calvin's theology is rather modest. Cf. Berkouwer, *Man: The Image of God*, J. Ries, *Die natürliche Gotteserkenntnis in der Theologie der Krisis im Zusammenhang mit dem Imagobegriff bei Calvin* (Bonn, 1939), and esp. Torrance, *Calvin's Doctrine of Man*.

In this section we will first consider Christ as the perfect image of the Father. At the same time he is God's image to us in the sense that in him we become God's image.

Then we note the implications of that communication in Christ with the Father. It is realistic and personal. By means of Calvin's comments on 2 Corinthians 4:6b, we will finally illustrate how in Christ, who is the image of God, we have a personal relation to the Father.

> Paul testifies that in the person of Christ the glory of God has become manifest to us. In other words, the knowledge of God's glory radiates from the face of Christ. Granted: faith is directed toward the one God; but be sure to add to this that this faith must acknowledge Jesus Christ whom he has sent. For God himself would have remained remote and hidden if the light of Christ had not dawned upon us. For this reason the Father entrusted everything he had to his only begotten Son. In him God wanted to make himself known. Christ partook of his riches. *In that way* God wanted to produce a faithful image of his glory.[173]

This passage, taken from a context in which faith is discussed, again brings to the fore the familiar motif that God is too great to be known without the go-between who is Christ. The invisible Father must not be sought anywhere but in this image.[174] Christ conveys who God is. He images God. When, then, we here testify of Christ that he is the image of God this must in the first place be understood in a cognitive sense. He is an image so that through him we might know the Father. On first hearing it, the familiar text of 2 Corinthians 4:6 does not have a soteriological sound to it, although other texts in its immediate vicinity do clearly speak of redemption. This passage in 2 Corinthians is one Calvin loves.[175] We will see in a moment that it definitely functions on a soteriological level.

Observe first that, according to Calvin, Christ is the image of God. Naturally this is said of the one person who is Lord, and no distinction is made between his deity and humanity. But upon

---

[173] *Institutes* 3.2.1 (CO 2:398): 'quicquid habebat Pater, apud unigenitum deposuit ut in eo se patefaceret: ut ipsa bonorum communicatione exprimeret veram gloriae suae imaginem'.

[174] Ibid.: 'invisibilem Patrem non alibi quam in hac imagine quaerendum est'.

[175] Cf. ibid., 2.9.1 (CO 2:310), 4.1.5 (CO 2:751).

reflection one has to say that this pronouncement especially touches Christ's humanity and lifts this humanity to a special height. Also man is God's image but Christ is this uniquely: He is the visible perfection of the [divine] splendour[176] and the most perfect image of God.[177] Thus he is the splendour of the glory of God and the exact imprint of the being of God the Father.[178] He is the image of the Father's glory, a glory which is visible in his person.[179] This is not the place to examine the actual content which the biblical term 'image' in all these passages brings with it,[180] although the cognitive function of the image of God is again conspicuous. Important, however, is that in Christ the image of God is extended toward humans. In the image of God in Christ and only in him and by this route, humans come to stand over against God as his image. It is clear, therefore, that the image of God simultaneously begins to function soteriologically. It is a term which shows how the salvation of God in Christ actually reaches people. Seeing the glory of God we are transformed into the same image.[181] It becomes clear in this text that the cognitive and soteriological components coincide. In Christ the face of this grace lights up.[182] This is even more compactly expressed in Calvin's statement that Christ is the compendium (*summa*) of our salvation.[183] Also the purpose of regeneration is that Christ must transform us into God's image.[184]

However scintillating the relation of people to God becomes through this reformation (*reformatio*) in Christ, when we put a number of texts from sources outside the *Institutes* alongside of

---

[176] Ibid., 1.13.26 (CO 2:114): 'conspicua splendoris perfectio'.

[177] Ibid., 1.15.4 (CO 2:138): 'perfectissima Dei imago'.

[178] Ibid., 2.9.1 (CO 2:310): 'splendor gloriae et character substantiae Dei Patris'.

[179] Ibid., 3.2.1 (CO 2:398): 'in eius persona nobis visibilis est Dei gloria'.

[180] H. Ridderbos, *Paul: An Outline of His Theology*, trans. J. de Witt (Grand Rapids, 1975), 68–78; Torrance, *Calvin's Doctrine of Man*, 35–82.

[181] 2 Corinthians 3:18; *Institutes* 1.15.4 (CO 2:138).

[182] *Institutes* 2.7.8 (CO 2:259): 'In Christo autem facies eius gratiae et lenitatis plena erga miseros etiam ac indignos peccatores relucet.'

[183] Ibid., 2.16.19 (CO 2:385): 'tota salutis nostrae summa'.

[184] Ibid., 1.15.4 (CO 2:138): 'regeneratio finis, ut nos Christus ad imaginem Dei reformet'. Cf. ibid., 3.3.9 (CO 2:440): 'poenitentiam interpretor, regenerationem, cuius non est alius scopus nisi ut imago Dei . . . in nobis reformetur'.

it, we learn how dynamically, vitally, and *personally* God and people get to face each other precisely in the light of this motif of being-the-image-of-God.

We want to illustrate this reality primarily by the use Calvin makes of the statement in 2 Corinthians 4:6 cited earlier: 'For the same God who said, "Let light shine out of darkness", has shone in our hearts to give the light of the knowledge of the glory of God in the face of Jesus Christ.'[185] In the *Institutes* of 1539 this text – to start with – is commented on by Calvin as follows:[186] 'Christ could not rightly call himself "the Light of the world" if the splendour of the Father's glory did not illumine the world by him.'[187] Not only true, therefore, is the apostle's teaching that Christ is the reflection of God's glory and the exact imprint of his very being,[188] but we must add that in him the glory of the Father lights up *for us* and the image of his very being appears.[189] This is the case because the Father willed to deliver everything he had to him[190] in order 'through him to communicate himself totally to us and to glorify his name'.[191] Since everything is governed from beginning to end by the theme of the glory of the Father, we are particularly interested in the communication effected by the Son between God and man. This is not a half-way measure: he communicates himself to us totally (*se nobis totum communicavit*).

In reading this passage, one thinks involuntarily of Colossians 2:9 and 10: 'For in him the whole fullness of deity dwells bodily and you have come to fullness in him. . . .' However this may be, the image of God that comes toward us in Christ acquires a heavily weighted content: in him God communicates himself to us totally (*se totum*). The essential riches which characterize this communication between God and man are further highlighted when alongside of it we also recall the expression Calvin uses in a similar connection when he speaks about the relation between the Father

---

[185] 'τῆς γνώσεως τῆς δόξης τοῦ Θεοῦ'.

[186] CO 1:477.

[187] John 8:12; 9:5; 12:46.

[188] Hebrews 1:3.

[189] John 14:9.

[190] Matthew 11:27; John 3:35; 5:20.

[191] *Institutes* (1539) 6 (CO 1:477): 'ut per ipsum et se nobis totum *communicaret*, et nomen suum illustraret'. In this passage too, the honour of God and human salvation go together. The latter is even mentioned first.

and the Son. There we also read: in order that especially by the communication of his benefits he might express the true image of his glory.[192] This *communicatione* has its parallel and continuation in the 'total self-communication' (*se totum communicaret*) of the *Institutes* of 1539. All this, in our opinion, characterizes the communication between God and man as being very real, one that is heavily packed with reality.

To complete this picture we will add a few passages from sources other than the *Institutes* in which the text cited from 2 Corinthians occurs. To our mind, from this angle something important can be said about the relation between God and man and their polarity especially in light of the image of God.

In many instances Calvin interprets the Pauline saying referred to as meaning *the light of the gospel* which has begun to shine as a result of Christ's coming.[193] In connection with the most significant passage, Calvin's commentary on 2 Corinthians 4:6, the author even twice mentions the light of the gospel.[194] In other passages the reference is not to the gospel but more generally to the salvation which has begun to shine in Christ.[195] The odd time the text is used metaphorically.[196] We mention all this to give an overview of the manner in which the text from 2 Corinthians is used. What we are really interested in is the text from the commentary on 2 Corinthians 4:6.[197] Commenting on the expression 'in the face of Jesus Christ', Calvin goes on to say (we will reproduce the entire passage):

> In the same sense in which he had previously said that Christ is the *image of the Father*, (verse 4) he now says that the glory of God is manifested to us *in his face*. Here we have a remarkable passage from

[192] *Institutes* 3.2.1 (CO 2:398): 'ut ipsa bonorum communicatione exprimeret veram gloriae suae imaginem'.

[193] CO 7:600: 'quare alibi Paulus, quam lucem evangelii commendat, dicit illic refulgere Dei gloriam in facie Christi' (2 Cor. 4:6); CO 9:533: '[dicit] scripturae lucem in tenebris quoque fulgere'; CO 47:219: 'Deus per evangelium in Christi facie resplenduerit'.

[194] CO 50:52–3.

[195] CO 8:357: 'salutem mirabiliter educit, atque ita tenebras convertet in lucem'; CO 51:182: 'ubi agatur de regno Christi'; CO 50:52: 'nunc spiritualiter in nobis illuminavit'.

[196] CO 12:697; 24:58: 'ipse [Deus] pro immensa sua bonitate ex vitio servi sui elicere voluit gratiae suae materiam: sicuti solet ex tenebris lucem educere'.

[197] CO 50:52–3.

which we learn that God is not to be *sought out* (Job xi. 7) in His unsearchable highness (*for He dwells in light that is inaccessible*, 1 Tim. vi. 16) but is to be known in so far as He manifests himself in Christ. Hence, whatever men desire to know respecting God apart from Christ is vain, for they are wandering off the road. Humbly, indeed, God appears in Christ in the beginning, but He appears gloriously finally in the view of those who manage to move from the cross to the resurrection. Again we see that in the word *person* there is a connection with us, because it is more advantageous for us to behold God as He appears in His only-begotten Son than to search out His secret essence.

Indeed, a remarkable passage (*insignis locus*), and that for more than one reason: in a few words much is said that is genuinely Calvinian. God's glory shines out in Christ, his image. We must not attempt to search out God in his unsearchable highness. He is only to be found in Christ. Here, therefore, we again encounter the theme of Christ's mediatorship in the light of God's majesty. God became small in Christ.[198] Then Calvin goes on by saying that by the word 'person' (*in voce personae*) a connection is made in our direction. 'By the word "person"': we would construe that to mean via the person, on the level of the relation from person to person a relation to us is established. It is senseless to attempt to search out God's secret essence. To know him is essentially bound up with a relation: as he is toward us, as he comes to us in the person of Christ.[199] Knowing God only functions in the person-to-person relation. To seek to know him apart from Christ as he is in himself (*qualis est in se*) is not only useless but also reckless. God's majesty is too high for that! Thus – let it be said – this whole passage reflects the intensity of God's majesty. At the same time, however, it reveals the *personal* character of Calvin's theology. In the final analysis it deals with the relation between God and man. That alone is what it deals with. This relation exists and is made possible only by a *person*: Jesus Christ. In the word 'person' there exists a relation to us (*in voce personae relatio ad nos*).

We believe that in this terse formulation something very essential is said about Calvin's theological thought. This idea,

[198] CO 50:53: 'humilis in Christo Deus'.
[199] Ibid.: 'Iterum videmus, in voce personae relationem ad nos statui quia nobis utilius est Deum conspicere qualis apparet in filio unigenito quam arcanam eius essentiam investigare.'

God's relation to us in the person of Christ, is one that Calvin had expressed even earlier in the same commentary, namely, in his discussion of verse 4 of the chapter referred to from the Second Letter to the Corinthians.[200] There he writes as follows:

> When, however, Christ is called the *image of the* invisible *God,* this is not meant merely of his essence, as being 'co-essential of the Father', (*coessentialis patri*) as they say, but rather has a reference to us, because he represents (*repraesentat*) the Father to us. The Father himself is represented as invisible, because he is in himself not apprehended by the human understanding (*humano sensu*). He exhibits himself, however, to us by his Son, and makes himself in a certain sense visible. I state this because the ancients in their vehement reaction to the Arians insisted more than was befitting on the point that the Son is inwardly (*intus*) the image of the Father by a secret unity of essence. They, however, passed over that which is mainly for edification, namely that he is the image of God to us, when he manifests to us what had otherwise been concealed in him (the Father). Hence the term *image* relates to us.[201]

From all this it should be clear that the image of God plays a large role in Calvin's theology. This could already be said of the way he approaches the creation and creatures (especially humans). It can with even greater validity be said of his doctrine of redemption. Man is saved by and in Christ who is God's image *par excellence* and into whose image man may unfold.[202]

This image-of-God theology is pregnant with a profound reality. We think we were able to point this out more or less in passing (not exhaustively) in the texts in which there is mention of 'communication' (*communicatio*). This last word already suggests a relation. We have illustrated the truth that human salvation is realized on the person-to-person level with a passage from Calvin's commentary on 2 Corinthians. In this manner the theme of the bipolarity of God and man finds an exponent, as

---

[200] CO 50:51–2.

[201] CO 50:52: 'Itaque nomen imaginis, relationem ad nos habet.'

[202] No one, in our judgment, has more clearly shown and analysed the bipolarity of God and man as contained in the idea of the image of God in Calvin's theology than Torrance, *Calvin's Doctrine of Man.* Two citations from this work will suffice: 'Calvin constantly thinks of man, and of the *imago dei*, in terms of this dynamic relation to God' (61). 'Calvin's doctrine of the *imago dei* in man sums up the whole of this relation between man and God' (59).

forceful as it is hopeful, above all in Calvin's theology of the image of God.

6. Christ's meritorious work of redemption

The matter of Christ's merit (*meritum*) is characterized by Calvin as an addition, an addition to the redemptive work of the Lord. This certainly is a most modest description of a matter whose importance far exceeds the level of an interesting theological issue. Logically this issue naturally follows from what we said about Christ as the image of God. At the same time possibilities are here assigned to a human being which put him on a high level in his relation to God.

In the matter of the meritorious character of the redemptive work of Christ man attains a high point of valuation and ability vis-à-vis the sovereign God. The reference, of course, is to Christ. It is his merit that counts and is decisive but this in no way detracts from the fact that the *incarnate* Son of God has been given this high possibility of *meriting*. It is a true man who was called – precisely by being man, by an entire God-devoted life which culminated in an obedient death, who was a means of salvation (*modus salutis*) – to merit salvation for us humans. It is clear that Calvin's addition can be important for the divine–human relation, an importance which reaches farther than the word 'addition' or 'supplement' would lead us to suspect. This section, for that matter, is in our opinion a fine specimen of Calvin's thinking. His formulations have been carefully chosen. His diction betrays fine-tuned attention to the large components which play a role in this question. It is a splendid piece; and for those interested in Calvin's thought about God and man an indispensable bonus.

It is clear that this question is closely intertwined with the doctrine of satisfaction. Still we wish to devote a separate section to the merit of Christ's work of redemption because the fact of Christ's really meriting is given a complete and separate treatment also in Calvin. In the plan of this study, moreover, this subject follows logically on the discussion of Christ as the image of God. It is, as it were, the pinnacle of it.

In this section, following 'the state of the question', we first of all consider that the primacy of God's grace leaves room for a real redemption by Christ. We show how Calvin attempts to ground this together (*simul*) in Scripture and observe that his formulations attempt to express this together in a balanced and fine-tuned way.

Next, we highlight the special accent which the doctrine of satisfaction acquires in connection with the real merit of Christ's work of redemption.

'By way of addition this question also should be explained. There are certain uselessly subtle men who – even though they confess that we receive salvation through Christ – cannot bear to hear the word "merit" for, in their opinion, the grace of God is obscured by it.'[203] The question of the merit of Christ belongs in the sphere of theological points of dispute. What Calvin brings up here is the product of his dispute with Laelius Socinus who raised precisely this objection to the merit of Christ.[204] In our case we could formulate the problem as follows: does not the merit of Christ clash with God's sovereignty? Does not God's sovereign grace render Christ's activity superfluous and does it not also render all effectual and salvific intervention by Christ impossible? Can God's effectual grace be truly combined with genuine salvific activity on the part of Christ? When we describe the issue in these terms (and we believe we should), it is clear that the entire divine–human relation passes through an important stage precisely in connection with the meritoriousness of Christ's redemptive work.

It is not difficult to identify in Calvin's answer precisely those components which are important for the divine–human bipolarity. To start with, Calvin resolutely situates everything, including Christ, within the circle of God's grace. He begins by making God's sovereignty primary and by maintaining its primacy in advance by drawing Christ within the domain of God's action. Everything is grace, including Christ; indeed he is actually its most powerful example: the most brilliant light of predestination and grace is the Saviour, the man Jesus Christ himself.[205] There is no more magnificent example of predestination than the Mediator himself. From time to time this primary position of God in the history of salvation, following this fundamental beginning, comes strikingly to the fore. God's decision (*ordinatio*) is the first cause:

[203] *Institutes* 2.17.1 (CO 2:386): 'Haec quaestio *vice auctarii* expedienda est'.
[204] *Socini quaestiones* (1555; CO 10a:160–5).
[205] Augustine, *De praedestinatione sanctorum* 15.30 (MSL 44:981).

it is only on the basis of God's good pleasure that Christ can merit anything. Christ's merit depends on God's grace alone.[206] But there is no reason to fear, with Wendel, that this ordinance of God hollows out Christ's activity and makes it a formality.[207] The fascinating aspect of these pages is precisely that God's sovereignty is given full measure – as is the work of Christ. Calvin does solid scholastic work in this connection. The love of God (*dilectio Dei*) is the supreme cause (*causa summa*). Faith in Christ is the second cause (*causa secunda*) but then also a true cause as such. If someone should object that Christ is merely the formal cause, that person diminishes his power more than words could suggest. 'Formal cause' here definitely shares the meaning of what we understand by a 'mere formality', only in name. No: Christ is truly the author of salvation (*auctor salutis*); he really effects our salvation.[208]

Thus within the circle of God's mercy, which is the origin of all salvation, there is room for Christ's effective redemptive activity; Christ's really meriting salvation for us is not in conflict with the supreme cause of the love of God.[209] What occurs here is a concurrence on the highest level of pure divine mercy and human merit. If only the latter is consistently subsumed under God's mercy there is no objection whatever against this together (*simul*).[210] This *simul* means a harmonious joint activity of the divine and the human pole, and that even in redemption, the sphere of our salvation. From this perspective – we repeat – this addition is a true high point in the relation between God and man and vice versa.

---

[206] *Institutes* 2.17.1 (CO 2:387): 'ex sola Dei gratia dependet meritum Christi'.

[207] Wendel, *Calvin*, 228.

[208] In the 1560 edition of the *Institutes*, *causa formalis* is described as follows: 'c'est à dire, qui n'emporte point en soy vray effect'. Each word here is important. The causality that Christ has carries a power in itself ('en soy'). This, of course, takes nothing away from the *causa prima*, but it is really able to bring about a real effect ('vray effect'). One can speak of a real effect only if the cause is really able to bring something about (CO 3:604–5); cf. *Serm. Eph.* 6:19–24 (CO 51:859).

[209] *Institutes* 2.17.1 (CO 2:386): 'inscite opponitur Christi meritum misericordiae Dei'.

[210] Ibid., 2.17.1 (CO 2:387): 'nihil obstat quominus gratuita sit hominum iustificatio ex mera Dei misericordia, et simul interveniat Christi meritum, quod Dei misericordiae subiicitur'.

Calvin finds Scriptural confirmation for this *simul*. Also holy Scripture knows a certain ranking, a certain hierarchy of causes which play a role in the realization of human salvation. Calvin, in the nature of the case, has no difficulty advancing a long series of texts all of which in their own way attest that Christ is really the author of our salvation, that he really merited this salvation for us.[211] It is interesting, however, to note how Calvin combines the love of God with the peculiar efficacy of Christ's redemptive work. He speaks of the power and efficacy of Christ's death;[212] but the love of God is the beginning, the effective source to which all salvation is traced. On account of that love he has located the means of reconciliation in Christ.[213]

The love of God pervades everything, even the time in which he was angry with us, *until* he became reconciled in Christ.[214] On the one hand, the atonement wrought by Christ is truly the cause of our salvation, yet not in the sense that it again made possible the love of God toward us. The atonement presupposes God's love. In that way God's love makes its way toward us, thus restoring the right order (*ordo*). A like fine-tuned formulation comes through in the following statement: 'How did God begin to embrace in his love those whom he had loved before the creation of the world? Only because he revealed his love *when* he was reconciled to us by Christ's blood.'[215] This *ubi* (when) again testifies to Calvin's sense of proportion. It has the same quality as *donec* (until).[216] Here too, the love of God which is all-pervasive is left unchallenged in its primacy. It is inviolably sovereign, while at the same time a fully-valid space is sought for the reconciliation by Christ. The love of God is the first principle (*principium*), even though it is immediately followed by the remarkable statement: 'therefore righteousness is the principle of love'.[217] God's love is

[211] Ibid., 2.17.2–5 (CO 2:387–90).

[212] Ibid., 2.17.4 (CO 2:388): 'mortis Christi vis et efficacia'.

[213] Ibid., 2.17.2 (CO 2:387): 'demonstratur, Deum, nequid suo erga nos amori obstaret, reconciliandi modum statuisse in Christo'.

[214] Ibid.: 'Deus ineffabili quodam modo, quo tempore nos amabat, simul tamen erat infensus nobis, donec reconcilatus est Christo.'

[215] Ibid.: 'quomodo coepit Deus favore suo complecti quos ante conditum mundum dilexerat, nisi quia amorem suum exeruit ubi reconciliatus est Christi sanguine'.

[216] See above, n. 214.

[217] Ibid.: 'principium amoris est iustitia'.

simultaneously righteousness; it is necessarily the right *order of God*.[218] It is completely contrary to this entire passage to subordinate the love of God to his righteousness (*iustitia*). The idea is to join the love of God to the grace of Christ.[219] It is by connecting the two that God's righteousness is realized. This is what Calvin attempts to do and in our opinion succeeds in doing.

In this decisive light of the love of God which is primary we must also read the numerous passages which work out the idea of satisfaction. Confirmed in these passages is what we wrote earlier about this doctrine of satisfaction.[220] It must be said, moreover, that all the assertions about this satisfaction are subservient to the reality of Christ's work of redemption. 'If the effect (*effectus*) of his shedding of blood is that our sins are not imputed to us, it follows that God's judgment was satisfied (*satisfactum*) by that ransom.' The doctrine of satisfaction here is a substantiation of the thesis that Christ really and effectively brought about redemption for us; that he truly merited it with the Father . . . ; 'Christ's grace is too much diminished unless we grant to his sacrifice the power of expiating, appeasing, and making satisfaction.'[221]

Thus Calvin's doctrine of the merit of Christ implies a harmonious concurrence of divinely sovereign grace and an effectual human commitment which really earns salvation. Is the human partner ever more highly valued anywhere else?

Question: Is Calvin's writing here completely exempt from all tension? Can we nowhere detect even for a moment a certain reserve with respect to the efficacy of Christ's meriting salvation?

There is one moment when we get the feeling that Calvin takes something back of what he first, in a most careful formulation, attributed to Christ's merit, namely when the scholastic question arose whether Christ merited anything for himself. We have the impression that modern theology does not so readily want to call

---

[218] What is meant is that the love of God does not operate blindly, but that it helps to build up the right *ordo Dei*. God's love is at the same time his righteousness. Only the context helps us to understand this adage correctly.

[219] *Institutes* 2.17.2 (CO 2:387): 'Dei charitas adiungitur Christi gratia.'

[220] See above, pp. 8off.

[221] *Institutes* 2.17.4 (CO 2:388): 'facile patet, nimis extenuari Christi gratia nisi eius sacrificio vim expiandi, placandi, et satisfaciendi concedimus'.

this a 'stupid curiosity' or an 'impudent assertion'.[222] This is not the place to augment or refute the arguments from Scripture which Calvin advances in the matter. When in this connection Philippians 2:9 ('therefore God also highly exalted him and gave him the name', etc.) is cited, Calvin's commentary on this point is, however, important.

> He asks himself by what merit could he as *human being* have achieved that he would become the judge of the world, the head of the angels, that he would acquire God's supreme dominion, and that in him would reside that majesty, to which not even a thousandth part of all the power and virtue of men and angels can attain?[223]

In fidelity to what he said before we would be inclined to answer: by that mercy of God which also enabled him to merit salvation for everyone. That love of God is as great as his majesty. But here, under the impression of the high majesty which Christ, seated at the right hand of God, possesses, Calvin seems to hesitate. Paul, he says, is not here discussing the reason why Christ was exalted but only the sequence of his humiliation and exaltation.[224]

Although this last part seems to us an inconsistency in the whole of Calvin's discussion of the merit of Christ, it is at the same time again typical for him that he really never escapes the impression of the enormousness of God's majesty. At the same time, this marginal issue in no way detracts from his fundamental view concerning the true meritoriousness of Christ's work of redemption.

---

[222] Ibid., 2.17.6 (CO 2:390): 'non minus stulta est curiositas quam temeraria definitio'. Of interest is Thomas Aquinas's view on this. He makes a harmonious connection between Christ's merits for himself and his merits for us. See *Summa Theologiae* 3, q. 19, art. 3. Thomas connects the glorification that Christ merits for himself with the perfection that is ascribed to the eternal high priest of the New Testament in the Epistle to the Hebrews. *Super Ep. ad Hebr.* ch. 2, lect. 3; ch. 3, lect. 2.

[223] *Institutes* 2.17.6 (CO 2:391–2).

[224] Ibid., 2.17.6 (CO 2:392): 'Sed facilis et plena solutio est, Paulum illic non disserere de causa exaltationis Christi: sed consequentiam duntaxat ostendere ut nobis esset exemplo.'

III

⋘⋙

God's Honour and the
Way to Salvation

BETWEEN God's gracious mercy and the merits of Christ there
is a going together. At this point there is no tension in the
divine–human relation. Christ's really meriting is not inconsistent
with the fact that God is the sole cause of salvation. We closed
the previous chapter with a discussion of precisely this point. There
we spoke of the bipolarity of God and man as it comes to expression especially in the figure of Christ.

But the salvation that started in Christ extends to humans. As
a result of the mysterious inner working of the Holy Spirit, humans
begin to receive Christ and his benefits.[1]

The question is what, in this process, is the role of God and his
honour, and what is the role of humans with whose salvation we
are concerned?

To answer this double question we will speak, in the first section
of this chapter, about justification by faith and, in the second,
about the new life of a reborn person.

The third section is devoted to a discussion of the doctrine of
predestination, the doctrine in which Calvin attempts to locate
the ultimate ground for the weal and woe of human beings. For
humans the road to salvation or its opposite begins in God's decree
of election or reprobation.

1. Justification by faith

In light of the preceding, the question we now face can be
formulated as follows: If by God's mercy Christ has really been

---

[1] *Institutes* 3.1.1 (CO 2:393): 'arcana Spiritus efficacia, qua fit ut Christo
bonisque eius omnibus fruamur'.

enabled to merit, can there not – by virtue of the same enabling grace, the same effectual and creative goodness of God – be room for true merits on the part of humans (*merita hominum*) as well? In the divine–human relation, which is uniquely present in Christ, humanity has reached an equally exceptional great height such that, on the basis of God's merciful initiative and in its power, that humanity has been enabled to merit salvation for others. Does this not – in dependence on the merit of Christ (*meritum Christi*) and on a mercy that points back to God – open up for other *persons* as well the possibility of really meriting?

While these ideas are recorded here as a question, it becomes clear at the same time that such considerations do not arise in Calvin. According to him, it would be completely inappropriate to raise questions about what God could possibly do. All talk of human merit with respect to salvation is to him an abomination. It is again to make an idol of humanity – to erect an image of merit (*meriti simulacrum*) Pelagian style. The good works of man are completely powerless to bring about salvation. Humans are not justified by their good works but by faith alone.[2] Thus, via the discussion of Christ's merit, we are as it were automatically led to the doctrine of justification – a focal point in Calvin's theology and at the same time most precious to all Reformational confession. We shall try in a few broad strokes to sketch how at this focal point God and man relate to each other. Again, it is an attempt to set forth their bipolarity.

We shall begin this discussion of 'justification by faith' with Calvin's own starting-point: the human situation before God (*coram Deo*). This makes it clear from the outset that in justification we are dealing with two poles: the honour of God and the peace of the human conscience (*duo spectanda*). We shall then bring out certain implications of this *coram Deo,* and, from the perspective of man's confrontation with the living God, illumine God's role in justification. Here his mercy and grandeur stand

---

[2] It is our judgment that, as in the case of the *liberum arbitrium*, the Reformation concept of *iustificatio fidei* is not essentially different in Calvin from the actual Roman Catholic position on this doctrine. Not only is the testimony in Scripture on this point absolutely clear, but the same thing is expressed by Catholic documents – if they are read and interpreted in their proper light and according to their intent. Cf. Küng, *Justification*, 99–122 ('The Theology of Justification Past and Present'), 249–63 ('Sola Fide').

out. It is he alone who brings about salvation: this is a matter of exclusively his honour. But in this connection we must always remember that there are two directions in which to look: *duo spectanda*. The second focus is human salvation. In this context we encounter human faith and its significance in justification. Good works are part of this discussion and so toward the end we offer an interpretation of Calvin's expression: the 'prize' of good works (*pretium bonorum operum*).

Justification by faith is both a focal point and a bone of contention. When in 1539 Calvin replied to Sadoleto's letter to the citizens of Geneva, this is one of the great themes.

> In the first place, you [Sadoleto] touch upon justification by faith, which to us is the most significant and hotly contested issue with you. Is this perhaps a subtle and useless point of controversy? On the contrary! Whenever the knowledge of it has disappeared, the honour of Christ is uprooted, religion abolished, the church destroyed, and the hope of salvation utterly overthrown.[3]

From this statement alone, and from the extremely compact formulation of the issue, it is very obvious how profoundly important 'justification by faith' is to Calvin. At the same time this formulation as such is highly typical for everything he says about this dogma (*dogmata nostra*). While the honour of Christ is mentioned first, human salvation is also at stake. Our thoughts instinctively turn to another text about justification in which the two poles stand out even more clearly. 'Here, indeed, we must note especially two things ... the honour of God must remain inviolate ... and in the presence of his judgment our consciences must be guaranteed peaceful rest and serene tranquillity.'[4] Justification is 'the primary hinge on which religion turns',[5] 'the first principle of the entire doctrine of salvation and the foundation of all religion'.[6] And so, while justification by faith is at the core

---

[3] *Sad. et Calv. epist.* (1539; CO 5:365–416).

[4] *Institutes* 3.13.1 (CO 2:559): 'Atque omnino quidem duo hic praecipue spectanda sunt, nempe ut Domino illibata constet ac veluti sarta tecta sua gloria, conscientiis vero nostris coram ipsius iudicio placida quies ac serena tranquillitas.'

[5] Ibid., 3.11.1 (CO 2:533): 'ut meminerimus praecipuum esse sustinendae religionis cardinem'.

[6] *Serm. Synopt.* 1:5–10 (CO 46:23): 'Et c'est le principe de toute la doctrine de salut et le fondement de toute religion.'

of all true religion, and though Calvin fights for God's role and God's honour with all the weapons at his disposal – as we will demonstrate at greater length below – he also remains steadfast in his concern for humans and their salvation, specifically their peace of conscience. Once we have become alert to this dimension as well, we observe how pastoral his treatment of this eminently *religious* issue is. Although his mind is continually focused on God's honour and glory, he does not for a moment lose sight of humankind. His interest remains bipolar. We are inclined also to read his definition of justification by faith in this way: 'that person shall be considered justified by faith who, excluded from the righteousness of works, grasps Christ's righteousness by faith, and, clothed in this righteousness, appears in God's sight not as sinner but as righteous'.[7]

This appearance in God's presence as a righteous person sounds like a liberation, a liberating possibility and reality which is absolutely granted only in the event of justification by faith. For the practice of leaning on and appealing to one's own works does not only violate God's honour while appropriating it for oneself (that in the first place) but is at the same time a singularly uncertain foundation on which in fact no one can remain standing. Just go and present yourself before God with your good works and see what will be left of them![8] It is as if he has the nerve to look continually into his own conscience and finds this confrontation – which takes place in the sight of God – discouraging. If we have the courage to be honest in God's light, our good works cannot furnish us an easy conscience. It is precisely at this point that Calvin's concern for the human side comes out. When in his letter to Sadoleto he brings up justification by faith, he *begins* his exposition with a look into the human heart.

> We believe, in the first place, that people must begin with the acknowledgment of who they themselves actually are. And this scrutiny of self must not be superficial and hasty; indeed, they must have the courage to set their conscience before the tribunal of God. Then, when they have become sufficiently convinced of their own

[7] *Institutes* 3.11.2 (CO 2:534): 'Contra iustificabitur ille fide, qui operum iustitia exclusus, Christi iustitiam per fidem apprehendit, qua vestitus in Dei conspectu non ut peccator, sed tanquam iustus apparet.'

[8] Ibid., 3.12.2 (CO 2:554): 'Huc huc attollendi erant oculi, ut trepidare potius diceremus, quam inaniter exultare.'

corruption, they must also and at the same time reflect on the severity of God's judgment, a judgment pronounced upon all sinners. Thus, shamed and crushed by their own misery, they must prostrate and humble themselves before God. It is well to abandon all confidence in themselves. In that state they can only still groan as though their final ruin were near.[9]

Striking in this connection is that Calvin is aware of people's own conscience and that, in addition and in an even greater measure, he confronts them with the living God. People, remember, stand before *God*. It is no accident that just in the passage cited from Calvin's letter to Sadoleto alone he thrice uses the expression *coram Deo*. This theme, for that matter, had already been sounded in the text from the *Institutes* we cited earlier: The issue is 'that in the presence of his judgment[10] our consciences may be at rest'.

In any case, this *coram Deo* plays a remarkable role in Calvin's thinking. It is characteristic for the way he speaks and even more for the background from which he speaks.[11] Also the definition cited above includes the phrase 'in God's sight' (*in Dei conspectu*). This is definitely more than a facile pious addition: it is an indispensable condition for knowing what justification is. It is only when we dare stand before God's face that our true identity comes through in God's light. It is only then that we come to know how vacuous every appeal to good works begins to sound. Our justification can never come from that situation. Salvation must come from somewhere else: from faith in the righteousness of Christ. The reference is to laying hold of Christ's righteousness by faith. 'Justification by faith' is a concept one can only grasp from within a personal confrontation. It is an existential term, the fruit of an encounter with God we have experienced in faith. It has *personal* colour, therefore, and has its source in personal experience. 'Of course it is easy and possible for everyone in his study to prattle about the value of works in justifying people. But

---

[9] CO 5:397. Lüttge (*Rechtfertigungslehre Calvins*, 81) has clearly pointed out the function of this knowledge of self in justification through faith.

[10] *Institutes* 3.13.1 (CO 2:559): 'coram ipsius iudicio'.

[11] J. T. Bakker (*Coram Deo: Bijdrage tot het onderzoek naar de structuur van Luthers Theologie* [Kampen, 1956]) places Luther's theology in the same light, as indicated in Luther's speaking of an *opus alienum* and *opus proprium*. This theme is not found in this form in Calvin; nevertheless, humanity is no less continually confronted with GOD, *coram Deo*.

when we come before the presence of God we must put away such pleasantries!'[12] The expression *coram Deo* in its own way describes the bipolar structure of Calvin's thought.

The term 'in God's presence', accordingly, obviously plays an important role in the section on justification by faith. But this is not the only section in which it occurs! In another context, namely that of Christ's mediatorship, it is said of all people: 'Like their father, all of them trembled before the face of God.'[13] The person of Christ is necessary to us humans so that, 'fully trusting in their Mediator, we may freely dare appear in God's presence'.[14] '... The splendour of God's face, which even the apostle calls "unapproachable" [1 Tim. 6:16], is to us an inexplicable labyrinth unless we are led into it by the thread of the Word.'[15] Thus the face of God shines forth upon us in the doctrine,[16] and is a very important pledge of our salvation.[17] Thus, in broad outline, one can hear the *Institutes* speak about God's presence (*coram Deo*).

When it concerns their justification, therefore, people are expressly viewed as standing before the face of God. Justification is conditioned by the divine–human relation. It is precisely in this light that we must regard Calvin's defensive posture toward the teaching of Osiander, who has an essentialist view of justification. According to him, it is effected by Christ's divine nature and our participation in it.[18] Calvin responds by saying: no, we must

[12] *Institutes* 3.12.1 (CO 2:553): 'sed ubi in conspectum Dei ventum est, facessant tales deliciae oportet'. Cf. ibid., 3.2.23 (CO 2:417).

[13] Ibid., 2.12.1 (CO 2:340): 'Atqui omnes cum parente suo ad conspectum Dei horrebant.'

[14] Ibid., 2.7.1 (CO 2:254): 'ut Mediatore suo freti, libere in Dei conspectum prodire audeant'.

[15] Ibid., 1.6.3 (CO 2:55): 'Sic enim cogitandum est: fulgorem divini vultus, quem et Apostolus inaccessum vocat, esse nobis instar inexplicabilis labyrinthi, nisi verbi linea in ipsum dirigamur.'

[16] Ibid., 4.1.5 (CO 2:750): 'Dei facies, quae nobis in doctrina affulget.'

[17] Ibid., 2.10.8 (CO 2:318): 'facies eius, simul atque illuxit, praesentissimum est salutis pignus'.

[18] Cf. Niesel, 'Calvin wider Osianders Rechtfertigungslehre', *Zeitschrift für Kirchengeschichte* 46 (1927): 410–30. Niesel, however, has not taken sufficient note of the fact that for Calvin Osiander's doctrine of justification endangers one's assurance of salvation. Cf. also Lüttge, *Rechtfertigungslehre Calvins*, 75–9. See *Institutes* 3.11.10 (CO 2:540–1).

keep our distance in the presence of God. Again he wants to underscore the radical distinction between the two natures of Christ and avoid any suggestion of the deification of man.[19] Thus, in the *Institutes* of 1536, he writes:

> We are made righteous by faith. . . . This is Christ's righteousness, not ours: it is lodged in him, not in us, but it becomes ours by imputation. . . . Thus, in reality, we are not truly righteous, but righteous by imputation and we are not righteous people, but are reckoned righteous by imputation insofar as we possess Christ's righteousness through faith.[20]

Alongside of this, one should read (in the *Institutes* of 1545) with what forceful phrases Calvin nevertheless dared to express our union with Christ: 'the apostle mentions the reason that Jesus Christ dwells in us and not only has an unbreakable connection with us but by a marvellous union which surpasses our understanding he daily and increasingly unites himself with us into one single substance'.[21]

These two statements, read side by side, at first sound strange and inconsistent. But Calvin's intention is clear. It is twofold. Actually and unexpectedly he elucidates the entire complex of problems surrounding the divine–human polarity. On the one hand, he wants to picture the union between Christ and the believer as realistically and intimately as he can. But this intimate union, however real, may never be construed as though God's being flowed over into that of humans. Calvin must have sensed this threat and been unable to grasp this as anything other than the deification of man. It is not clear how maintaining a respectful distance and reverence for God's uniqueness and grandeur can be harmoniously combined with an equally strong intention to make the union of the saved person with Christ as intimate as possible.

---

[19] Cf. Wendel, *Calvin*, 259.

[20] *Institutes* (1536) 2.60 (CO 1:60): 'Ita non vere nos esse iustos sed imputative vel non esse iustos, sed pro iustis imputatione haberi, quatenus Christi iustitiam per fidem possidemus, res plana erit et expedita.'

[21] *Institutes* (1545) 3.2.24 (CO 4:42): 'par une conionction admirable et surmontant nostre entendement, il s'unist iournellement de plus en plus à nous en une mesme substance'. *Institutes* (1559) 3.2.24 (CO 2:418): 'Christus . . . in unum corpus nobiscum coalescit in dies magis ac magis, donec unum penitus nobiscum fiat.'

One may characterize this as a defect and as a basic tension in the divine–human relation, especially from a soteriological perspective, but noting the intention behind the words, it seems to us even more important to acknowledge that Calvin's intent is pure and beyond reproach. Apparent inconsistency in one's thinking and formulation may betray a deeper insight than facile and smooth-sounding formulas!

As was to be expected, Calvin's portrayal of God's role in 'justification by faith' is most impressive. It is precisely in the process of redemption that God's sovereignty comes fully into its own. His omni-causality comes magnificently to the fore and his honour is profusely and incessantly proclaimed. Here, too, the mighty worker of salvation, who is God alone, is at no point deficient in his character as the Merciful One. *Mercy* is the background and driving force of his conduct. 'Over and over the same thought occurs to me, namely, that I run the danger of failing to do justice to God's mercy because I labour so hard and with such anxiety to defend it as if it were doubtful or obscure.'[22] What consistently strikes us is something of which Calvin was very definitely aware. He is a stubborn and persistent preacher of God's mercy: 'When Scripture speaks of the righteousness of faith, it leads us to something very different: namely, to turning us away from the contemplation of our own works to the contemplation solely of God's mercy and Christ's perfection.' Pivotal, here, is God's pure and freely-given goodness;[23] indeed, but never viewed in isolation. To speak of mercy by itself and of pure goodness always has a polemical flavour. These words were spoken to *persons* in order that they might know that it is not their excellence and goodness which produce anything. One simply cannot escape this feeling when listening to Calvin's fervent recommendation of God's mercy in the context of justification by faith. The faith which plays such a large role in this connection is dominated by a mercy described in similar terms: 'faith *without works* rests entirely upon God's mercy'.[24] The promises of the gospel are

[22] *Institutes* 3.14.6 (CO 2:567): 'Redit eadem mihi subinde cogitatio, periculum esse ne Dei misericordiae sim iniurius, qui tanta anxietate in ea asserenda laborem, perinde acsi dubia obscurave foret.'

[23] Ibid., 3.11.16 (CO 2:547): 'mera gratuitaque bonitas'.

[24] Ibid., 3.11.18 (CO 2:548): 'fides sine operum adminiculo tota in Dei misericordiam recumbit'.

unmerited and rest solely upon God's mercy, whereas the promises of the law depend on the conditions of works.[25] Actually Calvin's references to God's mercy are never devoid of that polemical tone of resistance to possible human pretensions. It is obviously for this reason that he cites Bernard of Clairvaux's commentary on the psalm verse (Ps. 71:16): 'O Lord, I will sing of your righteousness, yours alone.' Calvin clearly interprets the verse to imply a rejection of all purely human merit.[26] In justification, therefore, everything turns on God's mercy and God's mercy alone. 'We have now clearly settled the main issue in this discussion, namely, that righteousness lies solely in God's mercy, solely in communion with Christ, and therefore solely in faith.'[27] Here again the threefold 'sola', which has such a Reformational flavour to it, clearly bears the stamp of resistance, but it is equally important to remember that in justification it is God's mercy which dominates and defines the divine–human relation. *That* is what justification is all about. When God's grandeur and his being the sole cause of everything play their role, they are nevertheless always dominated and defined by his mercy. His is a merciful grandeur and a merciful sovereignty. Simply for this reason alone, God's relation to people is never that of a potentate. In this connection it seems to us extremely important, therefore, to point to God's mercy with such emphasis. Just as in the matter of 'satisfaction', so also here, God's entire conduct toward us humans in justification is permeated by mercy.

People face a divine grandeur that is merciful, but then also a grandeur that is real, when God justifies them. This awareness and experience of divine grandeur is inevitably implied in the reality of *coram Deo* from the moment this divine presence is taken seriously. In fact, the signs of that grandeur can be found (in Calvin) on every page which speaks of justification by faith.

How, indeed, is it possible that people dare to speak of the justification of good works when they are actually bursting with sins?[28] It is possible because they have no sense of God's *iustitia*,

---

[25] Ibid., 3.11.17 (CO 2:548): '[promissiones evangelicae] gratuitae sunt, ac sola Dei misericordia suffultae'.

[26] Ibid., 3.12.3 (CO 2:555).

[27] Ibid., 3.15.1 (CO 2:579): 'sola Dei misericordia'; cf. ibid., 3.16.4 (CO 2:589): 'ad solam Dei misericordiam confugiendum'.

[28] Ibid., 3.12.1 (CO 2:553): 'crepant vitiis'.

that is, God's justice, his inviolable holiness.[29] That holy justice is so perfect that nothing pleases it unless it is pure and complete in all respects and completely without stain of any kind. We must not indulge in fantasies about how God is, but rather let our thoughts be inspired by holy Scripture – by the image Scripture gives of God.

> He is a God by whose brightness the stars are darkened; by whose strength the mountains melt; by whose wrath the earth is shaken; by whose wisdom the wise are caught in their craftiness; before whose purity all things are defiled; whose righteousness not even the angels can bear; who does not excuse the guilty; whose vengeance, when once kindled, penetrates the darkest corners of hell. . . .[30]

That is the God with whom we have to do! The manner in which Calvin describes God's grandeur is directly derived from the Old Testament's witness to God. Not surprisingly, he quotes at length from the Old Testament.[31] What do we think will happen to human innocence when it is compared with God's purity?[32] asks Calvin; people will tremble rather than mindlessly boast of their own excellence.[33]

Striking, here, is that God's grandeur, which is thus pictured in cosmic terms, is simultaneously and suddenly viewed as morally without blemish. Just as in the case of mercy, so also in this description, the author never forgets the counter-pole to whom all this is said. God's grandeur is not an abstract term but a reality which functions in vital connection with human beings.

To highlight the effective power of God's grandeur Calvin adds the motif of the all-causing Agent. He thoroughly scrutinizes the whole field of causality in order to credit every form of causation to the grandeur that is God, naturally with a clear intention to withdraw them from man. He says this explicitly: 'when we look at the four causes to be observed, according to the philosophers, in the outworking of things, we will find that none of them has

[29] Sizoo (*Institutie* 2:261) translates *iustitia* as 'rechtvaardigheid' (righteousness), which seems to us less correct.

[30] *Institutes* 3.12.1 (CO 2:553).

[31] Ibid., 3.12.1 (CO 2:553–4).

[32] Ibid., 3.12.4 (CO 2:556): 'quid putamus vel rarissimae hominis innocentiae futurum, ubi ad Dei puritatem composita fuerit?'

[33] Ibid., 3.12.2 (CO 2:554): 'ut trepidare potius diceremus, quam inaniter exultare'.

anything to do with works in the establishment of our salvation'.[34] One can see operating here Calvin's method of fighting the theology of the scholastics with their own weapons. For a comparison of this pericope on the various forms of causation with an earlier model, see, for example, Thomas Aquinas.[35]

The efficient cause (*causa efficiens*) is God's mercy; the material cause (*causa materialis*) is Christ's obedience; the formal or instrumental cause (*causa formalis, instrumentalis*) is faith, while the final cause (*causa finalis*) is the demonstration of God's righteousness and the praise of his goodness.[36] Precisely what this terminology means in the mind of Calvin would require further research. Only a dogma-historical investigation can open the door to a hermeneutic – the 'art of understanding' – of the terms used in Calvin. In our opinion it is a mistake to make heavy weather of the terminology used here. Calvin's reservations about any philosophical approach to revelation is well known. Add to this that his use of such terms is far from consistent and raises questions. Whereas we read in the section on 'satisfaction' that Christ is not merely a formal cause of salvation but a genuine 'efficient cause',[37] we are told here that Christ's obedience is the 'material cause'. But more important than this lack of clarity and consistency in his use of words is Calvin's intent, which in fact is clear. The God who justifies is only merciful, only great, the only universal Agent. And when humans find themselves situated before One who can only be described in colossal cosmic imagery (and even then he remains elusive),[38] who is inviolable in the perfection of his purity and furthermore the sole causative Agent of everything, they cannot but shrink in fear and must lose all inclination to persist in self-sufficient boastfulness. So also in this context the motif of God's honour becomes the conclusive and culminating

---

[34] Ibid., 3.14.17 (CO 2:575).

[35] Aquinas, *Summa Theologiae* 3, q.64, 3c.

[36] *Institutes* 3.14.17 (CO 2:575): '*Efficientem* enim vitae aeternae nobis comparandae causam ubique Scriptura praedicat Patris caelestis misericordiam, et gratuitam erga nos dilectionem: *materialem* vero, Christum cum sua obedientia, per quam nobis iustitiam acquisivit; *formalem*, quoque vel *instrumentalem* quam esse dicemus nisi fidem? Porro *finalem* testatur Apostolus esse, et divinae iustitiae demonstrationem, et bonitatis laudem.'

[37] See above, p. 93.

[38] *Institutes* 3.12.1 (CO 2:554): 'incomprehensibilis'.

end of what the presence of God (*coram Deo*) actually implies. This end is filled with tension and aggressively charged against all human boasting in connection with justification. If ever, then certainly here, Calvin could know he was backed up by the biblical witness in its entirety and especially by Paul's letter to the Romans.

In emphasizing God's honour (something that happens very naturally in stressing justification), Calvin is again clearly inspired by Paul. Countless quotations from Scripture testify to this fact. It is obvious that he completely made Paul's dialectic between faith and good works his own. 'If we establish a righteousness of our own, we throw God's righteousness away; to gain the latter we must completely do away with the former. He [Paul] demonstrates this very thing when he states that our boasting is not excluded by law but by faith.'[39] 'From this it follows that so long as any particle, be it ever so small, of works righteousness remain, some occasion for boasting remains as well.'[40] Just as in the work of the apostle, so in Calvin all these texts have a polemical tone. They are directed against the people who seek to lay hold of the honour which belongs to God alone. As long as people have anything to say in their own defence they detract something from God's honour.[41] There is no middle way. There is no possibility of dividing: the least bit of honour ascribed to man in this connection is already too much.[42] On the point of honour the relation between God and man is extremely tense. It is as if Calvin here furnishes a lengthy commentary on Paul's struggle against all human boasting and eagerly amplifies this theme. 'In short, humans cannot without sacrilege claim for themselves even a crumb of righteousness, for precisely that much is plucked and taken away from the glory of divine righteousness.'[43] A sharper

---

[39] Romans 3:27; *Institutes* 3.11.13 (CO 2:545).

[40] *Institutes* 3.11.13 (CO 2:545): 'Unde sequitur, quantisper manet quantulacunque operum iustitia, manere nobis nonnullam gloriandi materiam.'

[41] Ibid., 3.13.1 (CO 2:560): 'quia quantisper habet homo quod in suam defensionem loquatur, Dei gloriae nonnihil decedit'.

[42] Ibid.: 'quid magno nostro malo tentamus vel ullam particulam ex ista gratuitae benignitatis laude Domino suffurari?'

[43] Ibid., 3.13.2 (CO 2:561): 'Summa haec est, non posse hominem sibi ullam iustitiae micam sine sacrilegio vendicare, quia tantunden ex divinae iustitiae gloria decerpitur ac delibatur.'

formulation is scarcely conceivable. Calvin takes this matter so seriously that he does not shrink from speaking of sacrilege.

Very well: not the smallest particle of honour and justification is due to man. But if that is true, do humans then do nothing at all? Is it not a human being who is justified by God and not a thing? In this connection, is there any evidence of human initiative or perhaps of a free human acceptance of unmerited divine goodness,[44] which is accorded to a person from the side of God in justification? Does God's sovereign volition go so far as to leave no room whatever for human volition? We posit such questions here, being at the same time very well aware that to Calvin these sort of questions must have sounded like intolerable human audacity. Just as in the matter of free will, so here too his aim is not to tear down people and their capacities. He does not, as in later years the Thomists and Molinists did, immerse himself in fruitless and disastrous theological contention – in the question how human volition and God's all-powerful grace can possibly go together.

The point at which the divine and human poles touch each other in justification is faith.[45] But to Calvin this is no reason to immerse himself with all his theological astuteness in this faith and in that context to analyse human insight alongside of the divine operation of grace. Indeed not: faith is above all a motive for not boasting; it is precisely the opposite of personal achievements which are supposed to be meritorious. Faith in its entirety, therefore, points back to God's mercy.[46] As stated above, in the process of justification faith functions as the instrumental cause. Again one would be disposed to reflect on that subject. A person who starts believing certainly does not ever function solely as an instrument, do they? If they do, that person is certainly no longer a human being who believes. . . . To Calvin such a comment must have sounded like a stubborn attempt yet again to snatch away from God something belonging to his work and honour in the process of justification. Yet we have the impression that he had an eye for the inexplicable going together of God and man in the

---

[44] Ibid., 3.13.1 (CO 2:560): 'gratuita benignitatis laus'.
[45] Cf. Lüttge, *Rechtfertigungslehre Calvins*, 80.
[46] *Institutes* 3.11.18 (CO 2:548): 'fides tota in Dei misericordiam recumbit'.

act of faith. Or is he only fighting opponents who even seize upon faith to give greater prominence to man at the expense of God's honour? We believe that precisely also on the point of faith we can clearly detect in Calvin a concern to safeguard this domain from any foray by human intruders looking for plunder. He wisely stays out of the question *how* a person starts to believe when at the same time this event is solely God's work and a matter of God's honour. Striking, however, is that he reacts against any attempt, either openly or secretly, to make faith an independent something in honour of human being.

We must recall here that to Calvin faith is much more than a factual knowledge of revealed truths.[47] It is rather 'a firm and certain knowledge of God's benevolence toward us'.[48] At issue is God's attitude towards us (*erga nos*). It is a relation of person-to-person. In other words, Calvin's definition sounds existential and personalistic.[49] Now then, in this relation there is a strong accent on the benevolence of God; the person who believes is subject to the powerful pressure of the God who alone accomplishes salvation. Imagine that faith should at some point become a reason for boasting! We repeatedly get this impression when Calvin speaks about faith. In this connection let us weigh the following statements: 'We say that faith justifies, not because it merits righteousness for us by its own worth but because it is an instrument whereby we obtain gratuitously the righteousness of Christ.' Merely an instrument without any *intrinsic* dignity or excellence of its own.[50] Evidently the instrumental activity of faith only consists in apprehension, a purely cognitive activity which with respect to our salvation is totally devoid of merit. One senses how Calvin struggled to give to the faith component a proper and secure

---

[47] *Institutes* (1536) 2 (CO 1:56): 'Hoc vero est, non modo verum reputare id omne, quod de Deo ac Christo vel scriptum est, vel dicitur, sed spem omnem ac fiduciam in uno Deo ac Christo reponere.'

[48] *Institutes* 3.2.7 (CO 2:403): 'Nunc iusta fidei definitio nobis constabit si dicamus esse divinae erga nos benevolentiae firmam certamque cognitionem.'

[49] In our opinion, it is also for this reason that Calvin rejects so-called *fides implicita*. With implicit faith a third party, namely the Church, is slid in between, through which one believes in Christ. Cf. *Institutes* 3.2.3 (CO 2:399): 'Fides enim in Dei et Christi cognitione [Joh. 17:3], non in Ecclesiae reverentia iacet'; ibid., 3.2.2 (CO 2:398): 'commentum implicitae fidei'.

[50] Ibid., 3.18.8 (CO 2:610): 'Sola Dei misericordia et merito Christi constat nostra iustificatio, quam dum fides apprehendit, iustificare dicitur.'

place in the process of justification. However this may be, this instrument derives its value solely from its content: namely Christ

> . . . I gladly concede . . . that faith of itself does not have the power of justifying but only insofar as it receives Christ. For if faith justified of itself or through some intrinsic power, as it is called, it would – because it is always weak and imperfect – effect this only in part. Thus [God's] righteousness would be defective and confer only a fragment of salvation.[51]

In this last clause the importance of personal assurance of salvation comes surprisingly to the fore. It is a concern we already pointed out earlier as the second great purpose of justification: peace of conscience. The latter, however, is totally based on the other pole which the believing person grasps: Christ. There is a linkage between the two. The assurance of salvation rests, not on our faith, but on its content: Christ. Thus Calvin serves humans by in fact snatching from them their means of constructing a right-eousness of their own. At the same time it is evident – no matter how vehemently he champions the exclusive glory and action of God – that he nevertheless, and precisely in that way, champions the cause of humanity. In the process of theologizing he simul-taneously stands up for humans, for their salvation, their peace of conscience. That is: his theology is pastoral. Every so often he shifts his focus from God to man and back again. From all this, he says elsewhere, do not conclude that we take away from Christ the power to justify! He does not, accordingly, stress faith or even the Word by which faith is generated.[52] Neither the operation of God's power, nor his honour, is excluded even when the Word is highlighted.[53]

One can tell that Calvin's way of thinking readily returns to the divine pole, expressly staying there for a long time. That is clearly the case in his discussion of justification by faith. Still the

---

[51] Ibid., 2.11.7 (CO 2:538): 'si per se, vel intrinseca, ut loquuntur, virtute iustificaret fides, ut est semper debilis et imperfecta, non efficeret hoc nisi ex parte; sic manca esset iustitia quae frustulum salutis nobis conferret'.

[52] Ibid., 3.2.31 (CO 2:422–23): 'Item, Speravi in verbo tuo, salvum me fac. Ubi notanda est fidei ad verbum relatio, deinde salutis, consequentia. Neque tamen interea potentiam Dei excludimus, cuius intuitu nisi se sustentet, nunquam Deo tribuet suum honorem.'

[53] Ibid., 3.2.35 (CO 2:427): 'Ideo precatur [Paulus] ut in Thessalonisensibus impleat Deus omne beneplacitum suum et opus fidei in virtute [2 Thess. 1:11].'

rule is always in effect: there are two perspectives (*duo spectanda*), God's honour and human peace of conscience. But in order to achieve this goal a complete bulwark of human certainties has to be demolished. If even faith has to be regarded with so many reservations and caution, purely as an instrument, only powerful to save because of its content: Christ, then we have to be even much more critical when it comes to human merit and all good works. In terms of their power to save, Calvin totally demolishes them. Indeed, but this demolition is not the demolition of *man*. On the contrary: it provides people with a solid footing when it comes to their salvation. In a few concluding comments we want to make this point clear.

Calvin devotes a large amount of space to *good works*. He has nothing against them but only against the practice of giving them independence, as though they had power in themselves to effect justification. Nothing is praiseworthy that is not rooted in God.[54] Power derives solely from grace. But good works are grounded in grace; they do not exist in isolation. They are part of the fabric of God's grace. In other words, the whole person is saved; the whole person is justified right down to his or her actions and activities. The mistake is to separate human activity from the one source of grace, which is faith in Christ.[55] It is wrong, therefore, shamelessly to hold onto the praise of grace which is due to God alone. That is the intolerable practice of making good works stand by themselves.[56] In the justified person they must be viewed as one harmonious whole with grace which is like the root by which the entire tree is made healthy and bears fruit.[57] Justifying grace – to use the familiar expression – is *sanatio in radice*: the healing of the very roots of a person, by which the whole person is made healthy, including his or her activity and good works. The whole

---

[54] Ibid., 3.14.2 (CO 2:565): 'nihil est ullo modo laudabile quod non ab ipso proficiscatur'.

[55] Ibid., 3.12.8 (CO 2:559): 'quia laudem gratiae per se transeuntis improbe retinent'.

[56] Ibid., 3.15.3 (CO 2:581): 'Bonorum, inquam, operum laudem non (ut sophistae faciunt) inter Deum et hominem partimur: sed totam, integram ac illibatam Domino servamus.'

[57] Ibid., 3.17.10 (CO 2:598): 'debet sub eam [fidem] includi, et tanquam effectus causae suae (ut ita loquar) subordinari . . . . Ita merito dicere possumus sola fide non tantum nos sed opera etiam nostra iustificari'.

person is restored, healed and renewed. That, ultimately, is the significance of the unbreakable unity between justification and sanctification which Calvin repeatedly posits.[58] And this is also the background of the following familiar formulation: 'Thus it is clear how true it is that we are not justified without works, neither by works, since in our sharing in Christ (*in Christi participatione*), which justifies us, sanctification is as much included as justification.'[59] God's mercy, which is the efficient cause of justification, permeates the whole person and energizes that person even in doing good works. For that reason, too, Calvin rejects the notion of a double justification.[60]

Why does Calvin agitate so fiercely against all human 'merit'? Because in this word of man something is made to stand by itself and placed outside the one grace of God. Because by it something is withdrawn by man from the grace of God who alone is the cause of our salvation. The word 'merit' is thoroughly corrupted because it is always seen apart from the mercy of God who alone justifies and sanctifies a person. Apparently the word 'merit' can only be understood in the sense that a person can effect his or her own salvation apart from the grace of God. From this point of view Calvin is absolutely right when he believes it is better to abolish the word. In this sense it is nothing more than a Pelagian word. 'What is said about the merit of works destroys the honour of God in bestowing righteousness, as well as our assurance of salvation.'[61]

Hence also in his polemic against merits Calvin has both poles in view. In his absolute rejection of human merit it is also humans he seeks to serve. 'Merit' is a prideful term and can only obscure the grace of God.[62] This, therefore, is his reason for rejecting it. 'Merit' irrevocably diminishes God's grace and endangers our

---

[58] Among other places, especially eloquently in the letter to Sadoleto (CO 5:398).

[59] *Institutes* 3.16.2 (CO 2:586): 'Ita liquet quam verum sit nos non sine operibus, neque tamen per opera iustificari, quoniam in Christi participatione, qua iustificamur, non minus sanctificatio continetur quam iustitia.'

[60] Ibid., 3.11.12 (CO 2:545): 'Denique quisquis duplicem iustitiam involvit, ne quiescant miserae animae in mera et unica Dei misericordia, Christum implexis spinis per ludibrium coronat.'

[61] Ibid., 3.15 (CO 2:579).

[62] Ibid., 3.15.1 (CO 2:580): 'Certe ut est fastuosissimum, nihil quam obscurare Dei gratiam et homines prava superbia imbuere potest.'

assurance of salvation. Why did people actually use the word 'merit', asks Calvin, when *crowning good works* could easily have been rendered by another word and used without offence?[63] Calvin does not actually tell us what word we should use instead, but it appears he can make his peace with the expression: *crowning good works*. This last comment is important to our special interest in the divine–human relation. Crowning good works is something Calvin can meaningfully fit into his theology of justification and sanctification. It means that the same grace which justifies believers and penetrates their good works has a final effect also in the crowning or completion of their life: awarding a prize in the form of good works. But this latter expression sounds more static and passive than 'meriting' and points more directly to the fullness of grace present in the starting-point which permeates the life of the regenerate person. What precisely is meant by 'crowning the good works'? I believe it means the final phase and flowering of the grace-filled beginning of God's mercy in the life of a person. Demonstrable here is an organic connectedness. God's righteousness and mercy is the beginning and justifies a person by faith. Justifying the entire person, that grace of God presses on into the doing of good works and the culmination or coronation of those good works which is their final offshoot.

From this vantage point two results are achieved: (1) Everything is consistently placed under the sponsorship of grace: full justice is done to God's sovereignty. (2) A mutual connectedness between faith, good works and the glorious completion of good works is recognized and actually has to be there inasmuch as the one grace of God lays hold of the whole person. As such the human, for that matter, is already a single unbreakable whole. People do not consist of loosely connected components but constitute a profound unity, both in the project and the pattern of their life. That life is an unbreakable unity of basic attitude, thought and conduct which culminates in a specific human image to which a value can be assigned. This *appraisal* can run through an entire spectrum of value judgments, from the idealistic to the

[63] Ibid., 3.15.2 (CO 2:579): 'Quorsum enim obsecro, opus fuit invehi nomen meriti, quum pretium bonorum operum significanter alio nomine citra offendiculum explicari posset?' It is difficult to find a satisfactory translation for this phrase *pretium bonorum operum*. 'Reward' sounds too much like 'merit', a word which Calvin rightly wishes to avoid.

grossly materialistic. This *appraisal* is, as it were, the culminating or crowning conclusion of a once-chosen life project which impacts and permeates a person's life and conduct throughout their entire active life. This 'crowning' ties in and is harmoniously bound up with the life project and life pattern of that person. It is their final flowering and completion.[64] The human being who herself selects her life project and the pattern of life that matches it, accordingly, merits the appraisal and the 'prize' which goes with her – consistently pursued – life choice.

We are aware that these anthropological comments may sound strange in the context of our discussion of the notion of merit. Calvin's real intent is that which we referred to under point 1: that justice be done to God's sovereignty above all in relation to every kind of human merit. But it has become clear to us that he deliberately seeks to situate the *whole* person in the light of God's grace. This is part of the main thrust of his rejection of the idea of humans 'meriting' things. Why? Again, because this falls outside of the sovereign rule of God's grace – because a piece of a person's life is pulled out of the orbit of God's sovereignty. If this were not the case, Calvin would have no objection, just as he had no objection to good works, provided they were assigned their proper place. Calvin knows of a rounding off of faith and good works in what he calls the 'prize' of good works.[65] Hence the idea of 'awarding a prize' takes the place here of 'merit'. To Calvin the latter word is too suggestive of a human initiative by which God's sovereignty and exclusive causality vis-à-vis salvation are compromised. Calvin sees no way of combining the two harmoniously. If he had been able to fit the meritorious conduct of humans into the structure of the single driving force of a divine grace which permeates everything he would probably not have had any objection to speaking of the 'merit' of good works.

At bottom, is not Calvin's view and that of the other Reformers that of the Catholic Church? This fundamental view is that no humans can earn salvation by their own efforts.[66] God's sovereignty can incorporate human meritorious conduct in its grace-filled

---

[64] Cf. with this Calvin's discussion of the relation between faith and good works (see above, pp. 112–16).

[65] Cf. O. Ritschl, *Dogmengeschichte des Protestantismus*, 3:207.

[66] DENZ 1521–2 (193–4); cf. *Canones de iustificatione*. DENZ 1551–3 (811–13).

activity, as indeed this happens also with good works.[67] Calvin very clearly agrees with the latter but hesitates when it comes to the former. Does a certain view of humanity perhaps play a role here? What in any case plays a role here is the bipolar tension between God and man. Anxiously he rejects all human initiative in order not to do an injustice to God. In his thinking the idea of a prize takes the place of the notion of merit. But just as he can incorporate good works in the grace of God, the same thing can be done with merit. Every biblically-inspired theology will register a serious protest against any attempt to make human merit self-sufficient and independent. No human being can earn his or her own salvation; human beings can only be enabled to attain salvation by God's mercy.[68] But if the whole person is apprehended by God's grace, then, as the crowning part of good works, also his or her merit can be included. In that way *merit* becomes a fruit of grace.

The fact that Calvin rejects the word 'merit' does not mean that he is thereby denying the thing intended by it. Mind you, Calvin clearly took over the idea of the merit of Christ and subordinated it to God's mercy. The matter intended, accordingly, is nothing other than the fact that the whole person is included in the working of God's grace, also the crowning piece of good works, namely merit. That this is Calvin's intention is clearly evident from his statement – cited above – that the term 'the prize of good works' could easily be expressed by another word. In that case at least there is no danger that God's grace will be obscured.[69] His aversion to the word 'merit' stems from a tension in the divine–human relation. It witnesses to his concern that God's sovereignty will be threatened by humans precisely at the point of God's saving work. From this point of view the question of the merit(s) of good works is highly significant for the bipolarity of God and man. The two viewpoints (*dua spectanda*), which could serve as the motto for his treatment of justification by faith, also

---

[67] Cf. E. Mersch, *La théologie du corps mystique* (Paris, 1949), 391–8 ('le mérite'). Cf. also Augustine's well-known expression: 'Deus coronat merita sua' (*In Psal.* 70:2, 5, MSL 36:895). DENZ 1548 (810): 'tanta est erga omnes homines bonitas, ut eorum velit esse merita, quae sunt ipsius dona'. Küng, *Justification*, 265.

[68] *Institutes* 3.14.5 (CO 2:567): 'sola misericordia in spem vitae aeternae'.

[69] Ibid., 3.15.2 (CO 2:580): 'obscurare Dei gratiam'.

have a peculiar resonance of their own in his rejection of merit. If a person has been totally apprehended by God's grace, when that person has embraced the righteousness of God in faith, then he or she is regenerate.[70]

2. The life of the 'new man'

It would seem that in the new life one can focus freely on the regenerate person. The road is clear to make a highly positive appraisal of the 'new man'. But this is true only if one constantly remembers the Other who made that person so and constantly creates that person anew.

In this section we want to sketch a clear picture of the 'new man' – hence above all from the perspective that this person's newness points continually to its Author. That new person is conceivable only in a vital relation to God – a relation to which every aspect of that newness testifies. We will illumine this by pointing out certain characteristics Calvin cites in his sketch of the Christian's life. Featured in this connection will be the liberty of the children of God.

Next, these positive qualities of the new person, qualities which at the same time point to God, turn out to be evinced in cross-bearing and self-denial.

Finally we will discuss the highest activity of the new life, namely prayer. All these activities of regenerate persons witness to their high value, while at the same time they continue to point steadfastly to him from whom this highly blessed situation flows. Precisely in their positive values they bear a bipolar character.

True of all the good that is demonstrable in the new person is the summary statement that 'all the gifts which God has given us – when we recount them in memory – are to us like so many bright rays from the face of God'.[71] This is even much more true, Calvin

---

[70] Calvin discusses *regeneratio* before *iustificatio*. The reason for this is not entirely clear. According to some, it can be found in the fact that Calvin wished to express the importance of the new life, which is realized in good works. For that see P. Wernle, *Der evangelische Glaube nach den Hauptschriften der Reformatoren*, vol. 3, *Johann Calvin* (Tübingen, 1919), 402ff.; Niesel, *Theologie Calvins*, 124; Wendel, *Calvin*, 233, 262.

[71] *Institutes* 3.14.18 (CO 2:577): 'quaecumque in nos dona Deus contulit, sunt nobis quodammodo instar radiorum divini vultus'.

immediately adds, of the grace of good works. It is God's face which shines out through all our good works – it is his grace which is refracted through them.[72] The new person can bear the title of conqueror but always in relation to him who loved that person.[73] It is precisely for that reason that God's children become pleasing and loveable to him: he can see in them the features and lines of his own face.[74] In our opinion, this bipolar character of the gifts of a person are most strikingly expressed in the following line: '[the good work] is performed when they [the persons in question] by their righteousness and holiness refer to their heavenly Father and thereby show that they are not degenerate children'.[75] Good works *as such* always refer to Another. They exist only as they point to the Father. The reference to the Father is essential.

This consistent reference to the Father can also be clearly discerned in Calvin's description of the liberty which Christians have regained. In sum, Christian liberty comes down to the following.[76]

1. The human conscience is freed from the rigorous demands of the law, for believers position themselves before God's face (*coram Deo*) and for their justification put all their trust in him (note the words *conscientia* and *coram Deo*: again the bipolarity which is basic in the concept of Christian liberty). It is a liberty, therefore, which exists and can originate only before the face of God. But even more important: the liberty in question is liberty before *God*.

2. The liberated conscience (again Calvin defines the issue in terms of this human starting-point) can now freely and promptly obey the will of God.[77] That liberty is oriented, on the one hand, to the inner self. It makes possible a cheerful readiness; it appeals to the heart.[78] In that way it makes a person inwardly free; indeed,

[72] Ibid.: 'bonorum operum gratia'. Much is said in these three words. Cf. ibid., 3.14.17 (CO 2:576): 'omnia in hunc finem, ut divinae bonitatis gloria ad plenum eluceat'.

[73] Ibid., 3.14.19 (CO 2:577); Romans 8:37.

[74] *Institutes* 3.17.5 (CO 2:593): '[filii], in quibus [Deus] notas et lineamenta vultus sui videt'.

[75] Ibid., 3.18.1 (CO 2:604): 'Perficitur porro, quum iustitia et sanctitate Patrem caelestem referentes, se filios eius non degeneres esse probant.'

[76] Ibid., 3.19 (CO 2:613–24).

[77] Ibid., 3.19.4 (CO 2:615): 'alacris promptitudo in obedientiam Dei'.

[78] Ibid.: 'ut diligamus Deum nostrum ex toto corde'.

but always before God's face. This liberty is oriented to God as well.

3. Liberty *in the use of indifferent matters*. Again this third part of Christian liberty is defined in terms of the tranquillity of the human conscience. One can even say that this aspect is particularly humane in character. But also this liberty stands before the face of God.[79] The issue here is whether a person can – with an untroubled conscience before God – eat ordinary bread when one could also maintain one's body with even more elementary foods.[80] Actually it is not a trifling battle one fights here inasmuch as the will of God himself is brought into play. If people are tormented by this question, they may easily learn to despise God. Christian liberty liberates a person from all the torments of such unimportant questions. All external matters are left to one's freedom, provided 'our minds are assured that the basis for this freedom is firmly established before God'.[81] The 'basis before God' is decisive for this last use of Christian liberty. Thus the entire field of liberty is framed in the divine–human relation.

But, having said this, amidst all the gifts which adorn the new person, we have not yet sufficiently attended to one characteristic of that regenerate person. That person must above all be intent on seeking the honour of God. That is his or her primary calling. 'The chief part of righteousness is to render to God his right and honour.'[82] But this honouring is not something which comes upon a person from above as an element that is alien to his or her life and world. Honouring God is a question of life-and-death in the sense that humans must honour God with their life and specifically with the new life granted them by God with all the good gifts connected with it. *It is in and through our life that we honour God.*[83] People cannot honour God apart from the life that has been given them. While this may seem obvious, upon further reflection it is particularly important. Honouring God and living

---

[79] Ibid., 3.19.7 (CO 2:616): 'coram Deo'.

[80] Ibid., 3.19.7 (CO 2:617): 'tranquillus coram Deo'.

[81] Ibid., 3.19.8 (CO 2:617): 'modo eius libertatis ratio animis nostris apud Deum constet'.

[82] Ibid., 3.3.7 (CO 2:439): 'praecipua iustitiae pars est, suum ius et honorem Deo reddere'. Cf. ibid., 3.14.9 (CO 2:570): 'Ut haec sit praecipua nostra voluntas, voluntati eius servire, ac eius duntaxat gloriam modis omnibus provehere.'

[83] Ibid., 3.16.3 (CO 2:588): 'ut Deus in nobis glorificetur'.

the regenerate life are reciprocally related. God's honour, therefore, is not situated somewhere outside of the creation, still less
outside of human life, for God's image is refracted in both. This
image, as we stated earlier, finds its decisive completion in Christ.[84]
Apart from him God cannot be honoured, just as apart from him
God cannot be sought either.[85] It has pleased God to link his
honour to the created world, specifically to humanity, and apart
from their own life people cannot give to God the honour due to
him.[86] Thus God positions himself squarely in the midst of our
life. In all our actions his will and wisdom must be our guide. As
though he were preaching a sermon, Calvin continues to hammer
home that we are not our own.[87] All parts of our life, therefore,
have to be directed towards him.

Thus through the entire fabric of our life we honour God, also
in *self-denial* and *crossbearing*. Particularly in self-denial it is
strikingly clear that in the new life of the Christian the two poles,
God and man, are not just vitally related to each other but that
their interests coincide. Self-denial relates in part to our fellow
human beings, in part to God.[88] But this way of speaking is not a
matter of dividing up God's honour. This honour is firmly
anchored in our entire life and all its parts are directed toward
God. *In* serving our fellow humans, in the humane character of
self-denial, God is served. Service to others implies submission to
his majesty.

In Calvin's thought this humane character of self-denial
is brought out as something beautiful and positive. Self-denial is

[84] See above, pp. 84ff.

[85] Cf. *Institutes* 3.20.17 (CO 2:643–4) and *Comm. II Cor.* 4:6 (CO 50:51).
See above, pp. 88–9.

[86] This idea is very close to Irenaeus's pronouncement, 'gloria Dei vivens
homo' (*Adversus haereses* 1.4, c.20, n.7, PG 7:103B); cf. *Institutes* 3.6.3 (CO
2:503): 'Ex quo nos spiritus sanctus templa Deo dedicavit, dandam operam ut
Dei gloria per nos illustretur.' Thus the sanctification of our lives has much to
do with the honour of God. Cf. ibid., 3.6.2 (CO 2:502): 'non quia sanctitatis
merito veniamus in eius communionem ... sed quoniam ad eius gloriam
magnopere pertinet'; and ibid., 3.7.1 (CO 2:505): 'nequid posthac cogitemus,
loquamur, meditemur, agamus, nisi in eius gloriam'. How intramundane this
picture of God is to our minds.

[87] *Institutes* 3.7.1 (CO 2:506): 'Nostri non sumus. ... Rursum Dei sumus.'

[88] Ibid., 3.7.4 (CO 2:508): 'Porro in his verbis perspicimus abnegationem
nostri partim quidem in homines respicere, partim vero (idque praecipue) in
Deum.'

oriented to the other *person*. It takes shape in practical benevolence to others. Considered by itself, people may not in any way deserve it if judged by their merits, but this must not be our starting-point. We must be willing to see in them – in everyone – the image of God to which we owe all honour and love.[89] Mortification of self consists in the fulfilment of the duties of love (*officia charitatis*). It is not a perfunctory thing in which the heart remains totally uninvolved. On the contrary! The work of love in which this mortification functions must be done from the heart.[90] Calvin here sees the service of God as being very much oriented to our fellow humans; at the same time, in pointing toward the image of God in humans he brings out the other part of self-denial: bowing to the will of God. In the image of God both parts of self-denial find their connectedness and unity.

Partly, and primarily, self-denial has to do with God. That person has only truly denied herself who has totally surrendered to God, who wants God to govern all the parts of her life.[91] This surrendering all – even trials and adversities – to God's discretion honours him.[92]

Bearing one's cross comes under the heading of self-denial: it is the ultimate implication of it. In crossbearing a person's surrender to God achieves its most painful but also its most perfect realization. Thus our heavenly Father wants to purify his own.[93] The person who accepts his or her cross enters into fellowship with Christ.[94] It means that Christ is glorified in us.[95] Not only does it bless our suffering but it also advances our salvation. This *wellbeing* of a person is achieved in the most paradoxical manner. The cross means the total surrender of the self in order by this act to put one's whole trust in God. To rely on him alone, to obey

[89] Ibid., 3.7.6 (CO 2:510): 'Scriptura ... docet ... imaginem Dei in cunctis considerandam, cui nihil non et honoris et dilectionis debeamus.' Cf. ibid., 3.7.6 (CO 2:511): 'digna est imago Dei'.

[90] Ibid., 3.7.7 (CO 2:511): 'ex sincero amoris affectu'.

[91] Ibid., 3.7.10 (CO 2:514): 'nemo se rite abnegavit, nisi qui se totum ita resignavit Domino ut omnes vitae suae partes eius arbitrio gubernari ferat'.

[92] Ibid.: 'ne sic quidem desinet benedicere Domino'; ibid., 3.8.1 (CO 2:515): 'Sic est caelestis Patris voluntas.'

[93] Ibid., 3.8.1 (CO 2:515): 'ut certum de suis experimentum capiat'.

[94] Ibid.: 'nostra cum Christo societas'.

[95] Ibid., 3.8.8 (CO 2:520): 'haec crucis species, qua vult Christus in nobis glorificari'.

only him, to put God's will above all else – thus, theocentrically, Calvin interprets crossbearing.[96] The person who so thoroughly renounces all trust in himself or herself, indeed abandons their very self, loses it, signs their own death sentence. But in this act of total self-surrender to God such a person is saved. This paradox comes from Christ himself.[97] Can the relation between God and man be approached more startlingly than that? At the cross God and man no longer stand side by side. God alone still stands. Man falls, but is secure in God.

Calvin devotes a long chapter in his *Institutes* to prayer.[98] One can expect this of him as a pastor. A second thing we may expect is that precisely in this connection the bipolarity of God and man will assume a vivid form. Prayer is the mutual orientation of God and man in practical experience. Existential communion between God and man finds its expression in prayer.

Calvin's lengthy treatment of prayer alone already prompts us to suspect the great vitality of this mutual orientation between God and man. How personal this relation is! In this concluding part we want to confirm this suspicion by pointing out a number of facets of this vital mutual relatedness.

We shall do this by inspecting – in terms of their bipolar relatedness – the rules for prayer as Calvin defines them. Every sketch of the human situation, every stipulation laid down for human prayer, is a reference to God. Conversely, in this setting God is viewed only as being turned to man, as he is experienced by humans in his grandeur and goodness. 'The moment the dreadful majesty of God comes to mind, we necessarily tremble and the recognition of our own unworthiness causes us to sink away until Christ intervenes: he who transforms the throne of awesome glory into a throne of grace.' With this lapidary sentence Calvin sketches in broad outline all the subject-matter of prayer. It is a back-and-forth movement. Expatiating on his basic point of departure, the knowledge of God and the knowledge of man, each implying the other, he posits God's dreadful majesty over

[96] Ibid., 3.8.2 (CO 2:516): 'ut parva carnis confidentia exuti, ad Dei gratiam se conferant'. Cf. ibid., 3.8.3 (CO 2:517): 'sic humiliatos, in Deum unum reclinare docet'; ibid., 3.8.11 (CO 2:522): 'praecipuam crucis tolerandae rationem a divinae voluntatis consideratione sumpsimus'.

[97] Matthew 16:24; *Institutes* 3.8.1 (CO 2:515).

[98] *Institutes* 3.20 (CO 2:625–79).

against the experience of one's own unworthiness. God's majesty is experienced as dreadful precisely because humans experience themselves as unworthy. On the other hand, that majesty brings out human littleness in the starkest possible way. This is the first thematic thread we can point out in Calvin's discourse on prayer. The second is Christ. Prayer does not occur apart from him. But this presupposes faith in him.[99] Praying is an activity of the regenerate. Only for them the throne of awesome glory has been transformed into the throne of grace. Praying is the work of those who believe.[100] In prayer our faith is put to the test, the test, that is, of whether faith has not deluded us with lies or vain things.[101] Thus Calvin sometimes most strikingly characterizes prayer 'as a sort of verification of the faith'.[102]

On the basis of faith in Christ prayer is mutual orientation between God and man. It is communication in the purest sense of the word between persons.[103] It concerns two persons, or rather the relation between the two. Personal prayer arises from those two poles. It refers back to an experience of one's own situation, one's own distress and helplessness, and is at the same time a knowledge of the grandeur and goodness of the God who can and will help.[104] How from this double experience (*ex utroque affectu*) the back-and-forth movement of the mutuality of God and man comes to expression is evident from the four rules of prayer which Calvin lays down:

[99] This view of faith is characterized here by Calvin with the words 'secreta absconditaque philosophia' (ibid., 3.20.1 [CO 2:625]). Cf. Wendel, *Calvin*, 253: 'To benefit by this privilege of being able to approach the divine majesty under the protection of Christ, we must of course have the faith, and have received grace in consequence of it.'

[100] *Institutes* 3.20.1 (CO 2:625): 'De oratione quae praecipuum est fidei exercitium' (the heading of chap. 20).

[101] Ibid., 3.20.2 (CO 2:626): 'ut quod verbo duntaxat annuenti crediderunt non fuisse vanum, ubi necessitas ita postulat, *experiantur*'. This last word refers again surprisingly to the knowledge of ourselves, which plays an ongoing role in Calvin.

[102] Wendel, *Calvin*, 253.

[103] *Institutes* 3.20.2 (CO 2:625): 'Est enim quaedam hominum cum Deo communicatio.'

[104] Ibid., 3.20.11 (CO 2:635): 'Ex *utroque* ergo affectu emergat pii hominis oratio convenit, *utrunque* etiam contineat et repraesentet: nempe ut malis praesentibus ingemat, et a novis sibi anxie timeat: tamen confugiat *simul ad Deum*, minime dubitans quin auxiliarem ille manum porrigere sit paratus.'

1. One who enters the dialogue of prayer to God (*Dei collo-quium*) must have the proper attitude of heart and mind. This means being free of all human cares and thoughts.[105] Why? Because one is appearing before the face of God.[106] For that reason one must be intact and focused in a way that is worthy of God. The proper attitude in prayer, accordingly, is determined and measured by God's purity, by the grandeur also of his majesty.[107] Only those can pray who are impressed by God's majesty. Then we will also desist from troubling God with all sorts of foolish things and from asking him for more than he allows.[108]

2. Further, in praying to God we must be truly convinced of *our poverty*. This is not a neutral and merely theoretical matter of observation but a truly experienced perception accompanied by a burning desire to obtain from God what we need. Praying is never a perfunctory activity as though we were paying God something.[109] Those who pray enter into God's presence.[110] The living presence of the Lord prevents us from mumbling formulas and inspires us to speak fervently with a sincere affection of the heart.[111] It is only in confrontation with God, there-fore, that one gains true knowledge of one's poverty; only then does one pray with a sense of fiery personal involvement to which all perfunctoriness is foreign. The praying person, with the disposition of a beggar, longs intensely for God's kingdom and its glory.[112]

3. The fact that humans are not viewed apart from God and that God continually affects them inwardly is graphically formulated in the third rule of prayer: all thought of one's own honour, all imagined excellence of one's own and all self-confidence must vanish in those who pray, in order *to give full honour* to God.[113]

---

[105] Ibid., 3.20.4 (CO 2:627): 'mente animoque compositi simus'.

[106] Ibid., 3.20.4 (CO 2:628): 'in Dei conspectum'.

[107] Ibid., 3.20.5 (CO 2:628): 'Sciamus ergo non alios rite probeque se accingere ad orandum, nisi quos afficit Dei maiestas.'

[108] Ibid.: 'sine reverentia Deum plerique de suis ineptiis interpellare audent'.

[109] Ibid., 3.20.6 (CO 2:630): 'acsi pensum Deo solverent'.

[110] The repeated use of the expression *coram Deo* characterizes Calvin's discussion of prayer.

[111] *Institutes* 3.20.6 (CO 2:630): 'serio animi affectu exardescunt'.

[112] Ibid., 3.20.7 (CO 2:631): 'regni Dei et gloriae studium; . . . induat mendici personam et affectum'.

[113] Ibid., 3.20.8 (CO 2:631): 'dans in abiectione sui gloriam Deo in solidum'.

The sensitive point of honour most pressingly marks the reciprocal relatedness between God and man in prayer. The reader has to be struck here by the large place the honour of God occupies when Calvin speaks of prayer.[114] Honour is a relational concept. It concerns the relation between two persons in which the one takes his or her place before the other with reverence and respect. Also in the context of prayer the idea of God's honour is never an isolated concept in Calvin but always has connections with man. The experience of God's grandeur is always accompanied by a sense of one's own littleness. It teaches a person to disregard his or her own honour in order to give honour to God alone. Precisely *because* people are conscious of God's love they begin to extol God in prayer. 'God will never delight in praises that do not flow from this sweetness of love.'[115] Prayer is born in the context of the kind of mutual contact which brings out human weakness and God's grandeur.[116] Also the prayer of praise.

4. Finally, Calvin lays down the requirement that we must pray with a *sure hope*.[117] Given all the feelings of littleness and true humility, this firm hope is the product of God's goodness, of which the prayer has become aware. Again we see here the mutual relatedness between God and man. In this relation, while a sense of our own unworthiness in light of God's majesty instills in us both humility and fear, God's goodness offers us a firm basis for hope.[118] God's goodness shines out upon those who believe precisely when they are beset by the greatest difficulties.[119]

Thus prayer is dialogue with God, the space in which the bi-polarity of God and man is experienced. It is especially evident from the rules Calvin has laid down for prayer how closely the

---

[114] Read, for example, Calvin's account of the Lord's Prayer (*Institutes* 3.20.36–51 (CO 2:662–78). There one constantly encounters such expressions as 'ad propagandam eius gloriam' (ibid., 3.20.28 (CO 2:653), 'malignum silentium, siquod eius beneficium sine laude praeterimus' (ibid., 3.20.28 (CO 2:654), 'in sacrificio laudis nulla interruptio' (ibid.), etc.

[115] *Institutes* 3.20.28 (CO 2:655): 'Nec vero unquam placebunt Deo laudes quae non fluent ex hac dulcedine amoris.'

[116] Baruch 2:18 (*Institutes* 3.20.8 [CO 2:632]): 'oculi deficientes dant tibi gloriam Domine'.

[117] *Institutes* 3.20.11 (CO 2:634): 'vera humilitas, certa spes'.

[118] Ibid.: 'Sub Dei bonitate fidem complectitur timorem interea non excludens.'

[119] Ibid., 3.20.11 (CO 2:635): 'inter tales angustias ita ipsis affulget Dei bonitas'.

two poles are related to each other. Indeed, prayer is possible only in this intense mutual contact.

3. Predestination in terms of its bipolar structure

God is actively occupied with his creation. While his providential care embraces everything, it extends especially and in a particular way to humankind. God is actively involved with every individual person from the cradle to the grave – indeed more than and more profoundly than that: from the first *moment* of predestination to the end. From that perspective, predestination is a special form of God's providence. It is a particular application of it. In the ongoing course of his providence the Lord looks down upon his human children. Faith implies the acknowledgment that God *personally* involves himself in human matters.[120] The tie-in between providence and predestination is particularly important and highly significant in itself. God is intensely occupied with humankind. It is unceasing activity of caring for and governing. From the very start this point of departure gives predestination a *human* accent. At issue is the human in whom God is personally interested.[121]

In predestination, however, the relatedness between God and man has a double manifestation. In both cases God sustains a person's entire existence. He actively encompasses the life of a person from beginning to end, from his decree of election or reprobation to either glorification or ruin. This is a difference like that between day and night, between pure light and utter darkness. It therefore sounds nasty and irritating to speak, as we have done, of the *human* accent of predestination. Our concern here, however, is not the validity of its biblical foundation. When we speak of the *human accent* of God's predestination, we have in mind the vital interrelatedness between God and man. Predestination is God's relation to people and vice versa from its first prehistorical beginning to its decisive and definitive end. The relation has this

---

[120] Cf. ibid., 1.16.1 (CO 2:144).
[121] Cf. Wendel, *Calvin*, 178. Reuter (*Grundverständnis der Theologie Calvins*, 168) connects the relation between providence and predestination with creation and redemption: 'Daß die Vorsehung mit dem Geschöpfsein des Menschen, die Rechtfertigung oder "Annahme" aber samt der doppelten Vorherbestimmung mit seinem Christsein verbunden wird.'

reciprocal character in both of its manifestations. The reprobate is totally enclosed within the circle of God's activity, the irresistibility of his will. But also on his part he is never devoid of reference toward God. Right into his ruin he continues to help build up God's honour. He remains – however contradictory this may sound – responsible.

In this part our aim is to describe the double manifestation of predestination in terms of its bipolar components. In the first section we take our point of departure on the human side. Precisely for pastoral and biblical reasons this seems to us a legitimate beginning. It will be apparent that from the outset this starting-point points toward God and is actually possible and called into existence only in light of and with a view to God's sovereign goodness. This is the domain of election and glorification, of consolation and the assurance of salvation.

In the second section we take our starting-point in God. Here all the emphasis is on his sovereign irresistible will. But precisely this reality comes to horrifying expression in the life of the reprobate. From this side the idea of God's disposing someone for death[122] is evoked by the fact of that person's rejection of Christ's message of salvation. Also in this domain the relation is at all points reciprocal. In this connection, too, the honour of God, which plays such a striking role in Calvin's doctrine of predestination, comes up for discussion.

Finally we will close this part with a few remarks about the background of Calvin's idea of sovereignty.

3.1. The issue of predestination is pre-eminently practical. It is not something about which one can indulge in calm and emotionless speculation. It is a practical and pastoral matter about which a pastor *may not* be silent. At stake here also, something which was expressed emphatically in connection with justification, is God's honour and human salvation. When we first discuss election here, we must say again that God and man are not two opposing and competing entities. It may often appear that way, but upon deeper reflection we discover that the struggle for God's honour serves human wellbeing or is in any case connected with man. God's honour is salutary for humans and human salvation

---

[122] *Institutes* 3.23.6 (CO 2:703): 'ab utero certae morti devoti'.

helps build up the honour of God. The two facets are inseparable. This double interest is something that has to be preached. What God has revealed to us is above all intended for our salvation, both for this and for eternal life.[123] Accordingly, that which at first blush seems only to serve God's honour, in fact simultaneously also serves the wellbeing of humans. For everything God reveals to people is revealed with a view to human salvation. In this light one simply cannot speak of God's honour except as it serves human salvation. This bipolar aspect of the divine glory is again very clearly evident in connection with predestination. Calvin knows of no dogmatic truths intended only for academic use. His dogmatics always seeks to be pastoral. The different ways in which the gospel – the covenant of life – is received by people[124] require that believers know what they have to know about predestination.[125] This knowledge, in the first place, serves the honour of God. The incomprehensible majesty of God comes to the fore precisely in the double manifestation of predestination.[126] It is sublime wisdom which one should adore and not attempt to understand.[127] One may reverently take notice of God's sovereign acts of disposition without irreverently wanting to fathom the ultimate reason for his decrees.[128] But taking notice of God's acts of disposition, which are above all human criticism, at the same time occurs for the benefit of the human person. Only when people may know of their eternal election can they be clearly persuaded

[123] *Serm. Job* 23:13–17: 'notons que Dieu a decreté de nous ce qu'il en veut faire quant au salut eternel de nos ames, et puis il l'a decreté aussi quant à la vie presente' (CO 34:355–68).

[124] *Institutes* 3.21.1 (CO 2:678): 'foedus vitae'.

[125] Ibid., 3.21.1 (CO 2:679): 'emergunt quaestiones quae aliter explicari nequeunt quam si de electione ac praedestinatione constitutum habeant piae mentes quod tenere convenit'.

[126] Ibid., 3.21.1 (CO 2:678–9): 'in ea diversitate mirabilis divini iudicii altitudo se profert'.

[127] Ibid., 3.21.1 (CO 2:680): 'sapientiae sublimitatem (quam adorari et non apprehendi voluit, ut per ipsam quoque admirabilis nobis foret) ab ipsa aeternitate evolvat'. Cf. ibid., 3.23.4 (CO 2:701): 'indicavit [apostolus] altiorem esse iustitia divinae rationem quam ut vel humano modo metienda sit, vel ingenii humani tenuitate possit comprehendi'.

[128] Ibid., 3.21.2 (CO 2:680): 'Sit igitur primum nobis hoc prae oculis, aliam praedestinationis notitiam appetere quam quae verbo Dei explicatur, non minoris esse insaniae, quam siquis vel per invium incedere, vel in tenebris cernere velit.'

that their salvation flows from the wellspring of God's completely gratuitous mercy.[129] This knowledge of God's firm and unchangeable decree, which is solely the product of his good pleasure,[130] may keep people from glorying in something by itself. They praise God alone.[131] The formulation is aggressively opposed to all human pretension but this is in the human interest. At the same time this knowledge bears abundant fruit for humans themselves. It is precisely because in election God's pure grace is irresistibly at work that human salvation is unshakably secure. It is therefore unjust both toward God *and* man when people keep silent about the doctrine of predestination.[132] The reference here is to God and man in their mutual connectedness. Because we are bound to God (*obstricti Deo*), says Calvin, we have the marvellous assurance that, whatever may happen, we are undefeated in the struggle and saved for glory. Thus the knowledge of our election, and this knowledge alone, furnishes an absolute basis for our trust.[133] It is not true, therefore, that predestination confuses our faith and strikes us with fear. The opposite is true! It is the ground for the strongest possible confirmation and assurance of our salvation.[134] In this way predestination is the basis of our salvation.[135] When properly examined and preached, it confers assurance of election, the fruit of consolation.[136] Calvin cites with approval Bernard's statement: 'That vision does not terrify but soothes; it does not arouse a restless curiosity but allays it; and it does not weary but calms the senses. Here true rest is felt. The God of peace renders all things peaceful and to behold him who himself is rest is to be at rest.'[137] Just as in the case of justification, so also in Calvin's

---

[129] Ibid., 3.21.1 (CO 2:679): 'salus nostra ex fonte gratuitae misericordiae Dei'.

[130] Ibid.: 'Clare testatur Paulus . . . Deum mero beneplacito servare quos vult.'

[131] Ibid., 3.23.13 (CO 2:709): 'Neque tamen impediatur praedestinationis cognitio, ut qui obediunt tanquam de suo superbiant, sed in Domino glorientur.'

[132] Ibid., 3.21.1 (CO 2:679): 'Qui fores occludunt, nequis ad gustum huius doctrinae accedere audeat, *non minorem hominibus quam Deo* faciunt iniuriam.'

[133] Ibid.: 'Nec vero alibi fiduciae fultura.'

[134] Ibid., 3.24.9 (CO 2:720): 'posuimus . . . praedestinationem, si rite cogitetur, non fidei convulsionem, sed optimam potius confirmationem afferre'.

[135] Ibid., 3.21.1 (CO 2:679): 'salutis nostrae fundamentum'.

[136] Ibid., 3.24.4 (CO 2:715): 'ita qui recte atque ordine ipsam investigant qualiter in verbo continetur, eximium inde referunt consolationis fructum'.

[137] Ibid., 3.24.2 (CO 2:715): 'Tranquillus Deus tranquillat omnia, et quietum aspicere quiescere est' (Bernard of Clairvaux, *In cant. serm.* 23.15, MSL 183:192C).

treatment of predestination, human peace of mind plays a remarkable role. He clearly wants to put the believer at rest by what he writes. The believer's peace of conscience concerns him deeply, for he knows from *experience* how people are tormented by the question whether they may be counted among the elect. Such a question can become a form of torture and an obsession.[138] He consistently fights for peace of conscience before God, for the tranquillity of a person's conscience.[139] This is one side of predestination: a concern for people and a kind of pastoral care which corresponds to an equally radical claim on all honour and glory for God, which is the other pole. The former is only possible in connection with the latter; there is a correlation between God's honour and human salvation and peace of conscience.

Calvin concentrates both interests – God's honour and personal assurance of salvation – in the figure of *Christ*. Jesus himself is the great example of predestination. Christ himself did not merit the honour to be allowed to be the Son of God. This is the pure grace of the Father, for which there was no antecedent merit. Christ is a mirror of unmerited election.[140] In the pronouncements of Augustine both motifs play a clear role: the pure grace of Christ's election, but also the tranquil assurance of the believer who belongs to Christ. Christ, accordingly, is at the centre of the doctrine of predestination.[141] 'If we seek God's fatherly tenderness and goodness of heart we must look up to Christ in whom alone the heart of the Father rests' [cf. Matt. 3:17]. 'If we seek the salvation, life, and immortality of the heavenly Kingdom, we must take refuge in no other place, because he alone is the fountain of life, the anchor of salvation, and the heir of the kingdom of

---

[138] Ibid., 3.24.4 (CO 2:714): 'diris tormentis miserum perpetuo excruciat aut reddit penitus attonitum'.

[139] Ibid., 3.24.4 (CO 2:715): 'siquidem nullo pestilentiori errore infici mens possit quam qui sua erga Deum pace ac tranquillitate conscientiam diruit ac deturbat'. Cf. ibid., 3.24.17 (CO 2:727): 'quo tutius piorum conscientiae acquiescant'.

[140] Ibid., 3.22.1 (CO 2:688): 'Hoc prudenter animadvertit Augustinus, in ipso Ecclesiae capite lucidissimum esse gratuitae electionis speculum, ne in membris nos conturbet' (Augustine, *De correptione et gratia* 11.30, MSL 44:934f.); 'nec iuste vivendo factum esse Filium Dei, sed gratis tanto honore fuisse donatum' (Augustine, *Sermones* 174.2, MSL 38:941).

[141] *Institutes* 2.17.1 (CO 2:386): 'clarissimum lumen praedestinationis et gratiae ipse est Salvator homo Christus Jesus'.

heaven.'[142] Both God's goodness and the assurance of our salvation are anchored in Christ. For the assurance of our salvation we need look no higher than in him.[143] In Christ God has chosen us as his children; only in him can he love us and make us heirs of his kingdom. In him we find the assurance of our election, not in ourselves.[144] With this in view Calvin works out that which can be said about the bipolarity of God and man in the doctrine of predestination. This also is the firm biblical basis outside of which he can and will not say a sensible word.

The initiative that comes completely from the Father and has no connection with merit of any kind is illustrated in Calvin's resistance to overemphasizing *faith in Christ* as if our assurance of salvation depended on it. However important this faith may be, it would be an all-too-shaky basis for giving us the assurance that God has chosen us for glory.[145] In addition, this could create the impression that people, by the consent which their faith supplies, should in some way be co-workers in effecting salvation. Credit for the latter is due only to God.[146] Of course, the fact that a person begins to believe is a sign of his or her election.[147] Believing belongs to being elect. Faith is correctly connected with election provided it only takes second place.[148] This applies, if possible, even more stringently to a person's good works. They

[142] Ibid., 3.24.5 (CO 2:715): 'quando ipse unus et vitae fons est, et salutis anchora, et regni caelorum haeres'.

[143] Ibid., 3.24.5 (CO 2:716): 'Proinde quos Deus sibi filios assumpsit, non in ipsis eos dicitur elegisse, sed in Christo suo.' Cf. *Congr. sur l'elect.* (CO 8:114).

[144] *Institutes* 3.24.5 (CO 2:716): 'quod si in eo sumus electi non in nobis ipsis reperiemus electionis nostrae *certitudinem*; . . . testimonium habemus, nos in libro vitae scriptos esse si cum Christo communicamus'.

[145] Cf. *Serm. Eph.* 1:3–4 (CO 51:265): 'Car si nostre foy dependoit de nous, il est certain qu'elle nous eschaperoit bien tost, elle nous pourroit estre escousse, sinon qu'elle fust gardee d'enhaut.'

[146] *Institutes* 3.24.3 (CO 2:713): 'nonnulli cooperarium Deo faciunt hominem, ut suffragio suo ratam electionem faciat. . . . Alii . . . nescio qua ratione inducti electionem a posteriori suspendunt: quasi dubia esset atque etiam inefficax, donec fide confirmetur'.

[147] Calvin sees as signs of election calling and justification through faith (ibid., 3.21.7 [CO 2:686]; 3.24.4 [CO 2:714–15]) and the fruit of good works (ibid., 3.14.18 [CO 2:577]: 'multo magis bonorum operum gratia quae Spiritum adoptionis nobis datum commonstrat').

[148] Ibid., 3.22.10 (CO 2:697): 'Ac electioni quidem apte coniungitur fides, modo secundum gradum teneat.'

also belong to election. They, too, are a sign of election, just as faith, of which they are the fruit, is such a sign, but they do not in any way underlie election as its basis. In this act humans are by no means involved; in this they are not fellow workers with God.[149] Part of Calvin's concern not to assign any role to humans in election, which might look like a human achievement, is also his resolute rejection of divine foreknowledge (*praescientia Dei*) as the cause of predestination. This idea as such already suggests that God, influenced by his knowledge of human behaviour, would make his decision either to elect or reject the person on that ground.[150] The issue of foreknowledge is linked, in the nature of the case, with the absolute sovereignty of God, about which we will speak more explicitly in the following section when we deal with reprobation. But it is clearly a point of entry for possible human achievement in a domain where only God's grace prevails. For the same reason Calvin calls talk of foreknowledge a 'cover'.[151]

By its reaction to faith, to works, and to the foreknowledge of God in connection with election, the pole which is God draws the entire work of election to itself. The entire disarmament of human beings, however, at the same time creates the human assurance of salvation. All this can be seen, as in a mirror, in Christ in whom the salvation of the elect is forever established.[152]

Accordingly, in election the bipolarity between God and man is marked by pure grace on the side of God and assurance of

[149] Ibid., 3.22.11 (CO 2:697): 'ut probet divinae praedestinationis fundamentum in operibus non esse'. Cf. ibid., 3.14.19 (CO 2:577); 3.21.5 (CO 2:683); 3.22.3 (CO 2:689); 3.22.6 (CO 2:692).

[150] Ibid., 3.22.8 (CO 2:694): 'vacat vana illorum ratiocinatio cui praescientiam Dei defendunt contra gratiam Dei: et ideo dicunt nos electos ante mundi constitutionem, quia praescivit Deus futuros nos bonos, non seipsum nos facturum bonos'.

[151] Ibid., 3.22.1 (CO 2:687): 'sic interposito praescientiae velo electionem non modo obscurant, sed originem aliunde habere fingunt'; ibid., 3.21.5 (CO 2:682): 'eam multis cavillis involvunt, praesertim vero qui praescientiam faciunt eius causam'. Cf. ibid., 3.22.1–3 (CO 2:687–9).

[152] Ibid., 3.21.7 (CO 2:685): 'ut efficax et vere stabilis sit electio, necesse est ascendere ad caput in quo electos suos caelestis Pater inter se colligavit, sibi insolubili nexu devinxit . . . : quia capiti suo insiti nunquam a salute excidunt'. Cf. *Comm. I Cor.* 3:11 (CO 49:51): 'quale istud est fundamentum? An quod Jesus Christus initium fuit nostrae salutis'. See O. Ritschl, *Dogmengeschichte des Protestantismus*, 3:166.

salvation on the human side.[153] Each one evokes the other. This bipolar structure pervades Calvin's discussion everywhere. Parallel to this gracious election and the firmness of a person's salvation is the goodness of God which brings humans to humility and causes them to experience their own smallness. We want to confine ourselves here to reproducing a text which clearly contraposes God's goodness and our human littleness in their interdependence: 'Scripture does not mention predestination with the intent to rouse us to boldness that we might try with shameful rashness to search out God's inaccessible secrets, but rather that, humbled and cast down, we might learn to tremble at his judgment and look up to his mercy.'[154] Here, too, a person experiences himself or herself as a small human being.[155]

3.2. In the subject of election the postulate of God's honour corresponds to the wellbeing of people. This thesis cannot be maintained, however, when the subject matter pertains to the reprobate about whom we are about to speak now. When we examine the bipolarity between God and the reprobate human, it will sound all too bitter if we continue to speak, as we did in the preceding section, of the *human* aspect of the doctrine of predestination. Here Calvin seems to opt for God's honour at the expense of humans. But is Calvin really making a choice? Is it not rather the case that he is forced, on biblical and theological grounds, to judge as he judges? In view of the pastoral compassion which drives his theological work, the latter speaks for itself, but also for other reasons it is likely that the Reformer simply had to resort to the solution of a double predestination, the solution which in the ears of numerous people has given his name such a harsh and uncongenial sound.

For the doctrine of double predestination we have to refer the reader to studies in this area.[156] What interests us here is how also

---

[153] *Institutes* 3.22.9 (CO 2:695): 'nihil in electione nisi meram bonitatem velit nos intueri Dominus'.
[154] Ibid., 3.23.12 (CO 2:708): 'ut humiliati ac deiecti, ad iudicium eius tremere, misericordiam suspicere discamus'.
[155] Ibid., 3.24.4 (CO 2:714): 'Extra viam inquirere voco, ubi in abditos divinae sapientiae recessus perrumpere homuncio conatur.'
[156] Niesel, *Calvin-Bibliographie, 1901–1959* (Munich, 1961), 1207–39. Cf. especially I. John Hesselink, 'Election and Predestination (Section 13)', chap. 7 in *Calvin's First Catechism. A Commentary* (Louisville: Westminster John Knox,

in the case of reprobation the bipolar connections are maintained in both directions. The bipolarity in this case (unlike that of election) may be evident from the following. We wish to approach the sovereignty of God, which stands out starkly here, by way of the free *good pleasure* of God and the all-penetrative power of his *will*. Both concepts (intended to characterize the one sovereign majesty of God) have their repercussions in the reprobate person. But in the case of this rejection or reprobation it is persons who themselves bear the *responsibility*. Alongside this paradoxical line of God's irrevocable decree of the reprobation of human beings who remain responsible, the divine honour also functions here in the bipolarity. The reprobate's existence is not without reference to God. Also reprobates, despite themselves, contribute to God's honour. Here too God's honour is built in and conceivable only in the divine–human relation.

> Because God chooses some and passes over others according to his own decision, they [insolent opponents of this doctrine] threaten him with legal action. But if the thing itself is well known, how will it profit them to contend with God? We teach nothing not borne out by *experience*: namely, that God has always been free to bestow his grace on whom he wills. . . . Let them answer why they are humans, and not oxen or donkeys. . . .[157]

With these words Calvin opens the defence of his doctrine of double predestination on the basis of Scripture. To him the freedom of God's good pleasure is clearly present in Scripture.[158] It is also a datum proved by experience.[159] At the same time he sharply brings out how improper and absurd it is to call God to account over this as though the distinction were unjust.[160] God's discretion is foremost. In the face of this reality a person can only

---

1997), 93–100. Hesselink presents here a lucid, well-documented introduction to this theme. Marijn de Kroon (*Martin Bucer und Johannes Calvin. Reformatorische Perspektiven. Einleitung und Texte* [Göttingen, 1991], 19–34, 229–31) compares Calvin's ideas on predestination with those of Martin Bucer.

[157] *Institutes* 3.22.1 (CO 2:687): 'Respondeant cur homines sint magis quam boves aut asini.'

[158] Ibid.: 'Verum si res ipsa nota est, quid proficient contra Deum iurgando?'

[159] Ibid.: 'Nihil docemus quod usu compertum non sit.'

[160] Ibid.: 'Concedentne brutis animalibus de sua sorte cum Deo expostulare, quasi iniustum sit discrimen?'

maintain silence. 'If one asks why God shows mercy to some and leaves others to their fate, there is no other answer than that this is his good pleasure.'[161] This is pre-eminently the area in which God's good pleasure prevails.[162] Repeatedly the predominant role of this incomprehensible divine good pleasure comes to the fore.[163]

This undiluted divine good pleasure is directed towards people but it is also clearly affirmed in relation to them. What it pleases God to do happens, no matter how or what people may think. All these passages betray Calvin's usual aversion to human meddlesomeness and pretensions. Where this divine good pleasure prevails, works play no role and people have no further right to ask questions.[164] God alone has rights.[165] This *good pleasure* is the domain of God's sovereign *freedom*. This freedom again is not abstractly viewed as a transcendent divine property about which humans can speculate, but freedom focused in the direction of people. God's freedom has ties with humanity. As a result of that freedom he can grant grace to some, whereas he relates to others solely as a righteous Judge.[166] He is completely free to do whatever he wills. The mere fact that he wills it by itself justifies it. Thus God's good pleasure leads us by way of his sovereign freedom to the contemplation of his will. Of course we view everything in the context of one single divine reality, but also the will of God is defined solely in relation to humans. In the case of the reprobate, the power of God's will is clear from the 'dreadful decree' of reprobation (*decretum horribile*).[167] Already in the case of the elect this will of God was introduced as all-embracing and contained within the mighty propulsion of God's mercy, clearly with the express design to deny all power to the human will or

---

[161] *Serm. Eph.* 1:3–4 (CO 51:259): 'Or là dessus si on demande pourquoi Dieu a pitie d'une partie, et pourquouy il laisse et quitte l'autre, il n'y a autre response, sinon qu'il luy plaist ainsi.'

[162] *Institutes* 3.22.3 (CO 2:689): 'ubicunque vero regnat hoc *Dei placitum*'.

[163] Ibid., 3.22.7 (CO 2:693): 'praecise negat se uni potius quam alteri fore misericordem nisi quia *lubuerit*'; ibid., 3.23.4 (CO 2:701): 'solum divinae voluntatis *arbitrium*'; ibid., 3.21.1 (CO 2:679): 'merum beneplacitum'.

[164] Ibid., 3.22.3 (CO 2:689).

[165] Ibid., 3.22.1 (CO 2:688): 'Deo liberum ius eligendi ac reprobandi.'

[166] Ibid., 3.23.11 (CO 2:707): 'Potest igitur Dominus etiam dare gratiam quibus vult, quia misericors est: non omnibus dare, quia iustus iudex'; ibid., 3.24.1 (CO 2:712): 'cuius vult miseretur, et quem vult obdurat'.

[167] Ibid., 3.23.7 (CO 2:704): 'Decretum quidem horribile, fateor.'

human intent.[168] Also in the case of reprobation God opposes the human will and intent, but here his mercy is manifestly lacking. But God's will, which penetrates everything, seems to leave nothing to human decision.[169] God comes to people in a *compelling* way. He compels obedience.[170] In my opinion this text may not be interpreted to say that God forced people to bring about their own ruin. God's energetic impact, to be sure, goes to the very limit. But efficiently he withdraws from them every impulse of the Spirit, an action by which their fall becomes inevitable.[171] However far-reaching the power of God's will is according to this sketch, all of Calvin's language nevertheless betrays a measure of reserve. The verb *subducere* (to draw out from under; to remove stealthily) brings God's will very close to a person but does not absorb him or her. Obviously some space is left to people in which, as we will show more clearly below, they themselves are responsible. But on other occasions one discerns nothing of such reserve, such wrestling with the paradox between God's willing and human responsibility. In that case it is as if God does everything and we do nothing.[172] Then it is said that God's power is in no way restricted, even though our mind cannot grasp this.[173] From all of Calvin's strong emphasis on the omnipotence of God's will it is also clear that Calvin is continually worried that even some small impulse of salvific initiative would be credited to humans.[174] This danger continues to threaten from the side of human good works. Calvin continually shifts his attention from God to man and vice versa. 'Why do you continually look back to works?' he asks.[175] 'Why do you always again want to make a

---

[168] Ibid., 3.24.1 (CO 2:712): 'non dubitemus Apostolum omnia misericordiae Domini dare, nostris autem voluntatibus aut studiis nihil relinquere'.

[169] Ibid., 1.13.14 (CO 2:102); see above, pp. 4ff.

[170] Ibid., 1.18.2 (CO 2:170): 'ut etiam reprobos in obsequium cogat'.

[171] Ibid., 3.24.2 (CO 2:713): 'Atque etiam Deus, illustrandae gloriae suae causa, Spiritus sui efficaciam ab illis subducit.'

[172] Cf. ibid., 1.17.2 (CO 2:155–6).

[173] Ibid., 3.23.5 (CO 2:702): 'velitne Dei potentiam sic limitatam esse, ut nequid plus ad agendum valeat quam mens sua capiat?'

[174] Ibid., 3.22.4 (CO 2:690): 'Iam si Dei voluntas ... alios ab aliis descernit ... frustra cuiusque conditio in ipso *initium* habere fingitur.' This passage clearly intends to deny any human initiative.

[175] Ibid., 3.22.6 (CO 2:692): 'cur ad operum tuorum intuitum partem reflectes?'

division between God's grace and human effort?'[176] There simply
would not be divine grace if in making his choice God would take
good works into account.[177] From this it is evident that all saving
power is denied to the human will.[178]

God's will, accordingly, proceeds from his good pleasure alone,
and is neither conditioned by works nor by foreknowledge. In
that will, by a special decree, God excludes some from the glory
which he has reserved for his children.[179]

In the face of God's good pleasure and his mighty will we must
keep silent, for God's wisdom is greater than one of us can grasp.
No human can attain to the sublimity of God's judgment.[180] His
wisdom, says Calvin, is too high for us humans.[181] We need not
be ashamed to have no insight here; not to know here is to be
wise.[182] It is the glory of God to conceal a matter,[183] for his judgment is as incomprehensible as it is irreproachable.[184] The nature
of divine righteousness is far too high for it to be measured by a
human standard.[185] To insist on nevertheless doing this is nothing
less than wickedness.[186]

---

[176] Ibid., 3.24.1 (CO 2:712): '. . . qui inter Dei gratiam, voluntatem, cursumque
hominis partiuntur'.

[177] Ibid., 3.22.3 (CO 2:689): 'Porro haec [gratia] gratuita non erit, si in suis
eligendis Deus ipse qualia sint futura cuiusque opera reputat.'

[178] For what we have already said about this in connection with *iustificatio
fidei*, see above, pp. 108ff.

[179] *Institutes* 3.23.1 (CO 2:698): 'Quos ergo Deus praeterit, reprobat: . . .
illos *vult* excludere'; ibid., 3.21.5 (CO 2:683): 'aliis damnatio aeterna
praeordinatur'. On this point also Calvin expressly rejects the distinction between
willing and permitting. Cf. ibid., 3.23.8 (CO 2:705): 'cur permittere dicemus
nisi quia ita *vult*?'

[180] Ibid., 3.21.1 (CO 2:679): 'mirabilis divini iudicii altitudo'.

[181] Ibid., 3.21.1 (CO 2:680): 'sapientiae sublimitas'.

[182] Ibid., 3.21.2 (CO 2:681): 'Neque vero pudeat aliquid in ea re nescire ubi
est aliqua docta ignorantia.'

[183] Proverbs 25:2 (*Institutes* 3.21.3 [CO 2:681]).

[184] *Institutes* 3.22.7 (CO 2:686): 'asserimus . . . quos vero damnationi addicit,
his iusto quidem et irreprehensibili, sed incomprehensibili ipsius iudicio, vitae
aditum praecludi'. Cf. ibid., 3.23.1 (CO 2:698): 'agitur de incomprehensibili
eius consilio'.

[185] Ibid., 3.23.4 (CO 2:701): 'iudicavit [apostolus] altiorem esse iustitiae
divinae rationem quam ut vel humano modo metienda sit, vel ingenii humani
tenuitate possit comprehendi'.

[186] Ibid., 3.23.2 (CO 2:699–700): 'quantae sit improbitatis, causas divinae
voluntatis duntaxat percontari'. Cf. ibid., 3.24.4 (CO 2:714).

Thus in his doctrine of predestination Calvin continually seeks to muzzle human mouths. But it is precisely the frequency with which he cautions people against immodesty in wanting to know things which are exclusively matters of divine good pleasure and will shows how he himself wrestled with the problem. He never loses sight of the human being, however ironic this may sound in connection with the reprobate. Precisely because God's good pleasure and will always extend to human beings, the latter continue to ask questions, especially when those human beings, as in the case of reprobation, are ruined. Calvin's passionate plea for modesty in matters theological is a sign of his consistent preoccupation with God *and* man and the relation between the two.

Corresponding to God's will in the bipolarity between God and the reprobate human is the responsibility of the latter which, paradoxically enough, continues to exist. God decides in favour of the reprobation of a human being; at the same time that same human being remains responsible for his or her fall. Indeed, Calvin does not hesitate to locate the *cause* of that person's perdition in that person himself and does so while for God's good pleasure he demands unlimited freedom and for God's will unlimited efficient power.[187] The downfall of the person depends totally on God's will, while at the same time that same person is the cause and occasion of their own fall. A person falls because God's providence so ordains it, but they fall by their own wickedness.[188] Humanity has corrupted its nature by its own wickedness (*malitia*). From this premise Calvin looks for a solution of the paradox. 'Accordingly, we should rather look for the evident cause of condemnation in the corrupt nature of the human race (which, after all, is close to us) than scrutinize the hidden and completely incomprehensible cause in God's predestination.' Here the emphasis of the author clearly lies on the human pole which is itself the cause of reprobation. But this construal actually makes the paradox – with the irrevocable and immutable separate decree

---

[187] Ibid., 3.23.8 (CO 2:705): 'Adhoc, sic ex Dei praedestinatione pendet eorum perditio ut causa et materia in ipsis reperiatur.'

[188] Ibid.: 'Cadit igitur homo, Dei *providentia* sic ordinante: sed suo vitio cadit' (the spontaneous use here of *providentia*, where one would expect *praedestinatio*, shows once again the connection between the two).

of God who effectually wants the reprobation[189] – only more acute. One gets the impression that Calvin locates the cause and guilt in humans in order to safeguard God from all guilt. The objection that, given such an irrevocable decree of reprobation, a person is necessarily blameless is explicitly cited in Calvin's argumentation.[190] No one, therefore, perishes undeservedly.[191] But one has not resolved the problem by pointing to humanity's own wickedness and perverseness as the deepest ground for its fall.[192] This is explicable only by reference to the absence of God's grace.[193]

Calvin would be the first to admit that he too lacks insight into the way the mighty will of God and man's own fault and responsibility fit together. The important thing is that, for whatever reason, he leaves room for human responsibility. Thus the relation between God and man, between the sovereign God and the reprobate human being, is determined by the irresistibility of the divine will and the reprobate's own fault. The irrevocability of the downfall brings out the sovereignty all the more impressively, yet at the same time the personal responsibility of the reprobate person continues to raise questions about the scope of God's intentionality with respect to that person.

Finally, the bipolarity between God and the reprobate is characterized by the honour of God which is also built into the relation between the two. Always, says Hunter, when the reason for God's action simply eludes us, Calvin is inclined to answer with the words: it serves the enhancement of his glory. Calvin, accordingly, loves to cite from Proverbs the saying that it is the glory of God to conceal a matter.[194]

However this may be, also in the case of the reprobate God's honour is attained only in a relation to a *human being*. His justice comes to expression [in that relation].[195]

---

[189] Ibid., 3.23.1 (CO 2:698): 'illos *vult* excludere'.

[190] Ibid., 3.23.8 (CO 2:705).

[191] Ibid., 3.24.12 (CO 2:722): 'afferimus nullos perire immerentes'.

[192] Ibid.: 'siquis respondeat, diversitatem ex eorum provenire malitia et perversitate, nondum satisfactum fuerit'.

[193] Ibid.: 'sola Dei gratia alios aliis praecellere'; cf. ibid., 3.21.6 (CO 2:685): 'vitio suo et culpa fateor, exciderunt ab adoptione'.

[194] Hunter, *Teaching of Calvin*, 58, 59.

[195] *Institutes* 3.21.7 (CO 2:686): 'quos vero damnationi addicit, his iusto quidem et irreprehensibili . . . iudicio vitae aditum praecludi'; ibid., 3.23.3 (CO 2:700): 'non tyrannica saevitia, sed aequissima iustitiae ratione'.

In all of Calvin's treatment of predestination the motif of God's honour plays a large role.[196] Election, to be sure, is more admirable on account of God's goodness which completely undeservedly shines forth to humans there.[197] It would have been more in keeping with his justice had God left humanity in its fatal state of condemnation. The response of the elect to God's goodness, a goodness which renders them small and humble, can only consist in an active commitment to God's glory in this world.[198] The elect must serve God's honour.[199]

But also the reprobate, despite themselves, help to build up the divine glory. In addition to the way indicated, this occurs also in a negative way. The inequality of God's decisions makes the undeservedness of the glory which awaits the elect stand out all the more sharply. It is as if darkness is needed to bring out the light of God's glory promised to the elect. Thus Calvin deems the inequality of God's grace in election useful in demonstrating the completely undeserved nature of that grace and to show that in his great generosity God is bound by no law and is free.[200] Worth mentioning here is a text from Calvin's commentary on Psalm 9, vs. 5: 'The goodness of God shines forth the more brightly in the fact that for the sake of the love which he bears toward one of his servants, *he did not even* spare entire nations.'[201]

Of the reprobate, then, it is said that God's glory avails itself of them: they illustrate it.[202] In their destruction these people who

[196] Cf. Lang, *Johannes Calvin*, 92: 'eines seiner wichtigsten Interessen'.

[197] *Institutes* 3.21.7 (CO 2:686): 'hoc consilium quoad electos in gratuita eius misericordia fundatum esse asserimus'. Cf. Hunter, *Teaching of Calvin*, 297.

[198] Hunter, *Teaching of Calvin*, 299: 'Predestination was the appointment of the few good to rule over the many bad in the interest of righteousness. . . . He had chosen them for his glory. . . . Nothing but their active participation in that work could give assurance of their election.'

[199] Cf. *Comm. Rom.* 12:11 (CO 49:241): 'vitam christianam actuosam esse oportet'.

[200] Cf. *Institutes* 3.23.1 (CO 2:698): 'quando ipsa electio nisi reprobationi opposita non staret'; ibid., 3.21.6 (CO 2:685): 'ut minime ab eo exigenda sit aequalis gratiae partitio: cuius inaequalitas ipsam vere esse gratuitam demonstrat'.

[201] *Comm. Psalm.* 9:5 (CO 31:98): 'Hinc autem melius refulget Dei bonitas, quod in unius servi favorem ne totis quidem populis pepercerit.'

[202] *Institutes* 3.22.11 (CO 2:698): 'in hunc finem excitentur reprobi ut Dei gloria per illos illustretur'.

have been devoted to death glorify the name of God.[203] In an almost heartrending way the honour of God and the ruin of those 'devoted to death' are connected. Calvin's language does not always suggest that the reprobate are inescapably doomed, but he never sees their doom apart from God's glory. For the sake of that glory God takes from them the power of his Spirit.[204]

So the entire doctrine of predestination is overshadowed, as it were, by the honour of God toward which, in its double manifestation, it is directed. By way of a summary Calvin formulates the reason for this double predestination: 'It now remains for us to see *why* God does that of which it is clear *that* he does it.'[205] He is clearly dealing here with the difference between God's action in the case of the elect and in the case of the reprobate.[206] In Calvin's answer he does not deny that the reprobate are rejected on account of their own wickedness but the reason for their stubbornness (*contumacia*) must be sought in God – in his immutable decree (*immutabile decretum*). From this premise he proceeds to open a wide path for the honour of God for which all these things have been so ordained. It is to show forth his name in all the earth. God's judgment is inscrutable, but the reprobate have been raised up to glorify his honour through their condemnation.[207] If all this remains obscure to us, we must be gladly ignorant when God's wisdom rises to such a sublime height.[208]

We believe we have demonstrated that in election as well as in reprobation this honour of God functions in the bipolarity between God and man. Pure sovereign goodness and the assurance of faith are the components which determine the divine–human relation in its mutual connectedness in the case of election. In the case of reprobation, the mere good pleasure of God and his all-controlling will, paradoxically enough, stand over against human

[203] Ibid., 3.23.6 (CO 2:703): 'consilio nutuque suo ita ordinat, ut inter homines nascantur, ab utero certae morti devoti, qui suo exitio ipsius nomen glorificent'.
[204] Ibid., 3.24.2 (CO 2:713): 'Atque etiam Deus, illustrandae gloriae suae causa, Spiritus sui efficaciam ab illis subducit.'
[205] Ibid., 3.24.14 (CO 2:724).
[206] Ibid.: 'quia nondum patet istius varietatis ratio, cur aliis in obedientiam flexis, isti obdurati persistant'.
[207] Ibid.: 'ad gloriam eius sua damnatione illustrandam'.
[208] Ibid., 3.24.14 (CO 2:725): 'aliquid nescire non recusemus, ubi se Dei sapientia in suam sublimitatem attollit'; cf. ibid., 3.23.5 (CO 2:702): 'melior est fidelis ignorantia'.

responsibility. Continual exhortation to practice the virtue of believing ignorance betrays the utter man-relatedness of Calvin's discourse on predestination. We can agree with Reuter that also in the doctrine of predestination the human being always remains *das Gegenüber Gottes* (God's counterpart).[209]

3.3. The linkage of the doctrine of predestination to the divine–human relation confirms that the honour of God (however large its role may be) cannot be called a first principle of Calvin's views on divine foreordination. God's honour is, of course, bound up with his sovereignty.[210] But that sovereignty (and the honour of God bound up with it) is never constructed apart from its relation to humankind. Its structure is essentially bipolar. God's honour is always correlated with the elect and the reprobate.[211]

From the perspective of the divine–human bipolarity also the question whether God's honour or predestination is the starting-point in Calvin's thinking will be seen in another light. Doumerque makes God's sovereignty, that is, God's honour, the governing principle of Calvin's entire theology. Also predestination is no more than a logical consequence of this principle.[212] O. Ritschl is probably the most outstanding representative of the opposing view which maintains that the doctrine of predestination is central in Calvin's thought.[213]

---

[209] Reuter, *Grundverständnis der Theologie Calvins*, 164.

[210] Hunter, *Teaching of Calvin*, 61: 'it becomes evident that what Calvin understood by the glory of God ultimately was what He attained and achieved by the exercise of his sovereignty'.

[211] Cf. *Institutes* 3.22.11 (CO 2:698); 3.24.2 (CO 2:713); 3.24.14 (CO 2:724).

[212] Doumergue, *Jean Calvin*, 4:362: 'C'est donc un malentendu de découvrir le caractère spécifique du calvinisme dans la doctrine de la prédestination, ou dans l'autorité des Ecritures, ou dans la doctrine des alliances ou dans le principe de la culpabilité héréditaire ou dans la correction de la vie, ou dans la forme presbytérienne du gouvernement ecclésiastique. Pour le calvinisme, tout cela ce sont des conséquences logique, rien de tout cela n'est le princpe initial.'

[213] O. Ritschl, *Dogmengeschichte des Protestantismus*, 3:163: 'Hätte Calvin jedoch die cognitio Dei creatoris und redemptoris nicht voneinander getrennt, so hätte er auch in der Ausgabe von 1559 die Lehre von der Prädestination im Zusammenhange mit der von der göttlichen Vorsehung gleich unter den ersten Themen der Lehre von Gott behandeln können, wie dies ja auch spätere reformierte Theologen getan haben. So aber ist im äuszeren Gefüge seiner Theologie die übergreifende Bedeutung, die seiner Lehre von der Prädestination zukommt, gar nicht entsprechend zum Ausdruck gelangt.'

In Calvin's theology we are ultimately dealing with God *and* man and, more precisely, with their reciprocal relationship. It is only in this framework that we can speak of God's honour. Also Calvin's entire discussion of predestination is governed by its bipolar background: neither God is viewed apart from man nor man apart from God. Questions such as whether God's honour or his acts of predestination must be considered primary are thereby shifted to a secondary level. This position is also in accord with the opinion of Walker and Dankbaar, both of whom expressly deny the centrality of Calvin's doctrine of predestination.[214]

Precisely because God is viewed as actively involved with human beings and they are viewed in the light of God's active involvement with them, any idea of divine arbitrariness is a misconstrual of Calvin's deepest motives. Calvin himself asserts, as is well known, that God is not *exlex* (lawless).[215] Nor is the fact of Calvin's having been influenced by nominalism and Duns Scotus a ground for speaking of divine arbitrariness in his thinking.[216] Reuter has demonstrated that the divine will in the theology of John Major and Gregory of Rimini, to whose influence Calvin was subject, is morally conditioned.[217] Also in the work of Gabriel Biel, who may certainly be regarded as one of the great representatives of nominalism, the will of God is normed by rectitude and justice.[218] God's will is not only irreproachable but morally aimed at the highest perfection.[219] His own goodness is law for him. In that

---

[214] Walker, *John Calvin*, 416: 'Yet it is an error to describe predestination as the "central doctrine" of Calvinism.' Dankbaar, *Calvijn*, 191: 'Aan de andere kant is de predestinatie ook niet het allesbeheersende dogma ... de verkiezing en de verwerping zijn voor Calvijn een conclusie achteraf, als hij nadenkt over Gods genade in Christus bewezen.' Cf. Wendel, *Calvin*, 264.

[215] *Institutes* 3.23.2 (CO 2:700): 'Non fingimus Deum exlegem qui ipsi lex est'; cf. *Comm. Exod.* 3:22 (CO 24:49–50).

[216] Wendel, *Calvin*, 126–9; Doumergue, *Jean Calvin*, 3:121–2: 'pas de caprice'; Walker, *John Calvin*, 149, 414; O. Ritschl, *Dogmengeschichte des Protestantismus*, 3:190; Hunter, *Teaching of Calvin*, 54–6.

[217] Reuter, *Grundverständnis der Theologie Calvins*, 143–51; 144: 'In dieser Schule hat Calvin gelernt, aus Gründen der Ehrfurcht vor Gott und der Verläßlichkeit seines Sagens und Handelns den Gedanken an eine absolute Macht Gottes als "gotteslästerliche", "unheilige", Erfindung zu verwerfen.'

[218] *Invent.* 2, dist. 20.

[219] Calvin disputes the notion of *potentia absoluta* in the sense of God's omnipotence without moral bounds. CO 8:361: 'Sorbonicum illud dogma.' Cf. *Institutes* 3.23.2 (CO 2:700): 'merito detestabile nobis esse debet'.

way and no other the active God is involved with human beings and only in that way is he known and experienced by them.[220]

Always God's honour is bound up with human salvation.[221] This pronouncement sounds like a principle of Calvin's theology,[222] but it is a principle to which Calvin was unfaithful in his doctrine of reprobation. In that doctrine it is indeed humanity but not human *salvation* that is bound up with God's honour. One cannot escape the impression that in Calvin's doctrine of double pre-destination the sovereignty of God weighs down on and oppresses people. Even though Calvin repeatedly and with striking emphasis assures his readers that he discerns honour for God in 'the dreadful decree of reprobation' (*decretum horribile reprobationis*), one has to ask whether at this point the Reformer does not detract from God's honour. In any case, we always detract from God's grandeur when we view it as competing with humanity.

Furthermore, whereas by his principle of learned ignorance (*docta ignorantia*) Calvin sets boundaries to believing thought, one gets the impression that at this point he himself crosses those boundaries.

Meanwhile, reprobation is the only point in Calvin's theology where human salvation does not serve the honour of God. Inasmuch as this occurs in violation of Calvin's own principle, it becomes easier to credit Hunter when he says that Calvin himself was far from happy with the doctrine of double predestination.[223]

But to Calvin's mind he had no choice. To him reprobation was a biblical given that is plainly and clearly taught. It is a

---

[220] The bipolar connections, which can be demonstrated throughout Calvin's discussions, testify to his pastoral fervour. As a result, this reference to a divine arbitrariness sounds strange to our ears.

[221] CO 5:391: 'ut cum nostra salute [nominis sui gloria] perpetuo coniuncta foret'.

[222] In other places, too, the honour of God is explicitly bound up with man's salvation. See, e.g., *Institutes* 1.14.15 (CO 2:127).

[223] Hunter, *Teaching of Calvin*, 297: 'Calvin was not more in love with the doctrine of reprobation than his critics.' For the position of the Nederlandse Hervormde Kerk on the doctrine of reprobation, see *De uitverkiezing, richtlijnen voor de behandeling van de leer der uitverkiezing, aanvaard door de Generale Synode der Nederlandse Hervormde Kerk* (The Hague, 1961), and *Enige aspecten van de leer der uitverkiezing. Rapport samengesteld op verzoek van de commissie tot de zaken der Remonstrantse Broederschap en van de Generale Synode der Nederlandse Hervormde Kerk* (The Hague, 1966).

postulate of Scripture. Accordingly, he repeatedly assures the reader that he is only interpreting the doctrine of Holy Scripture.[224]

It may, however, be deemed likely that, thanks to his thorough grounding in the nominalist mode of thinking, coupled with his practical, experience-oriented outlook, Calvin was strongly predisposed to interpret the witness of Scripture in this and in no other fashion.[225]

---

[224] *Institutes* 3.21.2 (CO 2:680): 'Sit igitur primum nobis hoc prae oculis, aliam praedestinationis notitiam appetere quam quae *verbo Dei* explicatur, non minoris esse insaniae, quam siquis vel per invium incedere, vel in tenebris cernere velit'; ibid., 3.21.3 (CO 2:681): 'redeundum erit ad verbum Domini, in quo habemus certam intelligentiae regulam. Est enim Scriptura schola Spiritus sancti'. The end of chap. 21, which is already interwoven with Scripture passages, reads: 'quod ergo Scriptura clare ostendit dicimus aeterno et immutabili consilio Deum semel constituisse, quos olim semel assumere vellet in salutem, quos rursum exitio devovere' (ibid., 3.21.7 [CO 2:686]). The heading of chap. 22 then also reads: 'Confirmatio huius doctrinae ex Scripturae testimoniis' (ibid., 3.22 [CO 2:687]).

[225] Ibid., 3.24.12 (CO 2:722): 'Alterius membri cum extant quotidiana documenta, tum multa in Scripturis continentur.'

IV

⟡

God's Honour and the
External Means of Salvation

THE last book of the *Institutes* discusses the external means of
salvation. The fourth chapter of this study is also devoted to
this subject. We will, however, view these means in the perspective
of the divine–human relation.

In this light we will deal in the first section with the church and
its discipline (*Ecclesiae disciplina*) and its ministers (*Ecclesiae
ministri*).

Second, we will examine the divine–human bipolarity as it
comes to expression in the sacraments, baptism and the Lord's
Supper.

In conclusion, in the third and final section of this chapter,
civil government and authority (*politica administratio*) will be
our focus.

1. The church of Christ

The church of Christ is rooted in divine election.[1] This is the
foundation of Calvin's ecclesiology.[2] It is impossible, therefore,

---

[1] *Institutes* (1536; CO 1:72–3): 'Primum credimus sanctam ecclesiam
catholicam, hoc est *universum electorum numerum* . . . unam esse ecclesiam ac
societatem et unum Dei populum cuius Christus, Dominus noster, dux sit et
princeps, ac tanquam corporis caput; prout in ipso divina bonitate *electi sunt*
. . . catholica est, id est universalis, quia . . . *electi Dei* sic omnes in Christo
uniuntur ac coadunantur, ut . . . in unum velut corpus coalescent. . . . Sancta
etiam est, quia quotquot *aeterna Dei providentia electi* sunt, ut in ecclesiae
membra cooptarentur, a Domino omnes sanctificantur (Joan. 17; Eph. 5).'

[2] *Institutes* 4.1.2 (CO 2:747): 'soli Deo permittenda est cognitio suae Ecclesiae
cuius fundamentum est arcana illius electio'. Cf. ibid., 3.24.6 (CO 2:716) and
3.21.1 (CO 2:679).

for those who are true members of Christ's church to be lost.[3] So also in connection with the church the theme we have singled out from the beginning returns: God's sovereign choice guarantees the salvation of believers. This salvation is secure and safe only when it points above all to the divine principle of election (*electio*). Election and salvation presuppose each other. Thus the reference to that choice of God by its very essence fits into Calvin's description of the church. But this highlights, in a surprising way, Calvin's preoccupation with the interpersonal relation between God and man, also when he deals with the church.

The church is an indispensable aid in securing human salvation, the salvation of the individual person who by faith has obtained a share in Christ and his benefits (Book III of the *Institutes*). It is fascinating to see how Calvin forges the link between the individual believer and the community which is the church. This line of communication runs by way of human weakness and laxity which cannot do without the help of others in the attainment of salvation. Underlying Calvin's views on the church, therefore, is his concern for the individual weak persons who make up its membership. Thus he constructs the bridge 'from his religious individualism to the church'.[4]

The relation between God and man, a relation from person to person, is not threatened by Calvin's ecclesiology. The bipolarity of the divine–human relation, however, does gain a new dimension: the connection with others, the communion of believers inasmuch as weak human beings cannot remain standing in the faith by themselves.

Given this starting-point, the idea of an institution which places itself between God and man has become impossible.[5] The church is above all the domain in which God's personal involvement

---

[3] *Institutes* (1536; CO 1:73): 'Cum autem ecclesia sit populus electorum Dei, fieri non potest ut qui vere eius sunt membra tandem pereant, aut malo exitio perdantur. Nititur enim eorum salus tam certis solidisque fulcris ut, etiamsi tota orbis machina labefacetur, concidere ipsa et corruere non possit. . . . Titubare ergo et fluctuari, cadere etiam possunt, sed non colliduntur, quia Dominus supponit manum suam.'

[4] Wernle, *Calvin*, 3:404.

[5] *Institutes* 4.1.2 (CO 2:746): 'In Symbolo, ubi profitemur nos credere Ecclesiam id non solum ad visibilem, de qua nunc agimus refertur, sed ad omnes quoque *electos Dei* in quorum numero comprehenduntur etiam qui morte defuncti sunt.'

with human beings is manifest in a particular way. God's special providence reaches out to believers.[6] The church, therefore, is a theatre of God's providence.[7] This express placement of the church at the centre of the guidance given by the caring Father gives to Calvin's language the directness of a person-to-person relationship. The well-known great importance Calvin attaches to church organization and discipline in no way detracts from this. Calvin's interest in the external church and its structures shows that his thinking about the church is consistently directed towards human beings. When – in his first rationale for the church – he begins to speak on this subject, the human pole is clearly foremost. On the basis of his experience and knowledge of what human beings are really like, he tries to make plain why exactly God willed a church. Because people are inexperienced, slothful and vain they need an external support system by which faith can take root and develop in them.[8] Thus human weakness is foremost where it concerns the great external means to salvation which is the church. This church, with its offices and regulations, does not form a contrast to the invisible community of the elect. Calvin knows nothing of two churches. Admittedly, the church must continually realize what it is essentially: the embodiment of the solidarity between God and man, a union of God and man in Christ.[9] It would be hard to speak more positively and appreciatively about the church than we see happening here. At the same time, by means of this expression 'the mystical union', full emphasis is given to the persons who, in the final analysis, are Calvin's pivotal concern. In our opinion this valuation even goes farther than that which

---

[6] Ibid., 1.17.6 (CO 2:159): 'singularem Dei providentiam in salutem fidelium excubare plurimae sunt et luculentissimae promissiones quae testentur'.

[7] CO 8:49 (*De scandalis*); cf. *Institutes* 1.16.4 (CO 2:147).

[8] *Institutes* 4.1.1 (CO 2:745): 'Quia autem ruditas nostra et segnities (addo etiam ingenii vanitatem) externis subsidiis indigent, quibus fides in nobis et gignatur et augescat, et suos faciat progressus usque ad metam: ea quoque Deus addidit, quo infirmitati nostrae consuleret.'

[9] The expression *mystica unio* is employed by Calvin in passing in a broader context in which he is disputing the Christology of Osiander. Nevertheless, this phrase is too striking not to mention it here: 'Quia non de mystica unione qua Ecclesiam dignatus est disserit . . .' (*Institutes* 2.12.7 [CO 2:347]). Cf. ibid., 3.11.10 (CO 2:540): 'Coniunctio igitur illa capitis et membrorum, habitatio Christi in cordibus nostris, mystica denique unio a nobis in summo gradu statuitur.'

Calvin assigns to the church when he calls it 'our mother'. The children whom God chooses are placed under her motherly care. In the church the Father's constant care has its continuation and concretization. In this regard God and the church go together, just as a husband and his wife belong together. 'For these things which God has joined together it is not lawful to put asunder [Mark 10:9], so that for those to whom he is a Father the church would also be the mother.'[10] The importance of this text, we believe, is generally not sufficiently highlighted. It signals a far-reaching going-together of God and man, the latter viewed in an ecclesial light. Whereas elsewhere Calvin categorically denies that a human being can ever be God's co-worker, this person, being a member of the church, participates in God's caring providence. We can understand this text only in the sense that the church as mother *participates* in the providence of God. While the *mystical union* between God and people already means a very personal and intimate conjunction of the two in ecclesial perspective, at this point we discover the important consequence of that union. The bipolarity of God and man in Calvin's thought is clearly dominated, to begin with, by a great tranquillity, an intimate being and working together. The reason why Calvin is frequently called an 'ecclesial man' is *not*, in the first place, the high value he assigns to the external side of the church with its offices and discipline, but the above mentioned high form of unity and solidarity between God and man. Following *this* beginning it can hardly still surprise us that Calvin sees divine and ecclesial authority as being all of one piece, as coincidental, so much so even that God's authority is violated when people detract from the authority of the church.

> For the Lord esteems the communion of his church so highly that he counts as turncoats and traitors of religion those who stubbornly alienate themselves from any Christian community which maintains the true ministry of the Word and the sacraments. He so esteems its authority that he regards his own authority destroyed when the church's authority is violated.[11]

[10] Ibid., 4.1.1 (CO 2:746): 'ut quibus ipse est Pater, Ecclesia etiam Mater sit'.

[11] Ibid., 4.1.10 (CO 2:754): 'Sic eius authoritatem commendat ut dum illa violatur, suam imminutam censeat.' Sizoo (*Institutie*, 3:19) translates this *censere* as 'het er voor houden' (takes it to be). This could suggest that God's *authoritas*, *creating distance* between himself and his church, actually remains

Neither can it still surprise us to read of the church that the heavenly glory of God can be found in it.[12]

In sum, we are saying that in Calvin's discussion of the church God and man are sketched as being in a mutual relationship, a relationship expressed in God's election and human salvation. Further, that God's special care above all concerns the church, by which the church becomes the theatre of God's providence and – as will be developed later – the workshop of his honour. Finally, that in the church of Christ God and man come very near to each other, establishing a profound and intimate bond (*the mystical union*). God's glory indwells the church: it is clothed with God's authority.

Thus, in broad strokes, we believe we have been able to depict the bipolarity between God and man in relation to the church. Within the framework of this outline, we can now visualize more concretely what Calvin says about discipline in the church and its ministers (office-bearers).

The elect are the people designated to serve God's honour and thus to give shape to the kingdom of Christ in this world.[13] Zeal to this end can be regarded as a mark of their election. They are animated by a genuine passion for God's honour. As we stated earlier in connection with predestination, this concern for the honour of God is most intimately tied in with the salvation of the elect themselves. The bipolar orientation in Calvin's thinking is also evident when he speaks of the church's discipline (*disciplina*). Correction and excommunication have precisely this *twofold* purpose: to secure God's honour and to ensure human

---

untouched. In our opinion, Calvin means that God judges that his authority is diminished. Then in reality this *is* also the case. The subjunctive form of the verb does not in any way detract from this.

[12] *Institutes* 4.5.17 (CO 2:810): 'Scimus enim Prophetas sub imagine rerum terrestrium, caelestem Dei gloriam, quae lucere in Ecclesia debet, nobis delineasse.'

[13] Ibid., 2.12.6 (CO 2:345): 'Iam in angelis quam in hominibus representari suam gloriam . . . voluit [scl. Deus].' Cf. O. Ritschl, *Dogmengeschichte des Protestantismus*, 3:227: 'Sondern gerade als Erwählten liegt ihnen immer auch die Pflicht ob in ihrer persönlichen Lebensführung sowohl wie in dem, was sie als Glieder an dem Leibe Christi im Interesse der Kirche zu leisten haben, direkt die Förderung des göttlichen Ruhms in der Welt mit allen Kräften zu erstreben.'

salvation. This is how one can summarize the three goals Calvin himself lists: 'The first goal [of church discipline] is that those not be called Christians – to the dishonour of God – who lead a disgraceful and sinful life.... The second goal is that the good themselves are not corrupted by continual association with bad people, as commonly happens.' Also the last motif of correction is directly addressed to human beings. 'The third goal is that they themselves, being ashamed, begin to repent of their shameful life.' It will scarcely be necessary to point out that here too the focus on the honour of God and the wellbeing of the person inter-lock. Correction and excommunication concern *human beings*. In these forms of discipline the honour of God is being served and at the same time human beings are being cared for. God's honour is involved in the failures of church members. But if this is clearly recognized in church discipline and correction or excommunication is taken very seriously, the church at the same time and *in this process* pursues the salvation of the member(s) in question.[14]

In the ministers (*ministri*) of the church – the office-bearers – the grandeur of the church assumes concrete form. But precisely because it is *humans* who are being clothed with divine authority, the bipolarity between God and man again acquires an element of tension. The old danger threatens that the persons who have been clothed with authority become independent agents, so that they begin to function apart from service to God and his Word. Calvin describes this danger very precisely. Nothing, not even the tiniest particle, may be credited to the ministers of the church apart from God. When in various places Paul declares himself to be a fellow worker with God and ascribes to himself the role of a messenger of salvation,[15] he in no way does this to credit himself

[14] It is interesting to compare the threefold purpose that Calvin gives for *fasting* with the three goals given for church discipline. In the former, *self-control* and *inwardness* come first! *Humbling oneself* before God is mentioned only as the last goal. Actually, in these purposes for fasting the great theme of the knowledge of God and the knowledge of self in mutual relation once again comes to the fore. To enter oneself in a self-controlled way, one finds one small over against the Creator. This seems to us both a positive and a biblically legitimate approach to fasting: 'Sanctum ac legitimum ieiunium tres habet fines: . . . ad macerandam ac subigendam carnem . . . ut ad preces ac sanctas mediationes melius simus comparati vel ut testimonium sit nostrae coram Deo humiliationis . . .' (*Institutes* 4.12.15 [CO 2:914]).

[15] 1 Corinthians 3:9.

with anything apart from God.[16] It would simply be blasphemous if a person were to credit to himself the enlightenment of the mind and the renewal of the heart.[17] The church must use its authority in the service of the Word.[18] To that authority also the ministers must cause all else to yield.[19] Although in the case of human office-bearers there is always the possibility of usurping that which belongs only to God and this is a continual source of tension in the divine–human relation, yet Calvin unhesitatingly accords to those ministers of the church a lot of esteem – esteem which instinctively brings to mind what has been said of the glory of the church in general. In their ministry, particularly the ministry of the Word, the very face of God shines forth. If there are people (and they have always existed, says Calvin) who just cannot bear to be instructed through the mouth of a human being, they really reject the face of God himself which shines out upon them in that teaching.[20] In the preaching of the Word the glory of God shines in the face of Christ[21] and precisely in connection with that glory the same motif surfaces which also played such a large role in connection with *Christ in the light of God's majesty*. If God were to speak to us directly, we would never be able to bear the overpowering nature of his glory. Were it not for ministers, we would be overwhelmed and dazzled. To us they are a human medium through which God can address us in a human manner.[22] Ministers are necessary on account of our human weakness. Through them God can speak to us in a familiar way (*familiaris docendi ratio*).

---

[16] *Institutes* 4.1.6 (CO 2:752): 'haec . . . nunquam eo protulit ut vel tantillum sibi *seorsum a Deo* tribueret'.

[17] Ibid.

[18] Ibid., 4.8.2 (CO 2:847).

[19] Ibid., 4.8.9 (CO 2:851): 'pastores . . . ut verbo Dei confidentes omnia audeant: eius maiestati omnem mundi virtutem . . . cedere atque obedire cogant'. Cf. ibid., 4.9.14 (CO 2:867) and ibid., 4.10.18 (CO 2:880): 'obedientiae laus'; ibid., 4.8.1 (CO 2:846): 'ministri ipsi suam Christo authoritatem conservare student'.

[20] Ibid., 4.1.5 (CO 2:750): 'Quod perinde est ac Dei faciem, quae nobis in doctrina affulget, delere.'

[21] 2 Corinthians 4:6.

[22] *Institutes* 4.1.5 (CO 2:750): 'etiam nostrae *infirmitati* consulit dum per interpretes humano more nos mavult alloqui. . . . Et certe quam nobis expedit haec familiaris docendi ratio, sentiunt omnes pii ex *formidine* qua merito illos consternat Dei *maiestas*'.

This is the directedness toward people which is manifested in the existence and life of ministers. Nor is the other directedness, the directedness toward God, lacking. To hear God speaking through human agents is the test of our obedience to him.[23] The usefulness of ministers, accordingly, has a double focus (*duplex est utilitas*). In the directedness toward God this implies for us an exercise in humility:

> when he accustoms us to obeying his Word even though it is preached by people like ourselves or even by people of lower standing than we. If he spoke from heaven it would not be surprising if his sacred pronouncements were to be reverently received without delay by the ears and minds of all. For who would not tremble before the power of his presence?

Precisely by listening to such a puny human being we evidence our piety and reverence toward God.[24]

In sum, we believe we can describe the bipolarity of God and man in connection with the ministers of the church as follows: in the first place they protect us from the intensity of God's glory which, through them, comes to us tempered and veiled, as it were. To this a person must respond with an attitude of reverence. By being permitted to encounter God in this way our humility is purified. In the second place, we have to say that God's glory only breaks through to us by way of human interpreters. God links the proclamation of his saving Word to the ministry of human agents. Also, it is only through the proclamation of the human minister that a person, having been humbled, can express reverence and obedience to God. Apart from human beings God's Word is not heard, nor is his glory known. Apart from human beings a person cannot draw near in obedience. In the ministers of the Word – and they belong to an array of external aids by which our salvation is achieved – we again see that the manner in which this salvation comes to us is essentially marked by a bipolar structure.

2. The sacraments

The sacraments which Calvin discusses under the heading of the external means of our salvation are defined by him in two ways.

---

[23] Ibid.: 'optimo examine obedientiam nostram probat'.
[24] Ibid., 4.3.1 (CO 2:777): 'homuncio quispiam ex pulvere emersus'.

Both definitions are of interest to us, for each in its own way shows the bipolar structure which also evidenced itself in the doctrine of the sacraments.

> It seems to me that this will be a simple and proper definition if we say that it is an outward sign in which the Lord seals *to our conscience* the promise of his goodness *toward us* in order to strengthen the *weakness of our faith*. And that we in turn attest our *piety toward him* in the presence of the angels and before human beings. It can also be defined more briefly, namely as a testimony of *God's grace toward us*, confirmed by an outward sign, by a mutual attestation of our piety toward him.[25]

What comes through powerfully in these two descriptive definitions is the interpersonal character of the divine–human relation. We are told of God's goodness *toward us* (*erga nos*)[26] and of our attitude *toward him* (*erga eum*), for also the sacrament(s) are designed to focus on the human person in God's light (*coram eo*). In both definitions the sacraments are clearly and explicitly defined in terms of a reciprocal relationship. The phrases 'toward us' (*erga nos*) and 'toward him' (*erga eum*) achieve express reciprocity in the adverb 'reciprocally' (*vicissim*). [27] Thus the external sign (*signum externum*) is completely embedded in the context of the interpersonal relationship. In that way Calvin's discourse on the sacraments from the very outset possesses a much more *personal* – rather than a merely matter-of-fact – character. Even though, according to his own testimony, his view completely agrees in meaning (*in sensu*) with that of Augustine, it is typical of his theology that he furnishes a definition of his own.[28] To the extent that here, too, he makes the personal divine–human relation primary, he is correct in saying that his definition explains the matter better and more precisely.[29] Thus in the sacrament God testifies to his grace in a personal way. Corresponding to this divine goodness on the side of man is a genuinely believing attitude. This, certainly, is how we must read the reference to

[25] Ibid., 4.14.1 (CO 2:942).
[26] Ibid.: 'divinae in nos gratiae testimonium'.
[27] Ibid.: cf. 'mutua nostrae erga ipsum pietatis testificatio'.
[28] 'rei sacrae visibile signum, aut invisibilis gratiae visibilis forma' (Augustine, *De catechizandis rudibus*, c. 26.50 [MSL 40:344].
[29] *Institutes* 4.14.1 (CO 2:942): 'rem vero ipsam melius ac certius explicat'.

pietas to which the believer witnesses before God. Again we observe here a reciprocal relation between God and man.

Clearly stated in the first definition is that the movement from God to man is an act of assistance by the Strong to the weak. The gracious God reinforces his promise as a concession to the human conscience. It is *for the sake of our conscience* that God seals his promise. Again it is the familiar glance into one's own conscience in which Calvin finds a motive for understanding the necessity of the sacrament. This human conscience reveals the weakness, the pathetic character, of our faith (*fidei nostrae imbecillitas*).[30] The *pietas* which is evoked on our part toward the goodness which is underscored for us in the signs expresses itself in witness. Again this witness is directed towards people, to heaven and earth. This *pietas*, which gratefully observes God confirming his promise, is also a sign to others of God's merciful faithfulness. It is oriented to the community and therefore of benefit to others as well.

The consciousness of human weakness is a recurrent motif in Calvin's discussion of the sacraments. In fact, the bipolar viewpoint always implies the component of human poverty. Thus the sacrament functions as an appendage which is added to the promise precisely to confirm and seal that promise with a view to the ignorance, dullness, and weakness of human beings.[31] In a passage from a sermon on Luke 4:20–21 this human weakness is related to the glory of Christ. Precisely because we cannot view this glory directly, we need the external signs of the sacraments.[32] By visible signs, which are an image of invisible things, we enter into contact with Christ. Human weakness points to God's glory. Manifested behind the veil of earthly signs, that glory evokes the

---

[30] The binding of the sacrament to faith is indispensable. In this respect, too, Calvin has in view the peace of the human conscience. Cf. ibid., 4.14.15 (CO 2:952): 'ut autem non signum veritate vacuum, sed rem cum signo habeas: verbum quod illic inclusum est, fide apprehendas oportet'.

[31] Ibid., 4.14.3 (CO 2:942–3): 'eo fine ut promissionem ipsam confirmet ac obsignet, nobisque testatiorem, imo ratam quodammodo faciat: quo modo nostrae ignorantiae ac tarditati primum, diende infirmitati opus esse Deus providet'. Cf. ibid., 4.14.7 (CO 2:946): 'fidem nostram . . . sustinent, alunt, confirmant, adaugent'; and also ibid., 4.14.6 (CO 2:945): 'pro tarditatis nostrae captu'.

[32] *Serm. Synopt.* 4:20-21 (CO 46:679): 'mais tant y a que nous le voyons entant qu'il nous est expedient, et selon nostre infirmite. Car si Iesus Christ ne cognoissoit que cela nous fust utile, il ouvriroit bien les cieux, et nous feroit appercevoir sa gloire manifestement'.

image of the weak human who cannot do without the external sign as a means of strengthening his or her faith.

From within that situation of weakness we gain a clear view of God's goodness and grandeur, which in veiled form manifest themselves in the sacrament. Our *pietas* in turn offers a testimony to God and to humans. Precisely because it is an expression of *pietas* this testimony or witness in the sight of other people is directed *toward God*. In fact, the witness before God and man coincide or flow together. This witness has two components: human weakness and God's glory. In our confession before other human beings God is honoured. The main accent falls on the divine glory. This is vividly experienced in baptism:

> Our confession before people is served in baptism (as follows). Indeed, it is a mark by which we publicly profess that we want to be reckoned as God's people, by which we testify that we agree with all our fellow Christians in honouring the one God, in the one religion, and by which, finally, we publicly give assurance of our faith, so that not only our hearts breathe the praise of God, but our tongues also and all the members of our body proclaim it in every possible way. For thus, as is fitting, all our faculties are employed in serving God's glory . . .[33]

Thus, in connection with human weakness, the divine pole is heavily accented precisely in human witness. But not just in this way alone. There are still other indications that God's grandeur and sovereignty stand out in the sacraments.

This is evident from the relation between the sacramental signs and the honour of God, the union of the earthly elements with God's grace and sovereignty. Perceptible in the relation between the two – which is ultimately reducible to the relation between God and creation – there is again some tension. Apparently Calvin has been accused from within the circle of Zwingli's followers of transferring God's honour to created realities in his doctrine of the sacraments.[34] Calvin answers it is not we who put power in created things;[35] rather it is God who uses means and instruments

---

[33] *Institutes* 4.15.13 (CO 2:969): 'nostra omnia in obsequium gloriae Dei'. A splendid formulation of what for Calvin was a precious idea.

[34] Wendel, *Calvin*, 314–15.

[35] *Institutes* 4.14.12 (CO 2:950): 'respondere promptum est, nullam in creaturis virtutem a nobis reponi'.

for his own purpose. In that way everything – God's entire creation – begins to work together for his honour.[36] It is therefore incorrect to put one's trust in the sacraments, nor may we transfer God's honour to them. The sacraments can only fulfill their function properly when the Holy Spirit, the inner Teacher, accomplishes his work through them.[37] One must see beyond these physical things; rather, by way of these we must look toward God.[38] Then we discover that only Christ is the cause of our salvation, the real *content* of the sacraments.[39] Calvin thus actually manages to relieve the tension and to achieve a harmonious view. The external signs of the sacraments are made subordinate; they are not brushed aside but their operation is made secondary to God's action which is primary.[40] Almost without a break Calvin then directs his attention away from the external signs (*signa externa*) to the ministers (*ministri*) who administer the sacrament. In connection with those human beings, however, the danger of defrauding God of his honour again becomes acute![41] For a moment Calvin abandons his harmonizing manner of speaking which he employed to construct a wholesome subordination of earthly means to the divine impulse of grace, and again the divine–human relation briefly reveals a moment of tension.[42]

The final factor which clearly puts God in the foreground in the bipolarity between God and man exhibited in the sacraments is the linkage between divine election and the efficacy of the external signs of the sacraments (*signa externa*). Calvin expressly states that in accordance with God's free decision the sacraments

[36] Ibid.: 'ut eius gloriae omnia obsequantur'.

[37] Ibid., 4.14.9 (CO 2:947): 'ubi interior magister Spiritus accesserit'. Cf. ibid., 4.14.17 (CO 2:954); S. van der Linde, *De leer van den Heiligen Geest bij Calvijn* (Wageningen, 1943), 177–83, esp. 179, 180.

[38] *Institutes* 4.14.14 (CO 2:951).

[39] Ibid., 4.14.16 (CO 2:952–3): 'Christum sacramentorum omnium materiam, vel (si mavis) substantiam esse dico.'

[40] Ibid., 4.14.17 (CO 2:954): 'Nos vero contendimus, quaecunque adhibeat organa, primariae eius operationi nihil decedere . . . praecipua illa vis.'

[41] Ibid.: 'ne ad hominem mortalem trahatur quod Deus sibi uni vendicat'.

[42] In the *Consens. Tigur.*, art. 15 (CO 7:740), one can find a defensive stance against any binding that wants to subordinate divinity to earthly, contingent things: 'Nam haec omnia sacramentorum attributa inferiori loco subsidunt, ut ne minima quidem salutis nostrae portio ab unico auctore ad creaturas vel elementa transferatur.'

are effectual only in the elect,[43] as only in them a true faith can be present.[44] Thus he firmly and completely places the sacraments under the absolute power of God's sovereign grace, thereby leading off the possibility of any human contribution to their saving effect.

Corresponding to the exclusive gloriousness of grace, there is only absolute spiritual poverty on the side of humans. Also in this area there is no possibility for humans to appropriate even the tiniest particle of God's honour. Man is driven out of the bulwark of the *opus operatum* in which he tried to rescue some of his independence with regard to salvation.[45] It lies outside the scope of this study to assess the validity of Calvin's assault on the theory of *opus operatum*. It does seem to us, however, that, in addition to the motif mentioned above, the interpersonal relation played a role as well. Through the works performed Calvin immediately saw the persons who performed them and of these persons he rightly saw that when receiving the sacraments also their hands are empty.[46]

In sum, we affirm that Calvin's definition of the sacraments is strikingly *personal* in character; that is, it is emphatically directed toward the ultimate relation at issue, that between God and man. It is precisely in the light of the sacraments that human weakness comes to the fore in this bipolarity. They are given for the confirmation and strengthening of the faith. Corresponding to this weakness is the glory and grandeur of God's grace. The

---

[43] *Institutes* 4.14.18 (CO 2:955): 'pro arbitrio suo'.

[44] *Consens. Tigur.*, art. 16 (CO 7:740).

[45] *Institutes* 4.14.26 (CO 2:962): 'quicquid de opere operato nugati sunt sophistae non modo Deo falsum esse, sed pugnare cum sacramentorum natura, quae instituit Deus ut fideles, vacui bonorum omnium et inopes, nihil praeter mendicitatem eo afferant. Unde sequitur, ea recipiendo nihil istos agere unde laudem mereantur'. The Sophists that are meant here are none other than Bonaventure, Thomas Aquinas, Duns Scotus, and Gabriël Biel (OS 5:285).

[46] The term *opus operatum* is intended to express that the 'operation' of the sacrament does not depend on the person administering it. This 'operation' inheres in the sacrament itself, simply because the *opus* (work) is accomplished (*operatum*). For a modern Catholic viewpoint on the *opus operatum*, see E. Schillebeeckx, *De Christusontmoeting als sacrament van de godsontmoeting* (Antwerp, 1957), 52–7, esp. 53: 'ex opere operato en kracht vanuit het Christusmysterie betekent hetzelfde'. Idem, *De sacramentele heilseconomie* 1:642–6.

sacraments create the possibility of entering into contact, in a veiled way, with the glory that is Christ.

The sovereign place of God is further accentuated by the *subordination* of all created things to God's primary operation, an order which to Calvin is imperative, and additionally by linking the sacraments to divine election (*electio Dei*), which makes the sacraments efficacious only in those who believe.

These lines of the bipolar structure of the sacraments apply without compromise to *Baptism* and the *Lord's Supper*. From our viewpoint, as we consider these two sacraments, we can further make the following comments.

> Baptism is a sign of the initiation by which we are received into the fellowship of the church, in order that, implanted in Christ, we may be counted among God's children. Now, baptism was given us by God for these ends (which, as I have taught, are common to all mysteries): first, to serve as a witness of our faith before him, and, second, as a confession before human beings.[47]

Here, in so many words, is mention of a double witness:[48] a witness *before God* and a witness *before people*. Upon closer scrutiny it seems to us more correct to speak of one single witness with a twofold focus: one towards God and one towards people. But what has to be considered more important is that the witness before God in all three facets Calvin mentions concerns human salvation. The witness is that [the sacrament of baptism is] a sign and proof of our cleansing.[49] Second, it is a token of our mortification in Christ and our new life in him.[50] Finally, our faith is given the assurance that we are sharers in all Christ's benefits.[51] This is a compendium of our salvation and sanctification. In other words, the object of our witness to God are we ourselves as

---

[47] *Institutes* 4.15.1 (CO 2:962).

[48] We already discussed earlier a passage about the witness character of baptism as an illustration of the witnessing character of the sacraments in general (see above, p. 157).

[49] *Institutes* 4.15.1 (CO 2:962): 'symbolum . . . nostrae purgationis ac documentum'.

[50] Ibid., 4.15.5 (CO 2:964): 'nostram in Christo mortificationem nobis ostendit, et novam in eo vitam'.

[51] Ibid., 4.15.6 (CO 2:965): 'sic ipsi Christo unitos ut omnium eius bonorum participes simus'.

those who are justified and sanctified in Christ. The content of our witness is the salvation that is accomplished in the lives of people.

While our witness before God is structured as outlined above, our confession before people is totally imbued with God's saving presence and action. About that, however, we have already said enough earlier. Thus the words 'in the first place before God' are as much oriented to man as the words 'in the second place before people' are directed towards God. The divine and the human pole are inseparably and reciprocally bound up with each other. There is simply no way one can speak about the one without involving the other.

God's sovereignty and his honour are especially accented in Calvin's rationale for infant baptism. If a person were not yet persuaded by the parallel Calvin sees in the Old Testament practice of circumcision, the motif of God's honour, a motif particularly supported by infant baptism, may tip the balance. One gets this impression from reading Calvin's extensive argumentation.[52] Whatever we may think of it,[53] God's honour does not hang in the air here but is realized in human beings. Infant baptism is above all a sign of the exceptional goodness of God. He furnishes abundant reason for us to proclaim his glory.[54] Calvin, accordingly, presents the case of infant baptism as one where the rejection of it violates God's honour because people fail to recognize his exceptional goodness which shines out here. *God* is deprived of his honour and *man* of the singular fruit of assurance and spiritual joy.[55] For that matter, who can tell God whom he may or may not sanctify?[56] Rather, there is every reason to be grateful for such goodness. . . .[57] 'Therefore, unless we wish spitefully to obscure God's generosity, let us offer him our children

[52] Ibid., 4.16 (CO 2:946–1002).

[53] Cf. Wendel, *Calvin*, 327–8.

[54] *Institutes* 4.16.9 (CO 2:982): 'ubi cum ingens sese proferat Dei benignitas primum amplissimam gloriae eius praedicandae materiam suppeditat'.

[55] Ibid., 4.16.32 (CO 2:1001): 'ut singularem fiduciae et spiritualis gaudii fructum, qui hinc colligendus est, nobis eripiat ac de bonitatis etiam divinae gloria tantundem delibet'.

[56] Ibid.: 'Ne ergo legem Deo imponere tentemus, quin sanctificet quos visum fuerit quo modo hunc sanctificavit, quando nihil eius virtuti decessit.'

[57] Ibid.: 'toto corde ad gratiarum actionem debemus exultare ut tali bonitatis specimine eius nomen sanctificetur'.

to whom he has given a place among his friends and in his household, that is, among the members of the church.'[58]

With respect to the Lord's Supper, we will limit ourselves to a couple of comments which are important for the divine–human relation. They concern Calvin's view of Christ's presence in this sacrament and his vehement opposition to the popish mass.[59]

To do justice to Calvin's discussion of Christ's presence, one must never forget the statement which so clearly betokens a reverent approach:

> now, if anyone asks me about the mode of his presence, I shall not be ashamed to admit that this is a mystery too high for either my mind to grasp or for my words to express. And, to put it even more plainly: I experience it rather than understand it.[60]

Yet it is precisely (how tragic!) about the mode of his presence that a bitter controversy was carried on. Despite the *Consensus Tigurinus*, the marks of this controversy have not been erased among Christians of the Reformation.[61]

Calvin confesses the real presence of the Lord at the Lord's Supper. The only things against which Calvin registers his protest are the things which appear to be either unworthy of his heavenly majesty or incompatible with the truth of his human nature.[62] This latter point concerns the *metaphysical* impossibility that something could at the same time be and not be. This demand may simply not be put to God's omnipotence.[63] If Calvin is then accused of failing in his respect to do justice to God's power and therefore robs him of his honour, his reply is that the reverse is

[58] Ibid., 4.16.32 (CO 2:1002): 'nisi maligne Dei beneficentiam obscurare libet'.

[59] Ibid., 4.17-18 (CO 2:1002–66).

[60] Ibid., 4.17.32 (CO 2:1032): 'experior magis quam intelligam'.

[61] For a concise summary of the points of difference, see Walker, *John Calvin*, 423.

[62] *Institutes* 4.17.32 (CO 2:1032): 'in sacra sua Coena iubet me sub symbolis panis ac vini corpus ac sanguinem suum sumere, manducare ac bibere; nihil dubito, quin et ipse vero porrigat, et ego recipiam. Tantum absurda reiicio quae aut caelesti Christi maiestate indigna, aut humanae eius naturae veritate aliena esse apparet'.

[63] Ibid., 4.17.24 (CO 2:1023): 'Insane, quid a Dei potentia postulas ut carnem faciat simul esse et non esse carnem?'

true.[64] Calvin's view of Christ's presence at the Lord's Supper, accordingly, is subject to the pressure exerted by the demands posed by divine omnipotence and the heavenly glory of Christ. In Calvin's interest in God's power and its limitation we think we can discern a clear reference to the views of the nominalist school on this subject.[65] God's omnipotence, accordingly, is always marked by that which is morally blameless and rationally possible. This is evidence that to an extraordinary degree God's power is directed toward human beings!

What is the role played by the majesty of Christ in the case of his real presence in the Lord's Supper, or – to define this norm in Calvin's words – what in this respect is unworthy of Christ's heavenly glory? This: that the glory of the heavenly Lord should be bound to a specific location. The glorified Christ is only in heaven and not locally situated within the bounds of the signs of bread and wine. Such restriction to a given location is incompatible with his heavenly majesty.[66] Calvin is not protesting against a true presence, therefore, but against a binding of the glorified Lord to any earthly creature.[67] *This* conjunction of the divine and the creaturely, the *reduction* of the One to the other, this binding (*alligatio*) is unacceptable. Voiced here is resistance to any fusion (*contaminatio*) of the divine with the earthly. Strictly speaking, we are not (yet) dealing here with friction between the divine and human pole. This friction only becomes really acute when what is created is personified. It is significant that precisely in this context Calvin offers a sharp definition of idolatry.[68] This fear of deification prompts him to protest against a form of veneration

[64] Ibid., 4.17.25 (CO 2:1024): 'Quicquam vero a nobis imminui de potentia Dei, usque eo falsum est ut nostra doctrina apprime magnificum sit eius elogium . . . semper nos insimulant, fraudari Deum suo honore.'

[65] Cf. Reuter, *Grundverständnis der Theologie Calvins*, 142–4, esp. 143, where John Major's view is treated.

[66] *Institutes* 4.17.19 (CO 2:1017): 'Nos vero talem Christi praesentiam in Coena statuere oportet quae nec panis elemento ipsum affigat, nec in panem includat, nec ullo modo circumscribat (quae omnia derogare caelesti eius gloriae palam est).'

[67] Ibid., 4.17.30 (CO 2:1031): 'prodigiosa ubiquitas'; '. . . nequid caelesti Christi gloriae derogatur: quod fit dum sub corruptibilia huius mundi elementa reducitur, vel alligatur ullis terrenis creaturis' (ibid., 4.17.19 [CO 2:1017]).

[68] Ibid., 4.17.36 (CO 2:1039): 'Quid enim est idololatria . . . dona pro datore ipso colere . . . nam et honor Deo raptus ad creaturam traductus est.'

concentrated on the sacramental signs.[69] Calvin's deepest intention is to protect the purity of the concept of God, to affect some distance between God and the created world, or, finally, between the *divine* and the *human* nature. 'If [the ability] to fill all things in an invisible manner is counted among the gifts of the glorified body, it is plain that the substance of the body is wiped out and that no distinction is left between the deity and the human nature.'[70] The word 'distinction' (*discrimen*) is decisive in the present context of the bipolarity between God and man.[71] For this reason the Lord's presence in the Lord's Supper, though real, is spiritual, not physical.[72] Against this background, Calvin's strong intention to maintain the distinction between Christ's divine and his human nature, one must also view the distinction between the presence of his majesty (*praesentia maiestatis*) and the presence of his body (*praesentia carnis*).[73]

It is Calvin's concern to preserve the distinction between the divine and the creaturely, between Christ's divine and his human nature! Actually, this is also the bipolar background of Calvin's protest against the popish mass.[74] But here the defence of this

---

[69] Ibid.: 'secundum hanc regulam [Col. 3:1] erat potius spiritualiter in coelesti gloria adorandus, quam excogitandum istud tam periculosum adorationis genus, plenum carnalis crassaeque de Deo opinionis'. Cf. also ibid., 4.17.37 (CO 2:1040): 'ut divinis honoribus signum afficerent'. It is for this reason, in our judgment, that Calvin pleads for a sober rite. Cf. ibid., 4.17.43 (CO 2:1045): 'istae frigidae et histrionicae nugae'.

[70] Ibid., 4.17.29 (CO 2:1029): 'nec discrimen ullum relinqui deitatis et humanae naturae'.

[71] Ibid., 4.17.30 (CO 2:1031): 'Verum ex Scriptura aperte colligitur, sic unicam Christi personam constare ex duabus naturis, ut cuique tamen sua maneat salva proprietas. . . . Quod discrimine inter naturas sublato, personae unitatem urgens, ex Deo hominem faceret, et ex homine Deum.'

[72] Fellowship with the Lord happens through the Spirit: ibid., 4.17.12 (CO 2:1011). Cf. van der Linde, *Heiligen Geest*, 190ff., and Wendel, *Calvin*, 348: 'He rejects the doctrine of the invisible corporeal presence of the Christ in this world. In this he sees an attack on the distinction between the two natures of Christ and, as Zwingli had taught it, an improper extension of the "communication of idioms".'

[73] *Institutes* 4.17.26 (CO 2:1026): 'Aliter secundum praesentiam maiestatis, semper habemus Christum; secundum praesentiam carnis recte dictum est, Me autem non semper habebitis.'

[74] We maintain the expression 'popish mass' in distinction from the Holy Eucharist as it is celebrated in the Roman Catholic Church.

distinction is so much more concrete in character and for that reason also much more vehement. Precisely for this reason friction between the two poles is so great: the human is shamelessly taking the place of God. This is *impietas* in the strict sense of the word and the popish mass is full of it.[75] In fact the *impietas* of the popish mass consists in human beings taking the place of Christ who is the only Priest and Mediator of the New Testament.[76] This Christ and his honour, accordingly, are central. The slander and disgrace inflicted on him in the mass are intolerable.[77] Among the objections raised by the Reformer the following statement, in our opinion, witnesses most sharply to the bipolar tension which controls all his thinking: '. . .who can think himself redeemed by the death of Christ when he has seen a new redemption in the mass? . . . What then remains of Christ's passion except that it is an example of redemption, so that from it we would learn *to be our own redeemers?*'[78] Calvin's entire 'discussion' of the mass can hardly be summed up more pithily than by the phrase 'our own redeemers'. Here humans take their place alongside the only Redeemer. Worse, human beings here take the place of the only Redeemer and become their own redeemers. This is absolutely how Calvin must also have viewed the priests as Christ's competitors, redeemers alongside of him, apart from him, independent, redeemers alongside the Redeemer, sacrificers alongside *the* Sacrificer. To Calvin the very word 'sacrificer' (*sacrificus*) has this unbearable Christ-dishonouring sound.[79] Any positive assessment, as in the case of the ministers of the church, is lacking here. Not a word is said about a possible *subordination*.

Thus in the case of the Lord's Supper all honour is redirected to Christ.[80] The only service the believers have to perform is to

[75] *Institutes* 4.18.18 (CO 2:1064): 'ut omnes intelligant, Missam ... omni genere impietatis, blasphemiae, idolatriae, sacrilegii scatere'.

[76] Ibid., 4.18.14 (CO 2:1061): 'Nam Christus unicus est Novi Testamenti Pontifex et Sacerdos.'

[77] Ibid., 4.18.2 (CO 2:1052): 'Ostendamus ergo quod primo loco propositum est, intolerabilem illic blasphemiam ac contumeliam Christo irrogari.'

[78] Ibid., 4.18.6 (CO 2:1056): 'quo discamus nostri esse redemptores'.

[79] Ibid., 4.17.48 (CO 2:1049): '[Scriptura] non ita Christi dignitatem obscurat ut sacrificos eos appellet.' Cf. ibid., 4.19.28 (CO 2:1086–7): 'victimarii'.

[80] Ibid., 4.18.14 (CO 2:1061). To speak of a repetition of the sacrifice for forgiveness of sins, which is supposed to take place in the Mass, is an intolerable slander against Christ and his sacrifice.

really give that honour. This is the only premise from which, in connection with the Lord's Supper, Calvin wants to speak of a sacrifice: a sacrifice of praise. 'The Lord's Supper cannot be without a sacrifice of this kind, for when in it we proclaim his death and give thanks to him, we do nothing but offer a sacrifice of praise.'[81] But how far-reaching is the scope of this *sacrifice of praise,* how deeply embedded in the structures of human life and how a whole existential world of human values corresponds to it! The honour which is rendered to Christ from the remembrance of him and which is a true sacrifice *does not bypass human involvement.* In the sacrifice of praise humans are intensely involved. Here, too, God's honour is directed in bipolar fashion toward humans. The sacrifice of praise makes an appeal to humans. Again, humanity and its world is integrated in God's honour. Also in connection with the Lord's Supper Calvin's utterances about God's honour have strong links with human beings. In conclusion, we can best convey this fact with the words of the *Institutes* themselves:

> In the other class of sacrifices, which we call thank offerings, are included *all the duties of love.* When we perform them to our brothers, *we honour the Lord himself in his members.* Also included are all our prayers, praises, and thanksgivings as well as all the other things we do in the service of God. All these things are interconnected with a greater sacrifice by which we are consecrated with soul and body to be a holy temple to the Lord. For it is not enough for us to apply our outward acts to obedience to him; but first we ourselves and then all that is ours must be consecrated and dedicated to him, so that all that is in us serves his glory and strives to increase it. This kind of sacrifice does not serve to appease God's wrath, to obtain the forgiveness of sins, or to merit righteousness but is concerned solely with glorifying and magnifying God. Thus all the good works of believers become a spiritual sacrifice.[82]

God is glorified in the sacrifice of praise by all the duties of love (*officia charitatis*) we perform to each other. Thus the sacrifice of praise serves the well-being of humans.

---

[81] Ibid., 4.18.17 (CO 2:1063): 'nihil aliud quam offerimus sacrificium laudis'.
[82] Ibid., 4.18.16 (CO 2:1063): 'sic omnia fidelium bona opera, spirituales hostiae'. In this light even good works can be called a sacrifice.

3. Civil authority

Calvin's attitude toward civil authority is marked, on the one hand, by a firm refusal to let it tell him anything about matters of faith or matters pertaining to the church order; and, on the other hand, his attitude testifies to a high level of esteem for the civil government.

The first aspect of this position constitutes the background of and explanation for the bitter struggle in which the Reformer had to engage with the civil government in Geneva.[83]

The other aspect of Calvin's attitude, the appreciation he had for civil authorities, has its roots in his firm conviction that all authority originates in God. This also explains his vehement opposition to the anarchistic tendencies which were ignited by the religious revolution of his day and threatened to confuse the cause of the true gospel.[84] By virtue of this regard for all authority Calvin continued to respect the French king, although the latter was far from doing his cause any favours.

Traces of Calvin's attitude toward the civil government contained in many pronouncements in his *Institutes* are perfectly clear.

Taught by hard experiences in Geneva, Calvin knows that government officials are frequently motivated more by political opportunism than by the honour of God. For that reason he by no means absolutizes political authority. The civil government must realize fully that the authority it has been given must be subject to Christ. In this connection Calvin cites the verse in the Psalms in which David commands all rulers to 'kiss' the Son.[85] All the kings and judges who have failed to do so will cringe in fear before the face of God and be destroyed.[86] Calvin knows the self-willed and self-serving conduct of persons put in positions of authority. But let them remember that tax revenues, much more than personal possessions, belong to the people as a whole. In fact they are almost, as he put it, 'the very blood of the people'.

---

[83] Cf. Dankbaar, *Calvijn*, 80–126, esp. 94–5. Walker (*John Calvin*, 245–324) provides an excellent account of Calvin's struggle and conflicts in Geneva.

[84] Cf. Calvin's treatise *Contre la Secte des Libertins* of 1545 (CO 7:145–252).

[85] Psalm 2:12; *Institutes* 4.20.5 (CO 2:1096).

[86] Ibid., 4.20.29 (CO 2:1115).

Not to respect this reality is harsh inhumanity.[87] But this harsh inhumanity goes hand in hand with godless self-confidence and contempt for God.[88]

Yet Calvin also knows of an exception to the rule that we must always obey the authorities set over us. This exceptional situation arises when this obedience would lead us away from obedience to him 'before whose majesty all royal sceptres should yield'.[89]

The true calling of the civil government consists in serving God's honour *and* in making human society livable. Calvin even mentions this second aspect first. He expresses this calling to make society livable in very human and concrete terms. 'Its function is to ensure that people can breathe, eat and drink, and are reasonably comfortable (all these activities belong to its task, because it must see to it that the people can live together). . . .'[90] But in addition the civil government must champion the honour of God and act against idolatry. It may not tolerate the desecration of God's name, blasphemy against the truth or other public offences against religion.[91] When he further demands that the civil authorities must act to protect the moral law, we again observe striking evidence of the twofold nature of that task. For basically the moral law has only two chapters: the honour of God and mutual love among people.[92] Thus the responsibility of the civil government faces both poles: it is directed towards God *and* towards human beings.

While all this as such already sounds very positive, Calvin's formulations become even more radical when he speaks of the human person who is clothed with authority. He successively calls

[87] Ibid., 4.20.13 (CO 2:1104): 'durissima inhumanitas'; 'tyrannica rapacitas'.

[88] Ibid.: 'impia confidentia in Dei contemptum'.

[89] Ibid., 4.20.32 (CO 2:1117).

[90] Ibid., 4.20.3 (CO 2:1094).

[91] Ibid., 4.20.9 (CO 2:1099): 'longe gravioris momenti . . . ut ipse pure coleretur ex Legis suae praescripto'. Although the tasks of the church and state are clearly separated in Calvin, one can hardly call him an advocate of the separation of church and state. According to Lang (*Johannes Calvin*, 112), Calvin continued to hold to the medieval theocratic view of the state: '. . . er verpflichtet auch sie für die Ehre Gottes einzutreten'.

[92] *Institutes* 4.20.15 (CO 2:1105): 'siquidem haec aeterna est et immutabilis eius voluntas ut a nobis ipse quidem omnibus colatur, nos vero mutuo inter nos diligamus'.

the civil authorities 'the deputies of God',[93] who 'provide guidance in his name',[94] are the 'servants and emissaries of God'[95] and even (Calvin uses the beloved phrase frequently) 'the image of God'.[96] One can guess the specific nuance associated with the image of God in his connection. The image of God which the magistracy must radiantly reflect is the image of God's majesty. Calvin even says so in so many words: God himself has impressed and engraved the function of the bearers of authority with the marks of an inviolable majesty.[97]

The implications of all this are clear: people who despise the civil authorities despise God himself. They reject not the government, but God.[98]

It is clear that throughout Calvin's entire discussion of the civil government God's honour is intimately associated with the noble characterizations the Reformer accords to the person of authority. Precisely because the person-in-authority is called to serve God's honour and promote the wellbeing of the community, that person is called God's deputy and marked with the stamp of God's own majesty. There is, accordingly, no tension between the bearer of authority and the God who might feel that his honour was threatened. Calvin himself builds the bridge between these two poles and does it in the following pithy formulation: 'Earthly power is not diminished when it is subject to its Author.'[99]

Nor on these pages is there any hint of competition or even tension between God's honour and human wellbeing. Both fall under the care and responsibility of the civil government. Ordained authority only answers to its calling to serve God's honour when it does not fail in its responsibility for people. It is also true that God's honour is only really served when the wellbeing of humans is assured. In building up a human and livable society the human authority is the servant of God's honour. Again we observe that

[93] Ibid., 4.20.6 (CO 2:1096): 'vicarii'.
[94] Ibid., 4.20.9 (CO 2:1099): 'praefectos'.
[95] Ibid., 4.20.22 (CO 2:1110): 'ministri et legati'.
[96] Ibid., 4.20.24 (CO 2:1112): 'species imaginis Dei'.
[97] Ibid., 4.20.29 (CO 2:1115): 'inviolabilem maiestatem impressit ipse et insculpsit'.
[98] Ibid., 4.20.7 (CO 2:1097).
[99] Ibid., 4.20.32 (CO 2:1118): 'quasi . . . minuatur terrena potestas, dum suo authori subiicitur'.

God and man, also on the level of the civil government, are reciprocally related. God's honour and human well-being presuppose each other.

In our opinion, this is the tenor of numerous passages in chapter 20 of Book IV of Calvin's *Institutes*. Let readers themselves judge the text to which we already referred earlier but which we now reproduce in its entirety by way of conclusion:

[The civil government] serves not only to ensure that people can breathe, eat, and drink, and feel reasonably at ease (all these activities, naturally, belong to its task when it sees to it that people can live together), but it has, I say, still another task as well. It must also see to it that no idolatry will raise its head; that God's name is not desecrated; that no blasphemies against his truth are allowed to pollute the air; that religion is not publicly insulted and that all these things are not spread among the people. Thus the public peace will not be disturbed; every person can safely and without injury possess their own things; people can quietly do business with each other. In this manner there can be room for an honourable and dignified lifestyle. In a word: The government must see to it, that Christians living together will be able in public to give shape to their lived faith and that the society of people living together will bear a human character.[100]

---

[100] Ibid., 4.20.3 (CO 2:1094): 'Denique, ut inter Christianos publica religionis facies existat, inter homines constet humanitas.' Calvin manages to formulate his meaning very compactly in this statement, but it is difficult to translate it in a satisfactory manner.

V

ᏃᏃᎧᏅ

God's Honour
and Human Salvation

A Reassessment

1. Perspectives and structures: a review

FOR the analysis of Calvin's theological thought world I proceeded in this study from the principle which he himself passed along with his main work. 'Almost the entire content of our wisdom . . . consists of two parts: the knowledge of God and the knowledge of ourselves.'[1] As a result of this statement his *Institutes* have become more than a collection of points of doctrine, more than a catechism, the form he had in mind for the first edition of 1536. Calvin's theology is contained in a dynamically charged framework. For the knowledge of God and the knowledge of ourselves are like two poles between which our knowledge restlessly oscillates. We do not know God without knowing ourselves; nor do we know ourselves without knowing God. We are dealing with two persons in a relationship that is both filled with tension and fascinating.

We devoted an entire section to tensions in Calvin's theology, tensions which continually characterize his word usage.[2] As we do in a human relationship, so here too we keep encountering expressions which convey certain moods: low points of dismal despair, deep oppressive anger, bitterness, desperation, even agonies of doubt take us by roads of hope, reconciliation and

---

[1] 'Tota fere sapientiae nostrae summa . . . duabus partibus constat, Dei cognitione et nostri' (*Institutes* 1.1.1 [CO 2:31]).

[2] See above, pp. 28–39.

trust, serenity of conscience and inner peace, to high points of tender love and supreme bliss.[3]

This arrangement tells us something about the author. It gives us a glimpse of his intense emotionality. It also says something about the document he wrote. It gives his book – at least if we dare to opt for a contemporary translation[4] – enduring freshness and vitality.

Calvin's principle concerning the sum of all our wisdom is the key which gives us access to the structure of his theology. Following Karl Reuter, I have called it the approach of bipolarity[5] and in connection with it I have repeatedly used the term 'bipolar structure' – a clear reaction to the system builders who, proceeding from a single principle, sought by logical deduction as it were to explain Calvin's entire theological oeuvre.

But does not the word 'structure' perhaps already claim too much? 'Structure' suggests to us the connectedness and order which authors introduce into their argumentation so that the reader is not just reduced to following the main outline but can also clearly and correctly distinguish the subjects which are being dealt with.

Such rigorous structuration is lacking in Calvin's *Institutes*. Admittedly, he always intended to bring about a clear and well-ordered division in the growing body of materials which constituted his life work. Finally, in the 1559 edition he explicitly stated that this was his goal. However, he did not succeed in accomplishing it. I will come back to this subject later.[6]

Therefore, in characterizing the principle with which Calvin launched his *Institutes* I would prefer the term 'perspective'. By this word one indicates the place from which a person looks out upon a given field. The knowledge of God and the knowledge of ourselves is the place from which Calvin wants to view his introduction to Christian doctrine. He does not posit his famous

---

[3] Cf. Texts C and D below and *Institutes* 3.2.18 (CO 2:413), where positive and negative experiences in faith (*suavitas* and *amaritudo*) are summed up. See above, p. 15, nn. 102, 103.

[4] For the interested reader, the original Latin text of important passages or parts of passages is quoted in the footnotes.

[5] See above, p. xvi and nn. 15, 16.

[6] See below, pp. 177–8.

adage with a view to announcing an epistemological treatise. He is not interested in philosophy. From the very outset he adopts the stance of the believer, also when he bases his knowledge of God on the glory of the creation, his observation of nature, and the experience of his own humanity.[7] In his mind knowledge of God is always embedded in the perspective of his honour and the knowledge of man is always oriented to human salvation. He is not interested in knowing either one abstractly.

The honour of God is illumined in a twofold way. Calvin sees God as a figure of awesome majesty before whom man – lethally crippled by sin (*deformitas*)[8] – becomes small and shrinks back in terror. He also views God as a figure of majesty who exerts an irresistible attraction. For God greatly loves humans. In traditional language: God is a figure of awesome and fascinating majesty acclaimed in Christian worship as the Father of immeasurable majesty.

Corresponding to this twofold illumination there is also a twofold perspective on humanity. On the one hand, the latter is a mere homunculus:[9] worse, as a result of sin man has become a failure, a monstrosity. At the same time, for Calvin the human person is also meant to be the crown jewel of God's entire creation,[10] an image of God, a divine person.[11]

This is how, from the perspective of his faith, Calvin puts content into the principle concerning the knowledge of God and ourselves. This theme is developed in chapter 1.

Calvin's theology, which on the basis of the *Institutes* is depicted here in chapters 2–4, is completely embedded in the same perspective of the interrelatedness of our knowledge of God and of ourselves. It bears an existential character. This means that Calvin's utterances are steeped in tensions, right into his Christology, or better: right into the person of Christ himself (chapter 2, sections 3–6), but there are also moments of rest and

---

[7] See below, pp. 181f.

[8] 'horrenda deformitas'. Cf. above, p. 11, n. 76.

[9] See above, p. 11, n. 81.

[10] 'praeclarissimum . . . suorum operum specimen' (*Institutes* 1.14.20 [CO 2:132]).

[11] Ibid., 1.5.5 (CO 2:44). So clever is the human that even in his sleep he remains active, coming up with ingenious ideas, reasoning, and even being able to foresee the future (ibid.).

harmony, for example, in the passages where the new life, rooted in faith, flourishes (chapter 3, section 2). But Calvin always theologizes 'in the presence of God',[12] and is therefore continually and painstakingly intent upon God's honour.

All these motifs stand out with striking clarity in what to Calvin and the entire Reformation was the crux of the Christian confession: justification by faith (chapter 3, section 1).

Calvin emphatically urges his readers to take special note of two things in this connection.[13] As always, his interest extends to two poles. First, to God whose honour is at stake. Second, to humankind whose peace of conscience is at issue. At bottom it sounds like an echo, a practical application of the rule which sees the highest wisdom in knowing God and ourselves. But this wisdom is not available in well-protected lecture halls.[14] It is obtained in the context of hard personal confrontation. In justification by faith alone the divine-human relation in Calvin's view is extremely tense. The tone in which Calvin addresses man is aggressive – almost derisive. Just look at your own inward self to see what kind of person you are, he writes. And if you know yourself well – not hastily or superficially – then take a stand, conscience and all, before God's tribunal. . . . This he says in his reply to James Sadoleto.[15] 'Looking at yourself. . . .' Certainly Calvin can only say this because he has looked at his own interior self. Surfacing here is something of his self-knowledge. This is the one pole: human beings having the courage to look into their own hearts. But they do so in continual confrontation with God. That is the second pole. The confrontation is played out between the two poles. By comparison to other people you may easily emerge somewhat favourably, he writes, but when you look up to God, that good impression collapses even before a word has crossed your lips. Not a straw remains of it.[16]

The image Calvin evokes of God in this confrontation is that of a majesty which is proclaimed throughout the creation and is exuberantly celebrated in the Scriptures, especially in the Psalms. These are the sources from which he draws his inspiration. From

[12] See above, pp. 100–2.
[13] See above, pp. 97ff., esp. p. 99, n. 4.
[14] 'in scholarum umbraculis' (*Institutes* 3.12.1 [CO 2:553]).
[15] CO 5:397.
[16] *Institutes* 3.12.2 (CO 2:554).

these sources God's high majesty gains its contours for him. But that again raises the question: How could he depict God in that way if he, with his testy, quick-tempered character, had not been extremely sensitive to the grandeur and beauty of creation and not been struck by it in his very soul? When God's honour is at stake, Calvin's temper flared as though his own honour had been violated. The way he describes God in cosmic images is not cool and detached but impetuous and passionate. This he could not possibly have learned in the lecture halls of the schools.

He draws the entire work of justification by faith in the direction of God.[17] *Good works?* Before the face of God absolutely nothing is left of them. The *four causes* from the scholastic doctrine of causation all point in the direction of God. The word 'merit' is only misleading and an occasion for people to congratulate themselves. Please abolish it, he says, and rather speak of prize, the awarding of a prize to good works. He is even afraid that people will boast of their *faith* as though it were their own achievement!

The question is whether in this one-sided vehement description of the process of justification by faith humans are not crowded into the background and do not totally vanish from our view. Absolutely not, says Calvin. It is only by our giving God all the honour for the work of justification by faith that human salvation is built upon a secure and firm foundation. The moment we begin to trust and build upon our own achievements and good works, that solid footing beneath our feet is gone. Human salvation rests solely and exclusively in God's mercy. It is in God's mercy that the human conscience finds rest. God's goodness can no more be captured in words than his grandeur. 'Am I unjust toward God's mercy? Over and over that thought returns to my mind. Continually, and with painstaking concern, I do my best to explain it as though one could possibly even doubt God's mercy!'[18] Both in the integrity conceived as original and perhaps even more, if possible, in the restoration of it, man is completely dependent on God. In justification by faith alone everything points to him, to his marvellous goodness.

[17] For what follows, see above, pp. 104–17.
[18] *Institutes* 3.14.6 (CO 2:567); cf. above, p. 104, n. 22. See below, p. 198, n. 134.

Conversely, God invested that honour in man, in the human being who is truly alive, in this divine human.[19] That is how God intended humanity to be. God's honour and human salvation are reciprocally related. And what we established with respect to justification by faith applies to every other topic we dealt with in this study.

There is only one exception: the doctrine of reprobation. Do not misunderstand: this point of doctrine too falls completely within the perspective in light of which Calvin's theological thinking unfolds – the knowledge of God and ourselves. Also in the case of reprobation there is a back-and-forth movement between God and human beings, a reciprocal relatedness. But here a horrendous breach occurs, for here, in reprobation, God's honour no longer conduces to human salvation. We need not mention here the complex of factors which combine to bring about this breach.[20] We merely observe here that Calvin's doctrine of reprobation implies a rupture in the pattern we have up until now been able to establish throughout his theology.

But if I am not mistaken, a tear, a paradox, even worse, a real contradiction becomes visible in Calvin's thought at this point. 'Always and forever', he argues in his reply to Sadoleto, 'the honour of God goes hand in hand with our salvation. It is my conviction that for this reason the Lord himself urgently recommends people to exert themselves for the honour of his name, to promote and to enlarge it.'[21]

2. Edward A. Dowey Jr, and the twofold knowledge of God

Among the scholars who have examined Calvin's theological world Edward Dowey occupies a special place. For he too can ground his study in Calvin's own words, words which serve as headings in the first and second book of his 1559 edition of the

[19] See above, p. 119 and n. 83; p. 120, n. 86.

[20] On the problem of predestination in Calvin, see Marijn de Kroon, *Martin Bucer en Johannes Calvijn. Reformatorische perspectieven. Teksten en inleiding* (Zoetermeer, 1991), esp. 20–35, 167–9. German title: *Martin Bucer und Johannes Calvin. Reformatorische Perspektiven. Einleitung und Texte* (Göttingen, 1991), pp. 19–34, 229–31.

[21] 'Sic quidem, fateor, Dominus ipse, quo nominis sui gloriam magis commendabilem hominibus faceret, eius promovendae atque amplificandae studium temperavit, ut cum nostra salute perpetuo coniunctum foret' (CO 5:391).

Institutes. They are the renowned titles concerning the twofold knowledge of God.[22] The classic text of these characterizations of Calvin's theology reads as follows:

> In the formation of the world but also in the general teaching of Scripture the Lord first makes himself known simply as Creator; afterward – in the appearance of Christ – as Redeemer.
>
> From this, then, arises a twofold knowledge of him. Of these two forms of knowledge the first is treated now; the second will follow in its proper order.[23]

To Dowey this directional pronouncement, according to which Calvin wants to organize and structure the *Institutes*, is the key giving access into the edifice of Calvin's thought, a door to an understanding of his theology. Supported by a broad and solid foundation in the Reformer's oeuvre, Dowey does precisely this in a thorough and thoughtful manner.

With this analysis of Calvin's ideas the author made his debut in his dissertation of 1951. A third and expanded edition appeared in 1994.[24]

While Calvin may have used the headings 'The Knowledge of God the Creator' for Book I and 'The Knowledge of God the Redeemer' for Book II for the first time in the 1559 edition, he actually had them in mind – as Dowey convincingly shows – already in preceding editions beginning in 1539. In terms of their material meaning, moreover, they are applicable to the entire text of the *Institutes*.[25] However, the two forms of knowledge do not result in a clear structure in Calvin's main work. He did not succeed, by means of the scheme of the twofold knowledge of God, in introducing a clear structure in his work, a structure by

---

[22] 'De cognitione Dei creatoris', 'De cognitione Dei redemptoris.'

[23] 'Quia ergo Dominus primum simpliciter creator tam in mundi opificio, quam in generali Scripturae doctrina, deinde in Christi facie redemptor apparet: hinc duplex emergit eius cognitio: quarum nunc prior tractanda est, altera deinde suo ordine sequetur' (*Institutes* 1.2.1 [CO 2:34]).

[24] Edward A. Dowey, *The Knowledge of God in Calvin's Theology* (Grand Rapids, 1994). In his discussion of my study of Calvin, D. Nauta rightly criticized the lack of any mention of Dowey's research. Cf. Richard A. Muller, *The Unaccommodated Calvin Studies in the Foundation of a Theological Tradition* (New York, 2000).

[25] Dowey, *Knowledge of God*, 40–9.

which the wealth of material distributed over a great many subjects would be properly divided. For the logical coherence of the great themes in Calvin's theology the headings concerning the knowledge of God the Creator and of God the Redeemer are not particularly illuminating. For example, Calvin develops his view of Scripture and in connection with it his view of the working of the Holy Spirit under the heading of 'The Knowledge of God the Creator' in Book I, chapters 6 and following.[26] A further development of this theme does not occur until Book II, chapters 1 and following.[27] Another important theme, the Law, fits equally well under both headings.[28] For Dowey this is the best example of the connection between the knowledge of God the Creator and of God the Redeemer.[29]

The starting-point selected by Dowey is undoubtedly helpful to an understanding of Calvin's theology. Dowey demonstrates this point and this gives permanent value to his study. In this 'perspective' – the term I personally prefer – of the twofold knowledge of God Dowey then proceeds to investigate Calvin's theology.

1. There are two sources from which we derive our knowledge of God: the first (a) is the revelation in creation itself; the second (b) is the general revelation in Scripture.[30]

(a) The Creator reveals himself in nature and in history. But he does not reveal himself as he is 'in himself'. People who want to know what God is (*quid sit Deus*) 'only play a game with speculations which leave a person cold'. What matters is how God is toward us (*qualis sit*).[31] Thus in his creation he reveals

---

[26] CO 2:53ff. On the working of the Holy Spirit in Calvin's theology, see W. Krusche, *Das Wirken des Hl. Geistes nach Calvin* (Göttingen, 1957).

[27] CO 2:393ff. In this connection, cf. T. H. L. Parker, who in the third, significantly revised version of his book *Calvin's Doctrine of the Knowledge of God* (Edinburgh, 1969) continues the controversy with Dowey undiminished. See pp. 1–12 (Introduction) and 55–7.

[28] *Institutes* 2.7ff. (CO 2:252ff.).

[29] Dowey, *Knowledge of God*, 221–38.

[30] Ibid., 50ff.

[31] 'frigidis tantum speculationibus ludunt, quibus in hac quaestione insistere propositum est, quid sit Deus: quum intersit nostra potius, qualis sit' (*Institutes* 1.2.2 [CO 2:34–5]). Cf. above, p. 41 and n. 297; *Institutes* 1.10.2 (CO 2:73): 'non quis sit apud se, sed qualis erga nos'; and n. 167 below.

himself in his attributes: his eternity, power, wisdom, goodness, faithfulness, righteousness, and mercy.[32] But this form of the Creator's revelation apparently also discloses something about human beings, and this is truly not little. Calvin makes three pronouncements, propositions which sound like axioms, all of which have great anthropological significance. I will briefly reproduce them in his own words:

1. 'I posit the following as being beyond all discussion: there is within the human mind an awareness of divinity. This has to do with a natural instinct (*divinitatis sensus*).'[33]

2. People have 'an awareness of divine judgment. This functions as a witness that is assigned to them. This awareness does not permit them to close their eyes to their own sins. It arraigns them as guilty before the tribunal of the Judge. This awareness is called conscience'.[34]

3. 'In the whole workmanship of the universe God has very clearly revealed himself and daily he reveals himself anew! We cannot open our eyes without seeing him. But it is true: his essence remains incomprehensible.'[35]

The universe is like a book in which we can read about God.[36] It is like a show (*spectaculum*)[37] in which his glory is displayed, and his works are like a mirror (*speculum*) 'in which he plainly and clearly depicts himself and his imperishable kingdom'.[38]

---

[32] *Comm. Rom.* 1:21 (CO 49:24). Cf. *Institutes* 1.10.2 (CO 2:73): 'in caelo et terra relucere: clementiam, bonitatem, misericordiam, iustitiam, iudicium, veritatem'.

[33] 'Quendam inesse humanae menti, et quidem naturali instinctu, divinitatis sensum, extra controversiam ponimus' (*Institutes* 1.3.1 [CO 2:36]).

[34] 'ita quum sensum habent divini iudicii quasi sibi adiunctum testem, qui sua peccata eos occultare non sinit quin ad iudicis tribunal rei pertrahantur, sensus ille vocatur conscientia' (ibid., 4.10.3 [CO 2:869]).

[35] 'se patefecit in toto mundi opificio, ac se quotidie palam offert, ut aperire oculos nequeant quin aspicere eum cogantur. Essentia quidem eius incomprehensibilis est' (ibid., 1.5.1 [CO 2:41]).

[36] *Sermon XXXV sur Job* 9:7–15 (CO 33:428).

[37] *Institutes* 1.5.5 (CO 2:45). See ch. 1 above, note 136.

[38] 'Atqui quantacunque claritate et se et immortale suum regnum Dominus in operum suorum speculo repraesentet' (ibid., 1.5.11 [CO 2:49]).

This third point describes the experience which God imparts to us. The great role which experience plays in our life will become clearer in the following.

(b) What the creation proclaims here is only confirmed by Holy Scripture. Particularly one psalm (Ps. 145) already proves this sufficiently, says Calvin,[39] and then, as compactly as clearly, he continues: 'With experience as our teacher (*experientia magistra*) we learn to know God precisely as he makes himself known in his Word.'[40]

It stands to reason, however, that with this we have not exhausted God's revelation in Scripture. There are three items of revelation about the Creator which are known to us only from Scripture: (1) that he is the triune God; (2) that he created the world; (3) the doctrine of providence.[41] Much more explicitly than creation Scripture proclaims the greatness of human beings: 'undeniable are the marks of divinity in human beings . . . ineradicable also the signs of immortality. Man is divine; and would he not acknowledge his Creator? What kind of logic is that?'[42] The word of God not only teaches but also guides us (*scriptura duce et magistra*).[43] But does not the parallel Calvin draws between Scripture and experience cast surprising light on the value he assigns to the latter?

2. But is the image of humanity given here from the perspective of the knowledge of God the Creator in fact realistic? The very question already suggests the answer. No: it is not. For something went radically wrong with humanity. In fact his original integrity did not remain intact. As a result of sin he toppled and was sidetracked, irreparably and without hope.[44] This would have been the last word had not the Creator also wanted to be a redeeming

---

[39] Ibid., 1.10.2 (CO 2:73).

[40] 'Adeo talem sentimus, experientia magistra, Deum, qualem se verbo declarat' (ibid.).

[41] Dowey, *Knowledge of God*, 126–31.

[42] *Institutes* 1.5.5 (CO 2:44): 'certa sunt divinitatis insignia in homine . . . deleri non posse quae in homine impressa sunt immortalitatis signa? Nunc quae ratio feret ut sit homo divinus, et creatorem non agnoscat?'

[43] Ibid., 1.6.1 (CO 2:53): the heading of ch. 6.

[44] Ibid., 2.6.1 (CO 2:247): 'excidimus a vita in mortem'. So radically that God could no longer recognize this humanity as his handiwork.

God. But he proved to be the latter in Christ's appearance in history.[45]

This is Calvin's position; this is where he stands. Actually he always thinks and reasons from the perspective of the knowledge of God the Redeemer even when, thinking about God the Creator, he tries to sketch the actual original setting (*genuinus ordo*) in which people, untouched and unblemished, would find and worship God from within their own world: humanity as a living tribute to God. In Calvin's own words: 'Now this was the optimal state of affairs. The work of art that is the universe should have been the school in which we would discover God. From that situation we were to have gone on our way to eternal life, our way to perfect felicity'.[46]

The great merit of Dowey's study is that, with penetration and persuasive power, he has demonstrated this connection in the twofold knowledge of God, the connection between the knowledge of God the Creator and the knowledge of God the Redeemer. In so doing he permanently disposed of the spectre of Calvin's 'natural theology'.[47] In essence, the relation between the two forms of knowledge is already contained in the two phrases cited: 'experience as teacher' (*experientia magistra*) as catch phrase for the knowledge of God the Creator; and Scripture as guide and teacher (*scriptura duce et magistra*), as catch phrase for the knowledge of God the Redeemer. Scripture guides us also with respect to our knowledge of the creating God. It is like a pair of glasses which enables us to discern things sharply.[48] Those who believe

[45] 'in facie Christi' (cf. 2 Cor. 4:6). Cf. above, pp. 177–8.

[46] 'Erat quidem hic genuinus ordo ut mundi fabrica nobis schola esset ad pietatem discendam: unde ad aeternam vitam et perfectam foelicitatem fieret transitus' (*Institutes* 2.6.1 [CO 2:247]).

[47] Dowey (*Knowledge of God*, 265–7 [Appendix III]), illustrates this on the basis of the classic debate between Emil Brunner and Karl Barth over the place and significance of 'theologia naturalis' in Calvin. Cf. *Natural Theology: Comprising 'Nature and Grace' by Professor Dr. Emil Brunner and the reply 'No!' by Dr. Karl Barth*, trans. Peter Fraenkel (London, 1946). Dowey shows that for Calvin the knowledge of the Creator is presupposed whenever he speaks of redemption, and, conversely, the knowledge of the Redeemer is presupposed whenever he speaks of creation. The very analysis of the twofold knowledge of God brings this to light.

[48] 'Specillis autem interpositis adiuti distincte legere incipient: ita Scriptura' (*Institutes* 1.6.1 [CO 2:53]).

can *see*. 'Now believers, to whom he has given eyes, see rays of his glory, as it were, which sparkle in every created thing.'[49]

This connection in the twofold knowledge of God is of eminent significance for the role of experience in Calvin's theology. Experience begins to function in the believer's field of vision, a field of vision which extends without limit over God's entire creation. There God lets himself be known. Daily the work of art that is creation becomes the school in which the believer is a pupil.[50] 'Daily he reveals himself anew. All you need to do is open your eyes.'[51] Truly, no lengthy and laborious proofs are needed as testimonies which tell us of God's majesty. 'Proofs are all around us – readily available for the taking. You can easily observe them with your eyes and touch them with your fingers.'[52] Thus graphically Calvin depicts the experience which causes him to speak continually and emphatically of God's majesty.

3. Naturally the specific area of the knowledge of God the Redeemer concerns Christ's work of redemption. Here Scripture is the sole source of revelation and 'faith' is the catchword which characterizes this event. Faith is the principal work of the Holy Spirit.[53] Faith unites all the theological topics which came up for discussion in the context of redemption. Dowey rightly devotes a generous section of his book to this theme.[54] 'Faith', his thesis reads, 'is the threshold of all Calvin's thought, because of the revelatory or cognitive priority of the soteriological.'[55] For Dowey knowledge is the fundamental and central category of Calvin's theological thought.[56] The doctrine of knowledge itself is the most important.[57]

The author consistently treats the entire complex of problems surrounding faith under the all-controlling heading of

[49] *Comm. Hebr.* 11:3 (CO 55:145–6).
[50] 'ut mundi fabrica nobis schola esset'; see above, p. 181.
[51] See above, p. 179.
[52] 'testimonia . . . adeo prompta et obvia esse constat, ut oculis designari, ac digitis notari facile queant' (*Institutes* 1.5.9 [CO 2:47]).
[53] 'fides praecipuum est eius opus' (ibid., 3.1.4 [CO 2:396]).
[54] Dowey, *Knowledge of God*, 153–204.
[55] Ibid., 255.
[56] Ibid., 247.
[57] Ibid., 254.

'knowledge'.[58] He sums up in interrogatory form the topics which are successively treated under the heading of faith as knowledge as follows:

What is the content of the knowledge of faith?

Have changes occurred in this knowledge over the course of the history of revelation?

Are there limitations in the knowledge of faith, limitations arising from the person who believes?

How certain is the knowledge of faith?

What connections are there between this knowledge and election and hope?

All this is given as an introduction *and* interpretation of Calvin's definition of faith.[59] Interestingly enough, Dowey finds himself compelled to add to this treatment of faith as knowledge two topics which, strictly speaking, fall outside the framework of Calvin's formal definition: (1) Calvin's sketch of 'existential' faith and (2) faith as mystical union with Christ.[60]

Dowey develops the theme of 'faith as knowledge' at great length and with extensive documentation. But precisely here the limitations which mark his analysis of Calvin's theology become clearly apparent.

He is so fixated on the term 'knowledge' (*cognitio*) that his translation and interpretation of the original text sometimes feel tendentious or are incorrect. In response to the question what the object of faith is, he ultimately refers to Christ as 'the core of explicit knowledge'.[61] For this interpretation he refers to Calvin's formulation '[apostolus] *explicitam requirit divinae bonitatis agnitionem*', that is, Paul calls for an explicit conscious acknowledgment of God's goodness.[62] The reference here is not to the knowledge (*cognitio*) of Christ by faith but simply to the acknowledgment (*agnitio*) of God's goodness. Therein, says Calvin, lies our righteousness. The word *agnitio* also occurs in a passage in

---

[58] 'Faith as Knowledge' (ibid., 153ff.).

[59] *Institutes* 3.2.7 (CO 2:403).

[60] Dowey, *Knowledge of God*, 192–7 ('Calvin's Picture of Existing Faith') and 197–204 ('Faith as Mystical Union with Christ').

[61] Ibid., 153.

[62] *Institutes* 3.2.3 (CO 2:399).

which Calvin sums up a number of expressions used for believing. Surprisingly, in a concluding sentence we encounter there the phrase *notitia fidei,* to be translated, in my opinion, by what we understand by 'faith' (*fidei* here as genitive of the object).[63] I reproduce this important passage under A.[64]

In still another far-reaching way Calvin nuances the knowledge of the believer. Those who believe are raised far above their understanding (*intelligentia*) of things by the working of the Holy Spirit. In connection with the text in question Dowey correctly uses the word 'supra-rational'.[65] But, typically enough, he adds that Calvin attempts to pin down this supra-rational element in terms of knowledge. In my opinion that is precisely *not* the case. By faith a person is touched in spirit and in mind, right down to soul and senses. He or she experiences it. To bring this supra-rational aspect of faith to expression Calvin takes refuge in this last domain, the world of the sense. But I will let the readers themselves judge the texts (Text B and C).[66]

With Dowey, who speaks in this connection of 'existing faith',[67] we do in fact find that also in the area of faith experience occupies a prominent place. The experience of God's goodness can penetrate a person's heart. In text C we read what believing *in optima forma* (in the sense of a full-orbed flourishing faith πληροφορίας) can bring about in a person.[68] What believers experience in their inmost self can hardly be expressed in words. 'I am only saying what every believer experiences. But words fall far short of explaining this in a satisfactory way.'[69] But also bitter experiences can be the lot of believers when their faith is tried and faith and unbelief vie with each other, a battle that is waged

[63] Cf. Dowey, *Knowledge of God,* 184. No critical study exists of the linguistic meaning of the terms that Calvin uses to define 'knowing', particularly in connection with faith.

[64] See below, pp. 186–8.

[65] Dowey, *Knowledge of God,* 183.

[66] See below, pp. 188–9.

[67] Dowey, *Knowledge of God,* 192.

[68] See below, p. 189.

[69] 'Non aliud loquor quam quod apud se experitur fidelium unusquisque, nisi quod longe infra iustam rei explicationem verba subsidunt' (*Institutes* 1.8.5 [CO 2:60]).

in their own deepest self. (A description of this faith-under-assault can be read in text D.)[70]

What takes place in the process of believing cannot be expressed in terms of knowledge. Calvin's definition itself indicates the context in which faith must be understood. In speaking of faith we are referring to 'a firm and certain knowledge of God's benevolence toward us'.[71] Believing refers to a relation or relationship between persons. The definition refers to a favourable, kind and affectionate disposition (on God's part) which elicits a wholehearted 'Yes' in response (on the part of humans). This is the content which the bipolar context assigns to believing.

Certainly the expression 'twofold knowledge of God' must be read and interpreted with the critical eye of Calvin himself. His focus is always a knowledge of God in relation to us humans (*erga nos*), never a knowledge of God as he is in himself (*Deus in se*).[72] Calvin is averse to all speculation about God. Also the twofold knowledge of God is embedded in a bipolar context. The four general characteristics of the knowledge of God with which Dowey, by way of prolegomena, introduces his discussion of the knowledge of God[73] all flow naturally, immediately, and logically, *not* from the twofold knowledge of God, but from the knowledge of God and ourselves in their reciprocal relatedness.[74] In fact, Dowey regularly appeals to this rule,[75]

[70] See below, p. 190.

[71] 'divinae erga nos benevolentiae firmam certamque cognitionem' (*Institutes* 3.2.7 [CO 2:403]).

[72] See above, p. 178.

[73] 'Its accommodated, correlative, existential character; its clarity and comprehensibility' (Dowey, *Knowledge of God*, 3–40).

[74] Thus the correlative character of our knowledge of God follows immediately from Calvin's principle of the knowledge of God and of ourselves. In Dowey's exposition, however, this starting-point is made subordinate to 'its correlative character'. It is reduced to being 'understood as one of Calvin's basic epistemological propositions' (ibid., 19). But along with that Dowey gives a tendentious interpretation and limits the meaning of the Latin wording in which Calvin's principle is contained (cf. above, p. 17, n. 1).

[75] Already in the treatment of the knowledge of God the Creator there are important anthropological statements that correspond to this knowledge from the side of man (see above, pp. 179–80). With the knowledge of God the Redeemer, the opposite pole, fallen humanity, comes even more clearly into view. 'It presents the "knowledge of God and ourselves"', Dowey also says, but then weakens it by adding, 'only in so far as its objective source is concerned'

recommended by Calvin as 'almost the entire content of our wisdom'.[76]

Most striking, however, is the remarkable difference between the physiognomy with which Calvin's theology presents itself in Dowey's study and the approach I favour. Dowey's analysis has a sober, almost a philosophical, cast to it. Indeed, it makes one think of an epistemological treatise. One perceives almost nothing here of the intense back-and-forth movement between God and man, of the tension and explosiveness which marks their relationship. Is this difference merely a matter of style and design, another way of approaching the subject? I think not. The difference in approach also touches the material content; it touches Calvin's theology right into his Christology.[77]

The twofold knowledge of God is a legitimate starting-point for the understanding of Calvin's theology. The manner in which Edward A. Dowey Jr has developed it, for all the criticism I have advanced against it on these pages, is enriching. It is my hope that this too is apparent from this section.

Text A

About faith as knowledge[78]

When I call faith a form of knowledge I do not mean comprehension of the sort which usually comes into being of things which are accessible to the human sense. For faith is so far above sense that the human mind has to go beyond and rise above itself in order to believe. And even when the mind has done this, it does not grasp what it knows. But once it is persuaded of what it does not understand, by the very certainty of this persuasion it definitely knows more than if it understood something about human life by its own intellectual capacity. Paul, accordingly, beautifully calls it an understanding of length, breadth, depth and height, and a

---

(*Knowledge of God*, 148). He speaks, as the occasion arises, of a preference for 'the correlate knowledge' (ibid., 215, 252–3), but in fact refers repeatedly to the knowledge of God and man in their reciprocal relatedness. Cf. ibid., 20 and n. 73, 154, 197, 205–6, 208, 215.

[76] 'tota fere sapientiae nostrae summa' (*Institutes* 1.1.1 [CO 2:31]).

[77] See above, pp. 72–96.

[78] *Institutes* 3.2.14f. (CO 2:409–10).

knowledge that surpasses all knowledge, the knowledge, that is, of the love of Christ.[79] By this he tries to express that what our human mind embraces in faith is boundless in all directions. This form of knowing far surpasses all our understanding. Nevertheless the Lord has disclosed to believers the secret of his will which had been hidden for ages and generations.[80] On very good grounds, therefore, faith is called 'acknowledgment' in the Scriptures and described by John as 'knowledge'. For he testifies that believers know they are children of God.[81]

And this they know with great certainty. But this is more because divine truth has strengthened them in this conviction than because they arrived at this insight on the basis of intellectual arguments. Also Paul's words suggest this: 'while we are at home in the body we are away from the Lord, for we walk by faith, not by sight'.[82] By these words he indicates that what we know by faith is still far removed from us. It is still hidden from our eyes. For that reason I say: what we understand by faith belongs more to the realm of certainty than to that of understanding.

The original text:

Cognitionem dum vocamus, non intelligimus comprehensionem, qualis esse solet earum rerum quae sub humanum sensum cadunt. Adeo enim superior est, ut mentem hominis seipsam excedere et superare oporteat, quo ad illam pertingat. Neque etiam ubi pertigit, quod sentit assequitur: sed dum persuasum habet quod non capit, plus ipsa persuasionis certitudine intelligit quam si humanum aliquid sua capacitate perspiceret. Quare eleganter Paulus, qui id vocat comprehendere quae sit longitudo, latitudo, profunditas et sublimitas, et cognoscere supereminentem cognitioni dilectionem Christi. Voluit enim significare, modis omnibus infinitum esse quod mens nostra fide complectitur. et genus hoc cognitionis esse omni intelligentia longe sublimius. Quia tamen arcanum voluntatis suae, quod a seculis et generationibus absconditum erat, Dominus sanctis patefecit, optima ratione fides subinde in Scripturis agnitio vocatur: ab Ioanne vero scientia: quum fideles testatur scire se esse filios Dei.

Et sane certo sciunt: sed divinae veritatis persuasione confirmati magis quam rationali demonstratione edocti. Id indicant et Pauli

---

[79] Cf. Ephesians 3:18.
[80] Cf. Colossians 1:26; 2:21.
[81] Cf. 1 John 3:2.
[82] Cf. 2 Corinthians 5:6, 7.

verba, nos in hoc corpore habitantes, a Domino peregrinari: quia per fidem ambulamus, non per aspectum: quibus ostendit, ea quae per fidem intelligimus a nobis tamen abesse, et aspectum nostrum latere. Unde statuimus, fidei notitiam certitudine magis quam apprehensione contineri.

Text B

Faith is the principal work of the Holy Spirit[83]

Therefore, we cannot possibly come to Christ unless we are drawn by the Spirit of God. When we are thus drawn by him we are lifted up in mind and heart above our own understanding. For the soul is illumined by him and receives as it were a new keenness of vision with which to contemplate the heavenly mysteries, whereas before it shrank at sight of their radiant brilliance. And when the mind of man has thus been illumined by the light of the Holy Spirit, it truly begins to develop a feeling for the things of the kingdom of God, while before it was so foolish and dull it could not even taste them. When Christ plainly and clearly interpreted the mysteries of his kingdom to two of his followers, his interpretation fell on deaf ears.[84] Only after he opened their eyes did they understand the Scriptures.

The original text:

Quemadmodum ergo nisi Spiritu Dei tracti, accedere ad Christum nequaquam possumus: ita ubi trahimur, mente et animo evehimur supra nostram ipsorum intelligentiam. Nam ab eo illustrata anima novam quasi aciem sumit, qua caelestia mysteria contempletur, quorum splendore ante in seipsa perstringebatur. Atque ita quidem Spiritus sancti lumine irradiatus hominis intellectus, tum vere demum ea quae ad regnum Dei pertinent gustare incipit: antea prorsus ad ea delibanda fatuus et insipidus. Quamobrem Christus regni sui mysteria duobus discipulis praeclare edisserens, nihil tamen proficit, donec sensum illis aperit ut intelligant Scripturas.

It is only with great difficulty that we allow ourselves to be persuaded by God's promises. . . . A great many people confine

---

[83] *Institutes* 3.2.34 (CO 2:426–7). Cf. John 6:44.
[84] Cf. Luke 24:27, 45.

God's goodness within the strict boundaries of their own narrowness.[85]

Text C
Faith and experience[86]

Far different is the feeling of full-orbed maturity that in the Scriptures is always attributed to faith. It is this faith which puts God's goodness squarely in front of us. It is impossible to doubt it. But when this is the case we always sense its delightful sweetness and experience it within ourselves.[87]

Therefore the apostle derives trust from faith and from trust, in turn, boldness.[88]

. . . Here, indeed, is the main hinge on which faith turns: we must not think that the promises – so full of mercy – which the Lord offers are only valid outside of ourselves and not within ourselves. No: the idea is much more that we should embrace them within our heart and make them our own.

The original text:

Longe est alius sensus πληροφορίας, quae fidei semper in Scripturis tribuitur: nempe qui Dei bonitatem perspicue nobis propositam extra dubium ponat. Id autem fieri nequit, quin eius suavitatem vere sentiamus, et experiamur in nobis ipsis. Quare Apostolus ex fide deducit fiduciam, et ex hac rursum audaciam. . . . Hic praecipuus fidei cardo vertitur, ne quas Dominus offert misericordiae promissiones, extra nos tantum veras esse arbitremur, in nobis minime: sed ut potius eas intus complectendo nostras faciamus.

In Romans 8:38 Paul expresses his unshakable confidence that nothing can separate believers from the love of Christ.[89]

---

[85] Cf. *Institutes* 3.2.15 (CO 2:410).

[86] Ibid., 3.2.15–16 (CO 2:410–11).

[87] Sizoo (*Institutie*, 2:33) translates this as follows: 'En dit kan geschieden, zonder dat wij haar liefelijkheid naar waarheid gevoelen en in onszelf ervaren' ('And this can happen, without our truly feeling its loveliness and experiencing it in ourselves'). This is precisely the opposite of what Calvin is saying, giving a distorted picture of the relation between faith and experience that is so important for Calvin's theology.

[88] Cf. Ephesians 3:12.

[89] *Institutes* 3.2.16 (CO 2:411).

Text D

Faith and experience[90]

But someone will say: believers experience this very differently. For all their recognition of God's grace toward them, they are tormented by disquiet – and this does not happen infrequently. Even more: sometimes they are racked by the most severe terrors. So dreadfully vehement are the assaults which disturb and confuse them. This, it would seem, is hard to square with the certainty which faith furnishes. This problem, accordingly, calls for a solution if I want to maintain my previous teaching.

When I state that faith must be certain and inviolable I do not of course have in mind the kind of certainty that is exempt from all doubt. Nor do I mean the kind of untroubled existence that is not disturbed by any anxiety. On the contrary! I say that believers are constantly at war with their own unbelief. I certainly have no intention of furnishing their conscience any kind of idyllic shelter unaffected by passing tumults. On the other hand, however seriously they may be assailed, I deny that they will lose and be detached from the rock-solid confidence they have received from God's mercy.

The original text:

Atqui (dicet quispiam) longe aliud experiuntur fideles, qui in recognoscenda erga se Dei gratia non modo inquietudine tentantur (quod saepe illis contingit) sed gravissimis etiam terroribus interdum quatefiunt; tanta est ad deturbandas eorum mentes tentationum vehementia: id quod non satis videtur cum illa fidei certitudine cohaerere. Proinde nodus hic solvendus est si superiorem illam doctrinam stare volumus. Nos certe, dum fidem docemus esse debere certam ac securam, non certitudinem aliquam imaginamur quae nulla tangatur dubitatione, nec securitatem quae nulla sollicitudine impetatur: quin potius dicimus perpetuum esse fidelibus certamen cum sua ipsorum diffidentia; tantum abest ut eorum conscientias in placida aliqua quiete collocemus, quae nullis omnino turbis interpelletur. Rursum tamen, qualemcunque in modum afflictentur, decidere ac desciscere negamus a certa illa, quam de misericordia Dei conceperunt, fiducia.

[90] Ibid., 3.2.17 (CO 2:411–12).

3. William J. Bouwsma's portrait of Calvin

I will leave aside the question whether the interest of theologians and Calvin specialists in the historical Calvin has been, as Bouwsma says, 'at best marginal'.[91] On this point, it seems to me, there exists a feeling of impotence and resignation. Fresh sources which picture the man Calvin in a new light are not being tapped and the French Reformer himself is intentionally and systematically silent about himself.

Bouwsma has broken this silence. That is sensational. No less surprising is where he gets the key which provides a new opening in the search campaign for the historical Calvin. This key is forged, on the one hand, in the workshop of the Reformer's own oeuvre – and that in its totality – ; on the other, it is modelled after the fractured era by which also the person of John Calvin is marked. Here we have the two sources from which the author has drawn the materials for his fascinating portrait. Calvin, in Bouwsma's book, becomes a man of his time, with all the contradictions of it, a complex personality. But to those who have an eye and an ear for 'oblique modes of communication',[92] Calvin does say a lot about himself. Bouwsma has this gift and therein, besides his thorough knowledge of the humanism of Calvin's day, lies the real strength of his monograph.

The image that results from Bouwsma's Calvin study is a portrait of two Calvins coexisting within the same historical personage. One of these Calvins was a philosopher, a rational person, a schoolman in the high Scholastic tradition whose most important representative was Thomas Aquinas, the other 'a sceptical fideist' in the lineage of William of Ockham, 'flexible to the point of opportunism and a revolutionary in spite of himself'.[93]

The building-blocks from which this double image is constructed are contained in the paradoxical analysis which the author has made of the complex personality of John Calvin. 'Paradoxical',

[91] William J. Bouwsma, *John Calvin: A Sixteenth-Century Portrait* (New York, 1988), 1. For reactions to Bouwsma's study, see I. J. Hesselink, 'Reactions to Bouwsma's Portrait of "John Calvin"', in *Calvinus Sacrae Scripturae Professor*, ed. W. H. Neuser (Grand Rapids, 1994), 209–13.

[92] Bouwsma, *John Calvin*, 5.

[93] Ibid., 230–1.

however, is too weak a word in this connection. Bouwsma's conclusion is the end of a journey which takes the reader past inconsistencies, past undeniable direct contradictions.

The following are a few striking examples:

- Calvin is reserved with respect to *artistic* wall embellishments. They violate 'the simple nature of things'.[94] He is against pomp and display in the worship service.[95] On the other hand, he asserts that 'sculpture and painting are gifts of God'.[96] He has special words of praise for religious music;[97] a person may without anxiety enjoy music. It is a gift of God.[98]

- Calvin expresses himself negatively about *women*. They continually threaten to disturb orderly, clearly marked boundaries.[99] All too often men are corrupted by their wives.[100] A wife is subject to her husband.[101] To Calvin, women in positions of leadership is an 'unnatural monstrosity'.[102] On the other hand, he speaks with deep respect about women.

[94] Ibid., 58. 'ac si appeterent homines mutare simplicem rerum naturam' (*Prael. Jer.* 22:14 [CO 38:385]).

[95] Bouwsma, *John Calvin*, 62. 'Toti . . . in puppis, tanquam pueri occupantur. At vera ecclesiae dignitas . . . interior est' (*Comm. Is.* 49:18 [CO 37:207]).

[96] Bouwsma, *John Calvin*, 135. 'Sed quia sculptura et pictura Dei dona sunt, purum et legitimum utriusque usum requiro' (*Institutes* 1.11.12 [CO 2:83]).

[97] Bouwsma, *John Calvin*, 225. 'quando nullum, melodiae genus vel tristis ac severi carminis Deus omittit, quo nos ad se trahat, nos vero saxei iacemus' (*Comm. Luc.* 7:33 [CO 45:307]).

[98] Bouwsma, *John Calvin*, 135. 'Artium enim et aliarum rerum inventio quae ad communem vitae usum et commoditatem valent, donum est Dei minime spernendum et virtus laude digna' (*Comm. Gen.* 4:20 [CO 23:99]).

[99] Bouwsma, *John Calvin*, 52–3. 'mais elle voudroit se faire valoir, comme si David tenoit la couronne d'elle, par manière dire. Et on en verra beaucoup de telles au monde' (*Sermon XIX sur II Sam.* 6:20, in *Predigten über das 2. Buch Samuelis*, ed. Hanns Rückert, vol. 1 of *Supplementa Calviniana: Sermons Inedits* [Neukirchen, 1936–61], 164:4–5). Cf. also *Sermon XII sur I Cor.* 11:4–10 (CO 49:733).

[100] Bouwsma, *John Calvin*, 53. 'Car on verra souuent que les maris sont corrompus par les femmes' (*Sermon XIX sur II Sam.*, 165:5–6).

[101] Bouwsma, *John Calvin*, 76. 'qu'il est chef. Et de qui? Des femmes' (*Sermon XII sur I Cor.* 11:4–10 [CO 49:724]).

[102] Bouwsma, *John Calvin*, 76. 'Nam γυναικοκρατίαν omnes prudentes semper instar portenti repudiarunt' (*Comm. I Tim.* 2:13 [CO 52:276]).

Spiritually they are equal to men;[103] in fact, in principle, he sees no objections to entrusting high church positions to women.[104]

- The human *body,* on the one hand, is a source of wickedness.[105] It is a hindrance to the recognition of God as the source of a well-ordered life.[106] It is not only the prison of the soul, but worse, 'carrion, trash, corruption', a source of infection that defiles the whole person.[107] On the other hand, Calvin states emphatically that 'our bodies are, in their essence, good creations of God'.[108] 'The body is a miracle attesting to God's wisdom and power.'[109] For that

[103] Bouwsma, *John Calvin,* 138. Bouwsma's reference to *Comm. Joh.* 1:13 is not convincing, for what is involved here is a statement of faith: 'quod filii Dei censemur, non esse hoc naturae nostrae proprium' (CO 47:12). This says nothing about the 'spiritual equality of women', unless by 'spiritual' the author means here 'in the perspective of faith'.

[104] Bouwsma, *John Calvin,* 138. But what is involved here is an exception: 'earum tamen infirmitati ignoscens [Christus] singulari honore dignatus est, munus apostolicum viris ereptum ad breve tempus resignans'. But what Calvin adds here is revealing: 'Atque hoc modo specimen eius, quod Paulus docet (1 Cor. 1:27) exhibuit, nempe quod eligat quae stulta sunt ac debilia in mundo, ut carnis altitudinem humiliet' (*Comm. Mc.* 16:1 [CO 45:792–3]).

[105] Bouwsma, *John Calvin,* 80. Bouwsma is completely wrong when he refers to *Sermon XXXIX sur Job* 10:7–15 (CO 33:483) in support of this statement. This passage proves the contrary earlier, when Calvin speaks of human propagation and marvels at it that from 'la semence humaine ... d'une chose honteuse et dont on n'ose parler' something so glorious as the human body appears. 'tant de miracles en un corps, et qu'il nous monstre là une si belle image et tant vive de sa maiesté'. It is beyond understanding.

[106] Bouwsma, *John Calvin,* 80. The reference to *Institutes* 3.10.3 is biased and incorrect. Calvin is criticizing there the *unbridled* desire to enjoy eating and drinking and expensive clothing. 'Ubi gratiarum actio, si te epulis aut vino ita ingurgites ... Ubi in vestibus gratitudo erga Deum etc'. (CO 2:530).

[107] Bouwsma, *John Calvin,* 80. 'en ceste prison de leur chair ... corps mortel, loge pleine de toute puantise et infection' (*Sermon XIII sur Job* [CO 33:170]). Cf. also G. Babelotzky, *Platonische Bilder und Gedankengänge in Calvins Lehre vom Menschen* (Wiesbaden, 1977).

[108] Bouwsma, *John Calvin,* 134. 'Il est vrai que nos corps en leur essence sont creatures de Dieu bonnes' (*Sermon LVIII sur Job* 15:11–16 [CO 33:728]).

[109] Bouwsma, *John Calvin,* 134. 'Iob donc veut ici exprimer la sagesse infinie de Dieu, laquelle se declare en la forme humaine: comme s'il disoit. Et Seigneur destruiras-tu un ouvrage si excellent, là où on peut voir ta sagesse, ta vertu, ta bonté inestimable pour te glorifier?' (*Sermon XXXIX sur Job* 10:7–15 [CO 33:481–2]).

reason humans are entitled to enjoy music (as we heard earlier)[110] but also sex and a good glass of wine, in a word, the good things of life.[111] For God 'delights us with his delicacies'.[112]

- Calvin articulates the nature of *faith* in two different ways. They suggest contrary ways of thinking. On the one hand, faith is intellectual assent to a body of doctrinal propositions.[113] Here we see the cerebral character of Calvin's theology coming to the fore.

  On the other hand, faith, according to him, is a matter of the heart.[114] It is wholistic, proceeding as it does from the spiritual centre of the entire person. Visible in the latter description is the influence of a biblically-oriented humanism.

- On the one hand, Calvin seems to regard *creatureliness* itself as culpable. This is how Bouwsma interprets a sermon by Calvin on Job.[115]

  On the other hand, Calvin is continually elated over nature which tells of God and his glory.[116]

---

[110] See above, nn. 97, 98.

[111] Bouwsma, *John Calvin*, 136. 'nostro vitio fieri si eius benignitas irritamentum est luxuriae' (*Comm. Joh.* 2:8 [CO 47:41]).

[112] Bouwsma, *John Calvin*, 135. 'sed ut nos coelestis pater suis delitiis suaviter oblectet' (*Comm. Gen.* 43:33 [CO 23:545]).

[113] Bouwsma, *John Calvin*, 99. 'quia supramodum noxia doctrinae vel minima deformatio' (*Comm. II Tim.* 1:13 [CO 52:356]).

[114] Bouwsma, *John Calvin*, 157–8. *Institutes* 3.2.1, 8. Cf. Text C above, p. 189.

[115] Bouwsma, *John Calvin*, 42: 'He saw guilt in creatureliness itself.' For this statement Bouwsma refers to *Sermon LI sur Job* 13:16–22 (CO 33:633). This passage talks about 'deux especes de la iustice de Dieu', which God's law demands, and 'une iustice plus haute en Dieu', according to which he would be able to condemn even the angels (cf. Job. 4:18). The aforementioned conclusion that Bouwsma draws from this indeed problematic passage, in my judgment goes too far. Even if humanity could fulfill God's law perfectly (which is impossible, says Calvin), there is still a justice in God that nothing can 'suffire ni satisfaire'. Calvin wants to emphasize God's absolute transcendence, not the sinfulness of the creature. Cf. Susan E. Schreiner, 'Exegesis and Double Justice in Calvin's Sermons on Job, *Church History* 58 (1989), 322–38.

[116] Bouwsma, *John Calvin*, 103–4, 174. 'multiplices avium cantus (qui tamen nos ad Deum glorificandum incitant)' (*Comm. Mt.* 26:75 [CO 45:744]).

- Calvin is devastatingly negative in his assessment of *humanity*. What we have inherited from our mother's womb is only common and despicable.[117]

  Alongside of these sentiments, however, he does not shrink from citing a saying from Ovid: 'Humans are by nature shaped to contemplate the heavens and so to learn to know their author.'[118] Even more strongly: Look within, says Calvin, and you will find God.[119]

These last two examples can be supplemented with numerous quotations from the preceding pages. But precisely in those instances where Calvin expresses himself in extremely negative terms on the creation and humanity, it is clear that we are dealing with pronouncements of faith which require theological reflection, an approach from which Bouwsma expressly dissociates himself.[120] This faith perspective, which takes sin with absolute seriousness, is different from the perspective from which the original intentions (*genuinus ordo*)[121] of the Creator vis-à-vis humanity must be viewed. I discussed this thematic complex in connection with free will[122] and in my discussion of Dowey's analysis of the twofold knowledge of God in Calvin's theological thought this view is confirmed.[123]

It is incorrect to view theologically intended statements (e.g. where Calvin contemptuously characterizes humanity in the light of sin as 'mere filth')[124] as being opposed to and contradictory of statements in which he expresses himself appreciatively and positively about humanity. We have given examples of the

---

[117] Bouwsma, *John Calvin*, 36. 'nos ex utero nihil afferre praeter meras sordes' (*Comm. Acta* 15:9 [CO 48:346]).

[118] Bouwsma, *John Calvin*, 73. 'Os homini sublime dedit, coelumque videre Iussit, et erectos ad sidera tollere vultus' (Ovid, *Metamorphoses* 1:84; cited in *Comm. Is.* 40:26 [CO 37:25]).

[119] Bouwsma, *John Calvin*, 104. *Institutes* 1.5.4 (CO 2:43): 'ut homo in corpore suo et anima centies Deum reperiens'. Cf. also n. 182 below.

[120] Bouwsma, *John Calvin*, 3.

[121] See above, p. 181.

[122] See above, pp. 46–62.

[123] See above, pp. 177–82.

[124] See above, n. 117.

latter category as well. This is not 'ambivalence',[125] because the perspective from which, and the context in which, these different-sounding pronouncements are made is different.

But, I ask, can one ignore the faith perspective when producing a 'portrait' of Calvin? Bouwsma's hypothesis concerning the role of anxiety in Calvin's life and thought inevitably, as will appear, triggers this question.

To a degree unknown until now, as we learn from countless passages, Calvin's life and thought were dominated by fear and anxiety. Bouwsma's Calvin is a man downright afflicted by anxiety, an anxiety which faithfully mirrors the brokenness of his own time.

To overcome his anxiety a supersensitive Calvin, on the one hand, took refuge in the established certainties handed down to him from the past. But this takes him into a labyrinth from which he can no longer escape. On the other hand, he felt powerfully drawn to the humanism which looks at man with new eyes and describes its knowledge as conviction (*persuasio*) based on experience.[126] But also this second road, a road which points to the future, is full of menace. It leads past an abyss of emptiness and meaninglessness. 'The Labyrinth' and 'the Abyss' are the famous metaphors which typically describe Bouwsma's work. These two metaphors underlie the picture of the two Calvins we encounter in this study. Both of them also serve to document the battle this reformer fought against anxiety.

The question is whether this anxiety was really that dominant in Calvin's life. The theme of anxiety is omnipresent, as it were, in this book and the author devotes a separate chapter to it.

Calvin nowhere speaks of his own anxiety in the I-form of the present tense. Nevertheless Bouwsma rightly refers to a number of statements which, though made in the first person plural,

---

[125] Bouwsma, *John Calvin*, 142. Statements like 'Emotionally, if not theologically, a large part of Calvin remained pagan' (ibid., 88) and '[Calvin's] relative confidence in the powers of human reason' (ibid., 104) give a distorted and misleading picture of Calvin's theological thinking.

[126] In humanist usage the term *persuasio* characterized faith also. The Strasbourg Reformer Martin Bucer characterized faith in this way, taking over this terminology from Laurentius Valla via Guillaume Budé. See de Kroon, *Martin Bucer*, 144–5, 121, n. 3.

unmistakably convey the author's own feelings of anxiety. The following is an example: 'The moment a suspicious noise occurs in the night a shudder of terror passes through our whole body.'[127]

Sometimes, however, these pronouncements are so general that they hardly mean anything, certainly with respect to Calvin's life, like the following: 'The greater the attachment of parents to their children, the more anxiously are they worried about them and do they watch over them.'[128]

Of much greater weight is a fundamental statement of Calvin which recurs no less than three times. It reads as follows: 'We know' – thus Calvin frequently introduces a strong and positive statement which cannot be challenged – 'that this is a benefit to be desired above all other things: to be free from every kind of fear, and not to be tormented or frightened by any care.'[129]

In listing the consequences of anxiety Bouwsma appeals to a text in which no mention of terror occurs but which does refer to people who devote themselves too vehemently and fanatically (*ad rem nimis attenti*) to a cause.[130] They are in a sense their own executioners. Ironically enough, the characterization of this sort of people strongly reminds the reader of the author's own character. . . .

In connection with the meaning of *anxietas, angustia* and *labyrinth* and in reference to the description of Noah's stay in the ark (*Comm. Ps.* 71:5; CO 31, 655ff. and *Inst.* II, 10,10; CO 2, 319), Bouwsma suggests (op. cit., 47) that Calvin was

---

[127] 'sed simul atque increpuit aliquid noctu, terror omnes sensus nostros occupat' (*Prael. Jer.* 20:14–16 [CO 38:355]). Cf. also the statements about anxiety in *Comm. Is.* 13:1 (CO 36:260): 'Conturbamur vel ad minimam mutationem, atque horrescimus'; ibid., 59:10 (CO 37:343): 'tanta anxietate premi'; *Prael. Jer.* 38:20–2 (CO 39:173): 'nemo est nostrum, quem non perturbant multae curae'; *Comm. Ps.* 30:6 (CO 31:295): 'fieri non potest quin assidue anxie simus et trepidi'.

[128] 'Nam quo maior est eorum indulgentia in liberos, eo magis anxie illis timent ac cavent' (*Comm. I Cor.* 7:36 [CO 49:424]). Cf. also *Prael. Jer.* 18:1–6 (CO 38:296): 'nihil stabile in hac vita'; *Comm. Ps.* 119:30 (CO 32:227): 'vitam hominum esse quasi in bivio'.

[129] 'Scimus autem bonum hoc prae aliis optabile, nempe vacuum esse omni metu, nec torqueri vel angi ulla cura' (*Comm. Ps.* 4:9 ([CO 31:64]). Cf. *Prael. Jer.* 30:10 (CO 38:619–22), and *Sermon LXVIII sur Job* 18:14–15 (CO 34:80).

[130] 'Scimus enim eos qui sunt ad rem nimis attenti se ipsos conficere, et quodammodo sibi esse carnifices. . . .' (*Prael. Jer.* 12:13 [CO 38:145]).

claustrophobic. Parallel to this, he similarly sees signs of claustrophobia in Calvin's description of the fetus in his mother's womb (*Comm. Ps.* 22:10; CO 31, 226). In my opinion, this ignores the context and intent of the places cited. This is especially true of the interpretation of *Ps.* 22:10 where Calvin speaks of 'the grave' of a mother's womb in order thereby to accentuate all the more strikingly the miracle of the birth (*vilescuit quidem hoc miraculum assiduo usu,* l.c.) and to highlight from the very first moment God's care which brings this about (*arcana et incomprehensibili virtute,* ibid.). Also Bouwsma's reference in this connection to Calvin's 'almost Manichean revulsion . . . toward human physicality' raises questions.[131]

Calvin calls *dread of conscience* a terror (*horror*). He knew the phenomenon himself. It comes over people when they have the courage to look at themselves before the face of God. 'Whenever I cast a glance at myself or raised my eyes to you, extreme terror seized me.' Calvin wrote this confession in his letter to Sadoleto,[132] But this is a once-for-all experience which often marks a conversion story. In time he apparently overcame this exceptional terror of conscience. But did he overcome all such terror?

'A more cruel executioner doesn't exist',[133] he says, and Bouwsma adds that Calvin continued to have an anxious conscience. To substantiate this he refers to two statements one of which – derived from his treatment of the question of predestination – is the more convincing:

> From time to time the same thought occurs to me, viz. that there is a danger that I am not doing justice to God's mercy. The truth is I stress it with such painstaking precision (*anxietas*)[134] as though it concerned something doubtful and obscure.

---

[131] See above, nn. 108, 109.

[132] 'Quoties . . . in me descendebam . . . extremus horror' (CO 5:412).

[133] 'nullus saevior carnifex esse potest' (*Comm. Is.* 57:20 [CO 37:321]).

[134] 'qui tanta anxietate in ea asserenda laborem' (*Institutes* 3.14.6 [CO 2:567]; cf. above, p. 175, n. 18). The other example is taken from Calvin's commentary on Joshua 2:1, where the Jewish leader takes extensive measures to scout the land and the city of Jericho. Calvin wavers between wondering whether he ought to approve of this behavior by Joshua and wondering whether Joshua's excessive anxiety (*nimia sollicitudo*) warrants disapproval (*Comm. Jos.* 2:1 [CO 25:438]).

In contrast to synonyms for anxiety (*timor, horror, terror, angor, metus*) Calvin not infrequently uses it in a metaphorical sense and then it means: 'oppressive and painful precision or intensity'. In the example before us, precisely from a literary viewpoint, the latter meaning is to be preferred.

This construal of a much-used term in a discussion of *Calvin's* anxiety is not unimportant. The examples cited below may confirm the metaphorical use of the expression in Calvin's diction.

- [Concerning the pastor] 'If anyone is responsible for such a large household he must apply himself with intense dedication (*anxio studio*) to this cause.'[135]

- 'There is not a single reason for us to start a vehement discussion (*anxie disputemus*) about the knowledge, competence, and wisdom of the Chaldeans.'[136]

- 'We know how intensely others labour (*anxie laborent*) to leave their whole fortune to their children.'[137]

- 'The more attached parents are to their children, the more they worry about them and watch over them.'[138]

- Sometimes the term *sollicitus* is used in this sense as well: 'It is necessary for us to practice patience with intense expectation (*sollicita expectatione*).'[139]

While it is possible that Calvin possessed a nervous anxious conscience, he certainly was meticulous and conscientious.

Anxiety and faith

Sometimes statements about fear and anxiety suddenly appear in the perspective of faith. Calvin regularly makes statements about the fear of death which sound like proverbial sayings. 'Countless deaths threaten us.'[140] 'The fear of death is worse than death

---

[135] *Comm. I Tim.* 3:15 (CO 52:287); cf. Bouwsma, *John Calvin*, 38.

[136] *Prael. Dan.* 1:4 (CO 40:539); Bouwsma, *John Calvin*, 39.

[137] *Comm. Gen.* 50:22 (CO 23:621); Bouwsma, *John Calvin*, 38.

[138] *Comm. I Cor.* 7:36 (CO 49:424); Bouwsma, *John Calvin*, 38.

[139] *Comm. Gen.* 24:21 (CO 23:335); Bouwsma, *John Calvin*, 44–5. Cf. also above, p. 198, n. 134.

[140] 'sunt innumerae ... quot mortes inde nobis impendent' (*Prael. Ez.* 5:18 [CO 40:135]).

itself.'[141] But then all a sudden we read this statement about the fear of death:

> Aversion to death is something natural. Human beings can never totally overcome this aversion. They want to escape death; they are afraid of it. Nevertheless they must overcome this fear by faith.[142]

Especially in his commentary on the Psalms this fear of death and the power of faith play a large role. Calvin identifies with King David who was threatened by death:

> David acknowledges his fear but adds that by his faith in the goodness of God he has managed to persevere. Now this is a real test of our faith: fears torment us – this is how it feels in our weakness – yet, inwardly, we remain undaunted. Indeed, fear and hope seem rather to be opposing emotions. How can they possibly dwell in the same heart! But experience proves that ultimately hope is in control where fear occupies a part of our heart.[143]

Faith is a fundamental reality. Calvin's genuine fear must be viewed in this perspective.

Anxiety and amazement

In studying the texts to which Bouwsma appeals in his chapter on Calvin's anxiety one is struck by the fact that Calvin forges a close connection between fear (or anxiety) and amazement. Bouwsma, having noted this connection, gives expression to it in the observation that 'there is awe as well as terror in his accounts of the turbulence of nature'.[144] But this connection, mind you, is of great importance. Does it not also cast a different light on Calvin's fears? Calvin fears, and has deep respect for, nature. He

---

[141] 'mirus horror, in quo plus mali quam in morte ipsa' (*Comm. Acta* 2:24 [CO 48:41]).

[142] 'fide tamen vincendus est metus' (*Comm. II. Tim.* 4:6 [CO 52:389]).

[143] '. . . fidei nostrae examen . . . sed experientia ostendit vere demum illic spem regnare ubi partem cordis occupat timor' (*Comm. Ps.* 56:4 [CO 31:548]). Cf. Richard A. Hasler, 'The Influence of David and the Psalms upon John Calvin's Life and Thought', in *The Biography of Calvin*, vol. 1 of *Articles on Calvin and Calvinism*, ed. Richard C. Gamble (New York, 1992), 87–98.

[144] Bouwsma, *John Calvin*, 33.

is particularly impressed by the threat of water, of the sea, 'It seems the sea threatens to plunge the earth into the abyss.'[145]

Calvin's cosmological insights are markedly unsecularized. He wants nothing to do with secondary causes or normativities which control natural processes. To focus on them, says Calvin, is to be like a person who only stares 'at the edges of another's fingernails but does not deign to look at his face'.[146] But that face is Calvin's concern. His awe at nature, the sudden changes which occur in it, invariably prompts him to marvel at the majesty of God. 'So then, let us not be so blind in contemplating the sky that we do not perceive this vivid image of the majesty of God.'[147]

And this perception, in turn, leads to encouragement, hope and confidence. The movement between God and man comes around full circle. It leads from fear, by way of awe and amazement, to admiration and thence back to hope and confidence.

In a lecture on Jeremiah 31, Calvin draws encouragement for the church from the contemplation of nature:

> The cycles of the sun and the moon, as well as those of the stars, run along fixed and certain courses . . . so certain will be the salvation in store for my church.[148]

Calvin can be amazed. This gift is part of his physiognomy. Without his amazement, an amazement which prompts him to create impressive formulations, some element of correct interpretation is lacking in his portrait.

The crossing of boundaries, pollution, and sin

Stability, order and harmony[149] – these are the properties Calvin admires so much in nature. 'This order of the providence of God

---

[145] 'Il semble que la mer menace la terre de l'abysmer' (*Sermon XCVI sur Job* 26:8-14 [CO 34:435]); 'une chose si effrayante' (ibid.).

[146] 'praeterita tota facie, intuitum in extremos tantum ungues defigat' (*Comm. Ps.* 29:5 [CO 31:289]).

[147] *Sermon XCVI sur Job* 26:8–14 (CO 34:434).

[148] *Prael. Jer.* 31:35-6 (CO 38:698–9): '. . . tam certa erit salus ecclesiae meae' (699).

[149] Through our sin, says Calvin, we have brought everything into disarray, heaven and earth. If we would really orient ourselves steadfastly in obedience to God, 'undoubtedly all the elements would strike up a song, and we would then hear in our world a heavenly melody [quasi angelicam melodiam]' (*Prael. Jer.* 5:25 [CO 38:635]). A phrase of great charm (cf. below, n. 187).

... so that each man has his rights, so that things are not jumbled together. ...'[150] Everything that threatens this divinely-willed order irritates and frightens him. In his thought 'the leaping over boundaries' is a standard formula with a negative connotation.[151] The consequence of leaping over boundaries is confusion, pollution, contagion, sin. For it is God's order that is being disturbed. This is also how he characterizes the fall: it is a horrendous muddle.[152]

Bouwsma has depicted – strikingly and comprehensively – this characteristic feature of Calvin's thought. In all sorts of areas the concepts cited above return. At the same time they lead us onto the track of Calvin's fears.

> Bouwsma even thinks he is spotting fear in Calvin's description of the escape of the two spies over the city walls of Jericho (*Comm. Jos.* 2, 14; CO 25, 444). This escape in some obscure way troubled Calvin, says Bouwsma, since, according to Calvin, 'it is criminal to leap over walls' (o.c., 35). In Calvin's thought, however, there is no sign of alarm or anxiety in this case, nor is this an obscure point. For it is clear from what follows in his commentary that Calvin here raised a well-known classic problem in connection with which the authority of Cicero is at stake and an appeal is made to the law which guarantees the security of city walls, obviously a matter of vital importance in those days (l.c. 445)

From *Prael. Jer.* 22:14 ('I will build me a grand house ... with windows ...') Bouwsma concludes that Calvin disliked Gothic churches 'because their walls were opened up by broad windows' (op. cit., 35)! And this while Calvin says no more than that in the circumstances of that day it was extravagant (*pars luxuriae*). Cf. CR 38, 384–5.

Calvin repeatedly shows his strong aversion to everything that pollutes and infects. In this connection Bouwsma speaks of an 'almost obsessive pollution imagery'.[153] Along with this he also

[150] *Sermon LXXXI sur Job* 22:16–21 (CO 34:246).
[151] *Comm. I Cor.* 7:25 (CO 49:417): 'limites transsilire'; *Comm. I. Tim.* 6:7 (CO 52:326): 'fines transsilire'; *Comm. Mt.* 6:27 (CO 45:210): 'fines suos transsilire'.
[152] 'ex lapsu primi hominis nihil praeter horrendam confusionem cernamus ...' (*Comm. Is.* 51:16 [CO 37:237]).
[153] Bouwsma, *John Calvin*, 36.

states that in using this imagery Calvin is referring to sin. The latter puts this in his own way as follows:

> From our mother's womb on we bring with us nothing in life that is not polluted. There is nothing in us that is fit to repair the breach between us and God.[154]

By reference to this total pollution Calvin articulates the radical breach with God that originated as a result of sin. Certainly this human catastrophe could hardly be described more succinctly. Bouwsma, referring to Calvin's 'almost obsessive pollution imagery', adds that it is 'inconsistent with much else in his understanding of the human condition'.[155]

Why inconsistent? In the perspective of faith, from the perspective of sin, a radical breach occurred in the divine–human relation, a breach no human being can heal. But this fact does not obliterate the excellent qualities which Calvin elsewhere attributes to humanity and which make humanity the crown jewel of creation.[156] The position from which these very different assessments of man are made by Calvin differs in each case.

But on this basis to speak of 'two Calvins' in the one historical person, as Bouwsma does, is devoid of all substance, however fascinating – and stimulating for further historical research – his portrait of Calvin may be. Moreover, on the basis of the above analysis, I want to observe by way of summary that, though anxiety in Calvin's work plays a remarkable role, it is not as dominant as Bouwsma sets out to demonstrate in his chapter on Calvin's anxiety.

4. In search of God: the majesty of God and Calvin's self-knowledge

> This is the true wisdom: we must in the first place look toward God and then, in the second place, each person must cast a look within himself and there examine himself thoroughly.[157]

---

[154] 'Quum dico pollutionis damnari totum humanum genus, intelligo nos ex utero nihil afferre praeter meras sordes, nec quidquam esse in natura nostra rectitudinis, quod nos Deo conciliet' (*Comm. Acta* 15:9 [CO 48:346]).

[155] Bouwsma, *John Calvin*, 36.

[156] See above, p. 173, nn. 10, 11.

[157] CO 33:221–32 (quotation from 227).

The knowledge of God and the knowledge of oneself – at this point the second principle, self-knowledge, is emphasized[158] – Calvin posits as a principle of wisdom in a sermon on Job 5:3–7.

This statement immediately brings to mind the basic rule or principle with which Calvin opens his *Institutes* and which also constitutes the starting-point and basis for this study.

Naturally the context as well as the setting is a different one here. Eliphaz remonstrates with Job about the nature of folly, sin, and malediction. Self-reflection is needed, says Calvin, before we judge others. Before God's face everyone must turn inward. People will then discover their own failure and their own poverty. Only then, according to Calvin, a person is sufficiently prepared to judge the conduct of foolish people.[159]

The wisdom Calvin recommends here is conspicuously ethical in character. It is practical wisdom, wisdom for living, which determines one's attitude toward God and one's fellow human beings.

This need for turning inward, for introspection and self-knowledge, is typical of Calvin. 'First, just take a look at your own inward self', he says, 'and when you then venture to stand before God, not much remains of the good impression you have of yourself.'[160] Calvin can only make such statements because he in fact practices the difficult art of self-knowledge. Particularly when in connection with questions of faith Calvin appeals to experience, we are listening to a man who has become wise through self-knowledge. If one believes with a full-orbed faith, he says, doubt is excluded. Then one experiences in person how utterly sweet God's goodness is. Then what he promises penetrates one's very heart.[161]

Bitter experiences of faith have purified him. He knows from personal experience about doubts, unrest, and continual struggle. But despite all this his confidence is intact.[162]

---

[158] '. . . un chacun doit entrer en soy, et examiner son etat et sa vie' (ibid., 223).

[159] Ibid., 227.

[160] See above, p. 174, nn. 15, 16.

[161] See above, p. 189 (Text C).

[162] See above, p. 190 (Text D).

Especially revelatory of his inner life is Calvin's commentary on the Psalms.[163] Aside from its introduction this work, too, is lacking in autobiographical data. It is rich, however, in detailing the experiences of faith. In his exposition of the Psalms he shows how impressed he is by the grandeur of God. In this connection he spontaneously refers to Psalm 145.[164] In translation or paraphrase – I will let the reader decide which it is – I will record here a few fragments of Calvin's commentary on this psalm and let him speak in the first person:

God's grandeur

God's greatness is immeasurable. Before his immeasurable power I am struck dumb. It makes me ecstatic.[165]

God's works! Inapprehensible! They are so many marvels which my senses cannot assimilate.[166]

God's grandeur is not concealed in his mysterious essence . . . for true religion has nothing to do with speculation. Its knowledge is directed toward the practice of life.[167]

God's goodness

Nothing moves me more than his goodness, the goodness with which he comes toward me and shows me: I am your Father.[168]

Nature – it is simply magnificent how everything has its place there! It lets God's goodness shine out plainly, even brilliantly. But the

---

[163] One sees in the book of Psalms, as in a mirror, what takes place in the innermost life. 'I have been accustomed to call this book . . . "An Anatomy of all the Parts of the Soul [ἀνατομὴν omnium animae partium]"' (Calvin, CO 31:15). Cf. James A. De Jong, '"An Anatomy of All Parts of the Soul": Insights into Calvin's Spirituality from His Psalms Commentary', in *Calvinus Sacrae Scripturae Professor*, ed. Neuser, 1–14.

[164] See above, p. 180, n. 39.

[165] 'Magnitudinem Dei immensam esse, ad immensitatem potentiae eius quasi obstupescimus, vel rapimur in ecstasin' (CO 32:413; comm. on v. 1).

[166] 'Verba mirabilium pro incomprehensibili operum Dei ratione accipio: quia totidem sunt miracula quae sensus nostros absorbent' (ibid., comm. on v. 5).

[167] 'Dei magnitudinem non latere in arcana eius essentia . . . : quum vera religio non speculativam, sed practicam notitiam requirat' (ibid.).

[168] 'nihil tamen magis nos afficit quam eius bonitas qua ad nos descendit, seque patrem exhibet' (CO 32:414; comm. on v. 7).

majority of people close their eyes to it and ignore it. For that reason the image David makes of it is so splendid: God who with his own hand distributes food to every living thing.[169]

That food is the work of his goodness: proofs of his love.[170]

Even though Calvin is ecstatic, his self-knowledge has not ceased to be sober:

God's indispensable help

How numerous are the questions still left which make me uncertain. How often do I have to beg God for help. And then how, with my feet dragging, I approach him. Sometimes I seem broken; then again I am so heavily afflicted that I threaten to perish. Sometimes my faith languishes and I am afraid. Therefore David proclaims with emphasis: all who call on God depend on him for help. To this rule there are no exceptions.[171]

This kind of text expresses better and more insistently than Calvin's other writings (including his doctrinal writings) what God meant to Calvin personally. They show us how he experienced God. This is also the category in which Calvin is most a 'theologian' and in which, in my opinion, he is also the most existential and current.

At the same time we cannot help noting that in these personal pronouncements, 'confessions', he spontaneously falls back on experience.[172] What comes through loud and clear is the voice of

---

[169] 'Concinna est hypothesis, quia enim miram Dei bonitatem quae in pulcerrimo hoc naturae ordine conspicua refulget, maior pars clausis oculis praeterit, Deum porrecta manu cibum animalibus distribuentem inducit David' (CO 32:417; comm. on v. 16).

[170] 'Alimenta enim effectus sunt huius beneplaciti, sicut χαρίσματα τῆς χάριτος' (ibid.).

[171] 'Iam vero quia multae nobis dubitationes obrepunt, quoties rogandus est Deus, atque ita vel trepide accedimus, vel fracti et examinati deficimus, vel metu languescit fides: ideo sine exceptione pronunciat David Deum omnibus qui ipsum invocant exorabilem esse (CO 32:418; comm. on v. 18)

[172] It is self-evident that the large role that *experience* plays in Calvin's theology has not escaped the notice of scholars. Cf. W. Balke, 'The Word of God and Experientia according to Calvin', in *Calvinus Ecclesiae Doctor*, ed. W. H. Neuser (Kampen, 1978), 19–31. On the basis of an etymological examination and – characteristically enough – with frequent reference to Calvin's Psalms commentary, Balke draws a comprehensive and vivid picture of the role of experience

nature, the witness of creation. Apparently here too the saying of the *Institutes experientia magistra* ('experience as teacher') is un-qualifiedly true.[173] These are statements of *faith* which Calvin makes (always he thinks and defines things from this perspective and is subject to the direction of the Word – *scriptura duce et magistra*)[174] but he nevertheless refers with warmth and conviction to 'the marvellous goodness of God which clearly and purely shines forth from the structure of creation. . . .'[175] My senses cannot assimilate it'.[176] I have extensively discussed the connectedness between Scripture and experience above.[177]

In this school of experience, the work of art which is God's creation,[178] he was introduced to God's majesty and speaks of it so frequently because he meets him there afresh every day. A person only needs to open their eyes.[179] As preacher of God's majesty, Calvin is not unique but he is certainly extraordinary. That majesty is utterly unimaginable and incomprehensible, but it *can be* experienced and perceived. The place of encounter with God, par excellence, is the human being himself:

> Humanity is divine. And would it not recognize its Creator? What kind of logic is that?[180]

> There is no need, says Paul, for us to step outside of ourselves. All those who meticulously examine themselves will find God within.[181]

> How utterly detestable, I ask you, is this nonsense that humans, finding God in their body and soul a hundred times over, on this very pretense of excellence deny that there is a God.[182]

---

in Calvin's theological thought, while recognizing at the same time that it is difficult to define clearly the place of experience within Calvin's theology.

[173] See above, p. 180, n. 40.

[174] See above, p. 180, n. 43.

[175] See above, p. 206, n. 169.

[176] See above, p. 205, n. 166.

[177] See above, pp. 178–82.

[178] See above, p. 182, n. 50.

[179] See above, p. 182, n. 51. Is this perhaps where the roots of Calvin's deep feelings of wonder before God's dreadful majesty lie? Cf. Ch. 1, 3.2 (pp. 25–6).

[180] See above, p. 180, n. 42.

[181] 'Sed non opus est exire a nobis, inquit Paulus. Quisquis excutiet se ipsum, intus reperiet Deum' (*Prael. Jer.* 10:10 [CO 38:71–2]).

[182] 'ut homo in corpore suo et anima centies Deum reperiens' (*Institutes* 1.5.4 [CO 2:43; OS 3:48, 1–3; n. 1]).

Also in these words – more vigorously expressed in the last quotation than ever – the world of experience is within reach and there one can encounter God, find and experience him personally in the microcosm[183] which is man.

But this search for God cannot be distressing and oppressive. On the contrary. In the well-known drawings which a student of Calvin made of him[184] one can see a man who – all too vehemently and fanatically – used himself up. Calvin was his own executioner.[185] The list of his ailments is a long one.[186] But during one of his lectures (in 1563) the following statements made by him were recorded:

> O if we were only truly committed to God! I assure you: all the elements would sing to us and we, we would get to hear in this world a melody made in heaven, so utterly beautiful.[187]

This, I submit, is a word of visionary power.

---

[183] Ibid., 1.5.3 (CO 2:43; OS 3:46 [and n. 4]; 33–47).
[184] Cf. Dankbaar, *Calvijn*, across from p. 135.
[185] Cf. above, p. 197, n. 130.
[186] Cf. Bouwsma, *John Calvin*, 30–1.
[187] *Prael. Jer.* 5:25 (CO 38:635): 'Nam si essemus rite compositi in Dei obsequio, certe omnia elementa nobis accinerent, atque ita cerneremus in mundo quasi angelicam melodiam.' Cf. above, p. 201, n. 149.

Bibliography

ANSELM OF CANTERBURY. *Cur Deus homo*. London, 1886.
——. *Fides quaerens intellectum id est Proslogion*. Edited and translated by Alexandre Koyré. 5th edn. Paris, 1978.
AQUINAS, THOMAS. *Summa theologiae*.
——. *Super Ep. ad Hebraeos*.
AUGUSTINE. *De catechizandis rudibus*. MSL 40.
——. *De correptione et gratia*. MSL 44.
——. *Epistola 130 (Ad Probam)*. MSL 33.
——. *De praedestinatione sanctorum*. MSL 44.
——. *In Ps. 70, sermo 2*. MSL 36.
——. *In Ps. 118, sermo 27*. MSL 37.
——. *Sermo 156*. MSL 38.
——. *Sermo 174*. MSL 38.
——. *Sermo 176*. MSL 38.

BABELOTZKY, G. *Platonische Bilder und Gedankengänge in Calvins Lehre vom Menschen*. Wiesbaden, 1977.
BAKKER, J. T. *Coram Deo. Bijdrage tot het onderzoek naar de structuur van Luthers Theologie*. Kampen, 1956.
BALKE, W. 'The Word of God and *Experientia* according to Calvin', in *Calvinus Ecclesiae Doctor*. Edited by W. H. Neuser. Kampen, 1978.
BARNIKOL, H. *Die Lehre Calvins vom unfreien Willen und ihr Verhältnis zur Lehre der übrigen Reformatoren und Augustins*. Neuwied, 1927.
BARTH, K. *Natural Theology: Comprising 'Nature and Grace' by Professor Dr. Emil Brunner and the reply 'No!' by Dr. Karl Barth*. Translated by Peter Fraenkel. London, 1946.

BAUR, F. *Lehrbuch der christlichen Dogmengeschichte.* 3rd edn. Stuttgart, 1867.

BERKOUWER, G. C. *Man: The Image of God.* Translated by D. Jellema. Grand Rapids, 1962.

——. *Sin.* Translated by P. Holtrop. Grand Rapids, 1971.

BERNARD OF CLAIRVAUX. *Tractatus de gratia et libero arbitrio.* MSL 182.

——. *In Cant. sermo* 23. MSL 183.

BEYERHAUS, G. *Studien zur Staatsanschauung Calvins mit besonderer Berücksichtigung seines Souveränitätsbegriffes.* Berlin, 1910.

BIEL, GABRIEL. *Collectorium circa quattuor libros Sententiarum.* Edited by W. Werbeck and U. Hofmann. 4 vols. Tübingen, 1973–84.

BOHATEC, J. *Budé und Calvin. Studien zur Gedankenwelt des französischen Frühhumanismus.* Graz, 1950.

——. 'Die Souveränität Gottes und der Staat nach der Auffassung Calvins', in *International Congres van Gereformeerden.* The Hague, 1934.

BOUWSMA, W. J. *John Calvin: A Sixteenth-Century Portrait.* New York, 1988.

BRUNNER, E. *Natural Theology: Comprising 'Nature and Grace' by Professor Dr. Emil Brunner and the reply 'No!' by Dr. Karl Barth.* Translated by Peter Fraenkel. London, 1946.

BUCER, M. *Metaphrases et enarrationes perpetuae epistolarum D. Pauli Apostoli . . . Tomus Primus. Continens metaphrasim et enarrationem in Epistolam ad Romanos . . . .* Strasbourg, 1536.

CALVIN, JOHN. 'Letter to Antoine de Bourbon, King of Navarre' (24 December 1561). CO 19.

——. 'Letter to Nicolas Duchemin' (1537). CO 5.

——. 'Letter to Guillaume Farel' (2 May 1564). CO 20.

——. 'Letter to Margaret of Navarre' (28 April 1545). CO 12.

——. *Catéchisme de l'Église de Genève* (1542). CO 6.

——. *Commentarius in Acta Apostolorum* (1554). CO 48.

——. *Commentarius in priorem Epistolam Pauli ad Corinthios* (1546). CO 49.

——. *Commentarius in Epistolam Pauli ad Corinthios II* (1548). CO 50. Also in *Ioannis Calvini Opera omnia,* Ser. 2: *Opera Exegetica* 15. Edited by H. Feld. Geneva, 1994.

CALVIN, JOHN. *Commentarius in Epistolam Pauli ad Ephesios* (1548). CO 51. Also in *Ioannis Calvini Opera omnia*, Ser. 2: *Opera Exegetica* 16. Edited by H. Feld. Geneva, 1992.

——. *Commentarius in Exodi* (1563). CO 24.

——. *Commentarius in Epistolam Pauli ad Galatas* (1548). CO 50.

——. *Commentarius in Genesin* (1550). CO 23.

——. *Commentarius in harmoniam evangelicam* (1555). CO 45.

——. *Commentarius in Epistolam ad Hebraeos* (1549). CO 55.

——. *Commentarius in librum Isaiae* (1551). CO 36, 37.

——. *Commentarius in Evangelium Johannis* (1553). CO 47.

——. *Commentarius in librum Josue* (1564). CO 25.

——. *Commentarius in priorem Epistolam Petri* (1551). CO 55.

——. *Commentarius in secundam Epistolam Petri* (1551). CO 55.

——. *Commentarius in Psalmos* (1557). CO 31, 32.

——. *Commentarius in Epistolam Pauli ad Romanos* (1540). CO 49. Also in *Studies in the History of Christian Thought*, vol. 22. Edited by T. H. L. Parker. Leiden, 1981.

——. *Commentarius in priorem Epistolam Pauli ad Timotheum* (1548). CO 52.

——. *Commentarius in secundam Epistolam Pauli ad Timotheum* (1548). CO 52.

——. *Confessio de Trinitate propter calumnias Petri Caroli* (1537). CO 9.

——. *Congrégation . . . de l'élection éternelle de Dieu* (1562). CO 8.

——. (*Consensus Tigurinus*) *Consensio mutua in re sacramentaria* (1549/1551). CO 7.

——. *Contre la Secte des Libertins* (1545). CO 7.

——. *Discours d'adieu aux ministres* (1564). CO 9.

——. Institutio: *Christianae religionis Institutio* (1536). CO 1.

——. *Institutio christianae religionis* (1539). CO 1.

——. *Institutio christianae religionis* (1545). CO 4.

——. *Institutio christianae religionis* (1559). CO 2.

——. *Institution de la religion chrestienne* (1560). CO 3.

——. *Institutie of onderwijzing in de christelijke godsdienst.* Translated by A. Sizoo. 3rd edn. Amsterdam, 1956.

——. *Petit Traicté . . . Que doit faire un homme fidèle . . . entre les papistes* (1543). CO 6.

CALVIN, JOHN. *Praelectiones in librum Danielis* (1561). CO 40.
——. *Praelectiones in librum Ezechielis* (1565). CO 40.
——. *Praelectiones in librum Hoseae* (1557). CO 42.
——. *Praelectiones in libruim Jonae* (1559). CO 43.
——. *Praelectiones in librum Jeremiae* (1563). CO 38, 39.
——. *Responsio ad Sadoletum* (1539). CO 5.
——. *De scandalis* (1550). CO 8.
——. *Sermons sur Deutéronome* (1555–56). CO 27, 28.
——. *Sermons sur Job* (1563). CO 33, 34.
——. *Sermons sur II Sam*, in *Predigten über das 2. Buch Samuelis*. Supplementa Calviniana, vol. 1. Edited by Hanns Rückert. Neukirchen, 1936–61.
——. *Sermons sur Luc* (1562). CO 46.
——. *Sermons sur I Cor.* (1558). CO 49.
——. *Sermons sur l'Épître aux Ephesiens* (1562). CO 51.
——. *Sermons sur la premiere Épître à Timothée.* CO 53.
——. *Sermons sur la seconde Épître à Timothée* (1561). CO 54.
——. *Socini quaestiones* (1555). CO 10a.
CHRYSOSTOM, JOHN. *Homilia de profectu Evangelii.* Opera Omnia. Edited by B. de Montfaucon. 2nd edn. Paris, 1834–40.

DANKBAAR, W. F. *Calvijn, zijn weg en werk.* Nijkerk, 1957.
DE JONG, J. A. '"An Anatomy of All Parts of the Soul": Insights into Calvin's Spirituality from his Psalms Commentary', in *Calvinus sacrae scripturae professor.* Edited by W. H. Neuser. Grand Rapids, 1994.
DE KROON, M. *Martin Bucer und Johannes Calvin. Reformatorische Perspektiven. Einleitung und Texte.* Translated from the Dutch by H. Rudolph. Göttingen, 1991.
DOUMERGUE, E. *Jean Calvin: Les hommes et les choses de son temps.* 7 vols. Lausanne, 1899–1927.
DOWEY, E. A. *The Knowledge of God in Calvin's Theology.* Grand Rapids, 1994.

FAVRE-DORSAZ, A. *Calvin et Loyola. Deux Réformes.* Paris, 1951.
FRIETHOFF, C. *Die Prädestinationslehre bei Thomas von Aquin und Calvin.* Freiburg (Switzerland), 1926.

GAMBLE, R. C., ed. *The Biography of Calvin.* Articles on Calvin and Calvinism, vol. 1. New York, 1992.

GANOCZY, A. *Calvin, théologien de l'Eglise et du ministère*. Paris, 1964.
——. *The Young Calvin*, trans. D. Foxgrover and W. Provo. Philadelphia, 1987.
GÖHLER, A. *Calvins Lehre von der Heiligung, dargestellt auf Grund der Institutio, exegetischer und homiletischer Schriften*. Munich, 1934.

HASLER, R. A. 'The Influence of David and the Psalms upon John Calvin's Life and Thought', in *The Biography of Calvin*. Articles on Calvin and Calvinism, vol. 1. Edited by R. C. Gamble. New York, 1992.
HAZART, C. *Triomph van de waerachtige Kercke*. Antwerpen, 1673.
HESSELINK, I. J. 'Reactions to Bouwsma's portrait of "John Calvin"', in *Calvinus sacrae scripturae professor*. Edited by W. H. Neuser. Grand Rapids, 1994.
——. *Calvin's First Catechism: A Commentary*. Louisville, 1997.
HUNTER, A. M. *The Teaching of Calvin: A Modern Interpretation*. 2nd edn. London, 1950.

IMBART DE LA TOUR, P. *Les Origines de la Réforme*. Vol. 4, *Calvin et l'institution chrétienne*. Paris, 1935.
——. 'Calvin'. *Revue des Deux Mondes* 23 (1934): 143–71.
IRENAEUS, *Adversus haereses*. MSG 7.

JACOBS, P. *Prädestination und Verantwortlichkeit bei Calvin*. Kassel, 1937.
JOEST, W. *Gesetz und Freiheit. Das Problem des Tertius usus legis bei Luther und der neutestamentlichen Parainese*. 2nd edn. Göttingen, 1956.

KRUSCHE, W. *Das Wirken des Hl. Geistes nach Calvin*. Göttingen, 1957.
KUITERT, H. M. *De realiteit van het geloof*. Kampen, 1967.
KÜNG, H. *Justification: The Doctrine of Karl Barth and a Catholic Reflection*. Translated by T. Collins, E. Tolk and D. Granskou. New York, 1964.
KUYPER, A. *Het Calvinisme. Zes Stone-lezingen*, 3rd edn. Kampen, 1959. English translation: *Lectures on Calvinism*. Grand Rapids, 1931.

LANG, A. *Johannes Calvin*. Leipzig, 1909.

LECERF, A. 'La souveraineté de Dieu d'après le calvinisme', in *Internationaal Congres van Gereformeerden*. The Hague, 1935.

LISTON, R. T. L. 'John Calvin's Doctrine of the Sovereignty of God'. PhD diss., University of Edinburgh, 1930.

LÜTTGE, W. *Die Rechtfertigungslehre Calvins und ihre Bedeutung für seine Frömmigkeit*. Berlin, 1909.

LUTHER, M. *De servo arbitrio* (1525). WA 18.

———. *Von den guten Werken* (1520). WA 6.

MERSCH, E. *La théologie du corps mystique*. 2 vols. Paris, 1949.

MULLER, RICHARD A. *The Unaccommodated Calvin: Studies in the Foundation of a Theological Tradition*. New York, 2000.

NAUTA, D. 'Calvijn's theologie'. *Elseviers Weekblad* 24 (1968): 33–4.

NIESEL, W. *Die Theologie Calvins*. 2nd edn. Munich, 1957.

———. 'Calvin wider Osianders Rechtfertigungslehre'. *Zeitschrift für Kirchengeschichte* 46 (1927): 410–30.

PARKER, T. H. L. *Calvin's Doctrine of the Knowledge of God*. Edinburgh, 1969.

POLMAN, A. D. R. *De predestinatieleer van Augustinus, Thomas van Aquino en Calvijn*. Franeker, 1936.

REUTER, K. *Das Grundverständnis der Theologie Calvins, unter Einbeziehung ihrer geschichtlichen Abhängigkeiten*. Beiträge zur Geschichte und Lehre der Reformierten Kirche, vol. 15. Neukirchen, 1963.

RIDDERBOS, H. *Paul: An Outline of His Theology*. Translated by J. de Witt. Grand Rapids, 1975.

RIES, J. *Die natürliche Gotteserkenntnis in der Theologie der Krisis im Zusammenhang mit dem Imagobegriff bei Calvin*. Bonn, 1939.

RITSCHL, A. *Geschichtliche Studien zur christlichen Lehre von Gott*. Jahrbücher für deutsche Theologie, vol. 13. Gotha, 1868.

RITSCHL, O. *Dogmengeschichte des Protestantismus*. Vol. 3, *Die reformierte Theologie des 16. und 17. Jahrhunderts in ihrer Entstehung und Entwicklung*. Göttingen, 1926.

SCHILLEBEECKX, E. *De Christusontmoeting als sacrament van de Godsontmoeting*. Antwerpen, 1957.
——. *De sacramentale heilseconomie*. Antwerpen, 1952.
SCHREINER, SUSAN E. 'Exegesis and Double Justice', in Calvin's Sermons on Job. *Church History* 58 (1989): 322–38.
SCHRENK, G. *Gottestreich und Bund im älteren Protestantismus vornehmlich bei Johannes Coccejus*. Gütersloh, 1923.
SCHULZE, M. *Meditatio futurae vitae. Ihr Begriff und ihre herrschende Stellung im System Calvins. Ein Beitrag zum Verständnis von dessen Institutio*. Leipzig, 1901.
SCHWEIZER, A. *Die Glaubenslehre der evangelisch-reformierten Kirche*. 2 vols. Zurich, 1844–5.
SMIDT, U. *Calvins Bezeugung der Ehre Gottes*. Berlin, 1927.
SMITS, L. *Saint Augustin dans l'oeuvre de Calvin*. 2 vols. Assen, 1957–8.
SPERNA WEILAND, J. *Orientatie*. Baarn, 1966.

TORRANCE, T. *Calvin's Doctrine of Man*. Grand Rapids, 1957.

De uitverkiezing, richtlijnen voor de behandeling van de leer der uitverkiezing, aanvaard door de Generale Synode der Nederlandse Hervormde Kerk. The Hague, 1961.

Enige aspecten van de leer der uitverkiezing. Rapport samengesteld op verzoek van de commissie tot de zaken der Remonstrantse Broederschap en van de Generale Synode der Nederlandse Hervormde Kerk. The Hague, 1966.

VAN DEN BERGH, W. *Calvijn over het genadeverbond*. The Hague, 1879.
VAN DER LINDE, S. *De leer van den Heiligen Geest bij Calvijn*. Wageningen, 1943.
VIGNAUX, P. *La pensée au moyen age*. Paris, 1938.

WALKER, W. *John Calvin: The Organizer of Reformed Protestantism, 1509–1564*. New York, 1969.
WENDEL, F. *Calvin: The Origins and Development of His Religious Thought*. Translated by P. Mairet. New York, 1963.
WERNLE, P. *Der evangelische Glaube nach den Hauptschriften der Reformatoren*. Vol. 3, *Calvin*. Tübingen, 1919.

WILKS, M. *The Problem of Sovereignty in the Later Middle Ages.* Cambridge, 1963.

WILLEMS, B. 'De verlossing als menselijke werkelijkheid'. *Tijdschrift voor Theologie* 5 (1965): 39–42.

WOLF, H. H. *Die Einheit des Bundes, Das Verhältnis von Altem und Neuem Testament bei Calvin.* 2nd edn. Neukirchen, 1958.

Index of Subjects

A. Citations from Calvin which mirror his thinking

ON GOD

I.   1.1.   *greatness*

'God's greatness is immeasurable. Before his immeasurable power I am struck dumb. It makes me ecstatic.' 205, n. 165

1.2.   *love*

'The affection which he bears toward us is far more ardent and vehement than the love of all mothers.' 12, n. 84

'That marvellous goodness of God which shines forth clearly and purely from the beautiful order of nature.' 206, n. 169

'There is nothing that is more peculiarly his own nature . . . than goodness. In it, especially, lies his honour.' 27, n. 187

'The delightful evidences of his Love.' 206, n. 170

ON CREATION

2.1.   *spectacle*

'Creation is a spectacle of God's glory.' 20, n. 136

'In it the knowledge of God shines forth.' 29, n. 191

2.2.   *school*

'The work of art which is the universe should be a school to us.' 182, n. 50

'God daily reveals himself anew. All you have to do [to see it] is open your eyes.' 179, n. 35

217

ON HUMANS

3.1.   *masterpiece*

'Man is the most brilliant masterpiece of creation.' 173, n. 10

'Humans are a mirror of God's glory.' 16, n. 108

'Man is divine.' 180, n. 42

'God's glory must shine out through us.' 120, n. 86

'Formerly some philosophers rightly called "man" a microcosm.' 16, n. 111

3.2.   *little humans*

'What do little humans mean by trying to break into the inner recesses of divine wisdom?' 11, n. 81

Man is 'weakness,' 'dullness,' 'coarseness,' 'poverty.' 10, n. 72; 11, nn. 79, 80; 124, n. 112

3.3.   *deformity*

'We bring nothing from our mother's womb but mere filthiness.' 195, n. 117

'The image of God is so mutilated in humans that they have become a hideous deformity.' 11, n. 76

ON CHRIST

4.1.   *honour of God*

'With his entire being he breathed the glory of God.' 26, n. 182

'In Christ God is inconsiderable.' 89, n. 197

4.2.   *image of God*

'Christ is the image of the Father to us. He represents the Father to us.' 90, nn. 200, 201

'The word *image* relates to us. In him the glory of the Father is manifested to us.' 87, n. 190

4.3.   *mystical union*

'That connectedness between the head and the members, Christ who dwells in our hearts, is a mysterious union which I value above all else.' 149, n. 9

4.4.   *one and the same substance*

'An amazing union which surpasses our understanding.' 103, n. 21

4.5.   *mediator*

'God dwells in inaccessible light. For that reason Christ has to intervene. That is necessarily so.' 75, n. 143

ON KNOWING GOD

II.   1.   *true wisdom*

'Almost the entire content of our wisdom ... consists of two parts: the knowledge of God and the knowledge of ourselves.' 1. n. 1

'This is the true wisdom: we must in the first place look toward God and then, in the second place, each person must look within himself and there examine himself thoroughly.' 171, n. 1; 203, n. 157

2.   *twofold knowledge*

'In the formation of the world but also in the general teaching of Scripture the Lord first makes himself known as Creator; afterward – in the appearance of Christ – as Redeemer. From this, then, springs a twofold knowledge of him.' 177, n. 23

3.   *God in himself*

'People intent on knowing *what* God is (*quid sit Deus*) play a game with speculations which leave a person cold.'

God for us

'How he relates to us (*qualis sit*) – that is much more important.' 178, n. 31

4.   *witnessing to God*

'He alone is able to witness concerning himself.' 7, n. 45

THE SOURCES OF OUR KNOWLEDGE

III. 1.1. *Experience as knowledge*

'With experience as our teacher we learn to know God precisely as he makes himself known in his Word.' 180, n. 40

'Nothing moves me more than his goodness.' 205, n. 168

'I experience Christ's presence in the Lord's Supper more than I understand it.' 162, n. 60

1.2.   *Scripture as source of knowledge*

'The Word not only leads but also teaches us.' 180, n. 43

'Scripture is like a pair of glasses which enables us to see things sharply.' 181, n. 48

'The Scriptures breathe something divine.' 21, n. 139

'Scripture has its own majesty.' 20, n. 138

ON BELIEVING

2.1.   *faith as knowledge*

'Faith consists in knowing Christ' (*Inst.* 3.2.8; *notitia fidei*). 184

2.2.   *conviction and certainty*

'You become persuaded of what you do not understand. But that conviction is so firm that you understand more about human life than you could by means of your own intellect.' 186, n. 78

2.3.   *the work of the Holy Spirit*

'The Holy Spirit lifts us up in mind and heart above our own understanding. Thus we get a new keenness of vision.' 188, n. 83

2.4.   *a fully matured faith*

'Very different is the experience of a fully matured faith. . . . It is this faith which makes God's goodness transparent to you. Doubt is excluded. You know and experience: how delightful this is!' 189, n. 86

2.5.   *a faith under assault*

'I am not dreaming of a kind of certainty that is exempt from all doubt. On the contrary! I am saying that believers are constantly at war with their own unbelief.' 190, n. 90

'NOTE ESPECIALLY TWO THINGS'

IV. 1.   *God's honour and peace of conscience*

'We are speaking of especially two things:
1. God's honour. It must remain inviolate and guaranteed.
2. Our conscience. In the presence of his judgment it must feel at rest and strictly secure.' 97–117, 174–6

On *justification by faith alone*, cf. 99, n. 4

2.   *God's goodness and our election*

'The Lord wills that in election we see nothing but his mere goodness.' 133, n. 153

3.   *God's providence and our culpability*

'Humanity falls. God's providence so ordains it. But humans fall by their own fault.' 138, n. 188

On *predestination* cf. 126–45 and under B.

A TWOFOLD PERSPECTIVE

V.   1.   *Weal and woe*

'The human mind has radically lost its wholeness. It has been corrupted, yet even now it is still clothed and ornamented with God's gifts.' 51, n. 18

2.   *true good*

'With the aid of numerous examples we can learn how much good God has left to human nature even after it has keen deprived of its true good.' 51, n. 19

'God is disturbed at the *corruption* of the work of his hands more than at the work itself.' 9, n. 69

3.   *the soundness of the will*

'Humans have not been robbed of their will . . . but of the soundness of their will.' 52, n. 26

4.1.   *optimal state* (*ordo genuinus*)

'This was the true, ideal state. The work of art that is the universe should have been the school in which we would be consecrated to God. From there we were to have gone on our way to an eternal life, to perfect happiness.' 181, n. 46

4.2.   *corruption*

'But God no longer recognizes us, violated as we are and ruined by sin, as his work. We have fallen "from life into death".' 180, n. 44

5.1.   *atonement by satisfaction*

'Always the wrath and curse weighs down upon us.' 179, n. 153

Cf. 3, 77–80 (*wrath, curse, vengeance*). 'The Intercessor intervened on behalf of this human being. He took upon himself and underwent his punishment.' 79, n. 154

THE HONOUR OF GOD IN CALVIN'S LIFE

VIII. 1.

'I have not written anything out of hatred against anyone. I have always faithfully set forth that which tended to the honour of God.' 24, n. 166

2.

'This life is both very short and very fragile – actually no more than a shadow. But the honour of God – that is the issue – must be much more precious to us.' 24, n. 165

B. Other characteristic pronouncements of John Calvin

abyss

'The admirable order of God's government is rightly called an abyss.' 7, n. 51

active life

'A Christian must lead an active life.' 140, n. 199

anxiety, anxiety of conscience

'A more cruel bully does not exist.' 198, n. 133

anxious precision

'From time to time the same thought occurs to me, namely, that I am in danger of failing to do justice to God's mercy.' 198, n. 134

coercion/necessity

'Is not God necessarily good?' 55, n. 41

'I gladly accept the distinction between coercion and necessity.' 55, n. 40

conscience

'Conscience is an awareness of God's judgment. It is, as it were, a witness who is constantly looking at you.' 179, n. 34

cosmology, secondary causes

'Those who try to explain natural events in the light of secondary causes are like a person who only stares at the edges of someone else's fingernails but does not deign to look at this face.' 201, n. 146

exlex

'We are not imagining a God who is above the law, for he is himself a law to himself.' 143, nn. 215, 219

fanaticism
>'People who work at something too fanatically burn themselves
>out and are in a sense their own executioners.' 197, n. 130

glorying in oneself
>'All grounds for glorying have been taken from us. For he alone
>must stand in the full light of his glory.' 10, n. 70

God's face
>'The splendour of God's face is to us an inexplicable labyrinth ...'
>102, n. 15
>Cf. the expression *coram Deo*. 98, 124, nn. 106, 110

God's majesty
>'God is awe-inspiring in his majesty but his goodness is as infinite
>as his power.' 41, n. 300

God, the Holy Spirit
>'The sacraments can only fulfill their function properly when the
>Holy Spirit, the inner teacher, accomplishes his work through
>them.' 158, n. 37. Cf. above A III 2.3.

good works
>'This is precisely how it is – that much is clear – : we are not
>justified *without* works. Neither, however, are we justified *by*
>works.' 113, n. 59

human body
>'What miracles are lodged in a human body! It offers us such a
>splendid and lively image of his majesty.' 193, n. 105.

ignorance – believing, learned
>'Believing ignorance is better than frivolous knowledge.' 141,
>n. 208; 137, n. 182 (derived from Augustine)

law (torah)
>'If you want to hold onto the true norm for the practice of love,
>you must first direct your eyes toward God.' 64, n. 86

merit
>'What a flashy word! It casts a shadow over God's grace and can
>cause people to perish in pernicious pride. I ask myself: was it
>necessary to introduce this word?' 113–14, nn. 62, 63
>*Of Christ*: 91–6.

opus operatum
>'All that those sophists have chattered about on *opus operatum* is
>not only false before God but also in conflict with the nature of
>the sacraments.' 159, nn. 45–6

predestination, permission

'Why should we speak of "permission"? Does he not *will* it to be so?' 137, n. 179

Cf. 5, n. 36 and A IV 3 above.

predestination

'The clearest example of predestination and grace is the Redeemer himself, the human being Jesus Christ.' 130, nn. 140–1 (derived from Augustine).

predestination, reprobation

'It is indeed a dreadful decree, I grant you.' 135, n. 167

Cf. A. IV 3 above.

psalms

'I usually call the book of Psalms an anatomy of all parts of the soul.' 205, n. 163

providence

'Providence does not mean that God idly observes [things down here] from heaven.' 6, nn. 41–2

Cf. A IV 3 and VII 1 above.

piety, true (*pietas*)

'Giving everything we have in the service of God's glory.' 157, n. 33

righteousness

'Whenever you hear mention of God's honour, think of "righteousness".' 27, n. 186

'Righteousness is the principle of love'. 94, n. 216

self-knowledge

'All those who thoroughly examine themselves will discover God within.' 207, n. 181. Cf. 195, n. 119

sin, fall into

'The fall of the first human being has resulted in horrible confusion.' 202, n. 152

will, free (*liberum arbitrium*)

'Free will is an idol.' 158, n. 47

Cf. A V 3 above.

C. Other Subjects

Index of Names